PEOPLE AND THEIR CONTEXTS

791-MOSH

PEOPLE AND THEIR CONTEXTS

A Chronology of the 16th Century World

Sally E. Mosher

To order additional copies of this book, contact:

Xlibris Corporation
1-888-7-XLIBRIS
www.Xlibris.com

Orders@Xlibris.com

CONTENTS

To my father, Judge Leslie J. Ekenberg, with happy memories of our many proof reading sessions for his wonderfully useful little book on government, Our Way.

PREFACE

This chronology was begun to fill my own needs. While preparing lectures and articles on Renaissance music, I sought general information on the period in order to place specific events in their context. I had already done considerable reading on 16th century subjects, but it had been specialized rather than general. Looking at existing chronologies, I found events listed in "bullet" format as one-liners with no explanation of names or terminology. The alternative was full-length books on the period, most of them extremely detailed and scholarly in tone. What I wanted was a cultural outline, with each entry self-explanatory, and containing as much information as possible about how people lived. Thus, I began to compile this cultural outline, and found the process so interesting that it continued to grow.

In its present form, the chronology is a convenient *vade mecum* for people either generally interested in the period or researching a specific aspect of it, and it can serve any reader as an introduction to this extraordinarily vivid age. It is not intended as a substitute for scholarly texts, but rather may be a launching pad for subsequent in-depth reading in them.

Throughout the 16th century, the Western world was beginning its rise to world dominance. Westerners have usually thought of the 16th century world as Euro-centered because we have relied on general histories written from the vantage point of the West, that haven't included much beyond Europe and its doings. The escalation of Western dominance during the following four centu-

9

ries was powered by advances in technology, spurred by insatiable curiosity, and morally undermined by a patronizing, sometimes truculent, belief in the superiority of Western civilization, race, and religion.

The reality is that a number of the civilizations encountered by the exploring, conquering 16th century Europeans deserved to be considered great. Some, indeed, considered themselves superior to the Europeans. However, the Europeans prevailed, and they wrote the books. Included in this chronology are significant people, events and achievements from the non-European world, including arguably the most enlightened monarch of the century, Akbar the Great, Mughal Emperor of India, who practiced religious toleration, reduced taxes and abolished slavery.

The 16th century was a time of discoveries; of firsts and the setting of precedents; of challenges to established paradigms in geography, religion and astronomy; of beauty juxtaposed with brutality and danger. Every year, a war was happening somewhere. Promises and treaties were made, and quickly abandoned as alliances shifted. The Pope was a political as well as a spiritual force, making treaties and sending armies into the field just like any other ruler. The Turks were a serious threat to Europe for the first seventy years of the century; in 1529 they laid unsuccessful siege to Vienna. The cities of Rome and Antwerp were both sacked by European armies. London suffered a serious earthquake, and Constantinople (now Istanbul) was destroyed by one. Moscow was destroyed by fire. Jews in most places and Muslims living in Spain (known to history as Moors) were persecuted. Torture was generally acceptable to both church and state, as was slavery. Under both Catholics and Protestants, witches were persecuted when witch-hunting crazes erupted sporadically throughout Europe.

If the 16th century was notably the century of geography—as the world was encompassed by four circumnavigations, as mapmakers enlarged people's knowledge of the world's vastness and shape, as navigators ventured onto vast, hitherto uncharted bodies of water—so also was it notably the century of religion. At the century's beginning, Europe was Catholic, and Christians dominated the Western world. At the century's end, many Protestant sects had gained important footholds all over Europe and a few countries could be considered entirely Protestant, although the Western world would continue to be dominated by Christianity through the 20th century. Between 1500 and 1600 lay Martin Luther and the Protestant Reformation, Henry VIII and England's secession from Roman Catholicism, seven bloody French wars of religion between Catholics and Protestant Huguenots, the Catholic Counter Reformation, the *Index Librorum Prohibitorum* (List of Forbidden Books), and the founding of the most famous of the Catholic religious orders—the Jesuits.

A significant number of people were burned at the stake for disagreeing with the prevailing religion, whatever it was. One definition of a heretic was someone whose religious views didn't agree with your own. The Catholic Inquisition's burning in 1600 of the peripatetic anti-establishment heretic philosopher Giordano Bruno is an apposite conclusion to a century of religious intolerance and turmoil. Bruno's burning is partly the result of one paradigm shift that *didn't* happen during the 16th century: a change of belief in an earth-centered to a sun-centered universe. Nicholas Copernicus was reluctant to admit he was serious about this theory, phrasing his statements about heliocentricity as scientific speculation, and having the publication of his discoveries deferred until after his death in 1543. Giordano Bruno was open about *his* belief that the sun was the center of our planetary system, and this was cited as a paramount reason for his condemnation. Bruno also believed there were many other inhabited planets in the universe, a unique point of view at that time.

The financial power base of Europe shifted from Antwerp in the Low Countries (the massacre and burning of the city by the Spanish in 1576 probably didn't help matters any) to Genoa in Italy by the last quarter of the century. The control of the seas passed from the Portuguese and Spanish to the English, who developed a new type of fast-moving, maneuverable ship and a new concept of command: putting seamen, rather than soldiers or other landsmen, in charge. Initially, the Portuguese and Spanish, and later the English and Dutch, took to the seas looking for a way to the fabled wealth of east Asia, although pious sentiments about saving pagan souls were regularly expressed. No doubt these lofty sentiments were believed by the priests who went along with the Spanish and Portuguese expeditions. Bernal Diaz, one of the Spanish conquistadores, said he "desired to serve God and His Majesty, and to grow rich as all men desire to do."

Almost no one among the first Europeans visiting the Americas, or anywhere else, was seeking to found a family-oriented colony, or to become prosperous gradually through sensible agriculture. Toward the end of the century, the English began to try to establish colonies for families, and some persecuted French Protestants also fled to the New World as family groups. There was little exploring for the sake of adventure or curiosity. Many of the explorers were rough, avaricious, wantonly cruel sociopaths, although at the same time they might also be brave, ingenious, charming and smart. Greed supplied perhaps the strongest impetus for discovery. In a cultural parallel, many of the 16th century firsts in literature and the arts sprang not from intellectual curiosity or a spirit of aesthetic adventure so much as from an effort to evoke the supposed glory days of the ancient Greeks and Romans. Thus, many of the century's firsts were inadvertent.

The long voyages of exploration are particularly impressive when one considers the total dependence on sail for locomotion through oceans with as yet unknown wind patterns and currents, and the inability to calculate longitude (east/west measurement). Because of these exploratory expeditions, especially the four voyages of circumnavigation beginning with Magellan in 1519, some navigators, among them Amerigo Vespucci, though not Columbus, came to realize that the Americas were separate continents rather than the eastern parts of Asia, and that the world was a far larger globe than had been supposed. The Flemish geographer Gerardus Mercator is credited with developing a projection that shows this great globe on a two-dimensional flat surface. By the end of the century, the Dutch were the best cartographers in Europe.

Enormous wealth in gold, silver, emeralds, and pearls poured out of the southern parts of the New World into the Old, most of it into Spain, from the 1520's on. Those riches contributed to a drastically spiraling inflation throughout Europe as the century progressed, and made luxuries available to a burgeoning middle class as well as an increasingly luxurious upper class. All sorts of new plants and substances—including tobacco, potatoes, and chocolate—also made the journey, changing European eating and lifestyle habits forever.

However, a number of substances often thought to have arrived in Europe in the 16th century, didn't make their first appearance there until the 17th century, among them coffee and tea. Coffee may have been cultivated first in southern Arabia in the ninth century. By 1510, it was being drunk in Cairo, and by 1517 in Istanbul (still Constantinople to Europe's Christians), and as the century progressed its use spread throughout the Islamic world. The Turks supposedly had some in their baggage when they besieged Vienna in 1529, but the date of its first appearance in Europe is generally given as 1615, when it was brought by Venetian traders. Tea was written about by a Venetian traveler in 1559, and was first introduced in Amsterdam by the Dutch East India Company in about 1610. The first English importation of tea, by the English East India Company, was from Java in 1669.

While a great deal of wine, beer and ale were consumed all over Europe during the 16th century, as they had been throughout the Middle Ages, the process of clarifying and bottling wine was still unknown, as was the regular use of corks. Since wine could not be effectively stored, the best, and therefore most expensive wine throughout the century, was newly produced. Beer remained a daily staple drink on all levels of society. Contraband correspondence was delivered to the imprisoned Mary Queen of Scots in the weekly beer deliveries.

Winters were unusually cold in Europe for much of the century, although England had one summer hotter than anyone could remember. Overland travel was still entirely by foot, horseback or open cart for most people, and occasionally by closed carriage for the well-to-do, and few roads had any paving. Except for professional couriers who used relay stations to provide fresh horses and riders, the maximum distance a traveler covered was usually about twenty-five miles per day. The few exceptions are related as colorful anecdotes: Thomas (later Cardinal) Wolsey's youthful 96 hour round trip between London and the Low Countries to deliver a message for King Henry VII, and a 2,500 mile voyage of galleys (boats propelled by oarsmen) accomplished in 31 days. The Incas of Peru, however, who lacked both wheels and horses (having only the Andean pack animals llamas and alpacas), had created a network of ultra smooth roads on which runners transported information throughout their enormous empire several times faster than anything moved around the Europe of their conquerors.

There was a great use of rivers and waterways for getting around all over Europe. Boats functioned as both private and public transportation, although there was no public transportation as we understand it. Bridges were few. London Bridge remained the only span across the River Thames, while the English were still using roads built by the Romans to get around the countryside, where there were as yet none of the hedgerows for which England later became so well known. Most sailing in the Mediterranean Sea and the ocean was still of a type called "coasting," which emphasized, and mapped, routes between seaports, without ever going far out into the ocean.

At present we think of literacy as including both reading comprehension and the ability to write. However, during the 16th century many more people could read a bit than were able to write. Even people of means sufficient to require the execution of legal documents often had to sign them with "marks," or penned a signature revealing how unfamiliar the process of writing was. As the century progressed, the number of books printed each year dramatically increased, while reading literacy increased in tandem. One manifestation of the spirit of the Protestant reformation was the printing of an ever-increasing number of books, including the Bible, in the vernacular languages, while well-known older works were translated out of the original Latin. Moreover, Protestants were actually reading the Bible, rather than accepting explanations of it from their betters.

The new religions had some unanticipated social side effects. Under Catholic regimes, prostitution and camp following had been legal, and were regulated by the government. The great 13th century Catholic theologian, St Thomas Aquinas, whose teachings continued to permeate Catholic thinking throughout the 16th century, had regarded brothels as an unfortunate necessity, but not so 16th century Protestant leaders John Calvin and Martin Luther. Unregulated, illegal prostitution, however, produced an increase in both disease and violence in Protestant cities. Catholic Venice, where prostitution remained legal, escaped this problem, and produced two directories of its choicest courtesans, including information on their specialties.

The plague still erupted from time to time, killing thousands as it ran its course. Most diseases were left to run their course. Physicians were seldom able to cure, and quite frequently killed. Most people treated themselves at home with folk or herbal remedies, and consulted a physician with considerable reluctance. However, there were some advances in medical procedure and the knowledge of human anatomy. Tens of millions of indigenous people died in the New World from diseases brought by their European conquerors, although syphilis was a lethal New World export. Even the teeth of royalty often rotted at an early age, and the only remedy was extraction, but there were little tooth whisks or cloths for cleaning, and mouth washes for sweetening the breath.

In an age of sharp contrasts and the irony that results from them, while most women were left uneducated and were expected to be subordinate to men, six of them were rulers of nations. Among the politically successful were Queens Isabella of Castile, who died at the beginning of the century in 1504, Elizabeth Tudor of England, who died three years after its end, and Catherine de' Medici, Regent and behind-the-scenes manipulator in Valois France until her death in 1589. The others were the Catholic Queen Mary Tudor of England (known to history as "Bloody Mary" for her persecution of Protestants in an increasingly Protestant country); Mary Queen of Scots (another Catholic in another increasingly Protestant country, whose second and third marriages were politically disastrous); and Juana of Castile (who never reigned because she was diagnosed as insane . . . by those who then ruled in her stead).

France was considered the center of elegance in costume and was known for gallant manners, although many luxury goods, like knit silk stockings and perfumed leather gloves, originated in Italy. Since rank and occupation were still indicated by a person's appearance, large sums were expended on clothing and jewels in order to make a good show. A nation's wealth and stability was expressed through the magnificence of its rulers, and crown jewels were occasionally used as collateral for loans to finance some of the many wars. The 16th century is known to jewelry historians as the Great Age of the Goldsmith, partly because techniques for cutting (faceting) diamonds and other hard gem-stones were still undeveloped. Thus, jewelers concentrated on making elaborate, often magnificently opulent, gold and enamel settings for stones with few or no facets. Although "sumptuary" laws limited the choice of color, fabric and type of fur for all but the highest nobility, people in general bought and wore what they pleased.

Italy continued to be the place to go for exposure to the "cutting edge" in the arts, both visual and musical. Most European painters and musicians spent years studying and working in Italy, and a few remained for life. This was the century of Italy's greatest painters and sculptors, including Leonardo da Vinci and

Michelangelo. While Italy and the Netherlands continued to be the prime artistic centers for music, the English were developing a distinctive compositional style, with William Byrd as the principal mover and innovator. However, the most famous and honored composer of the century, the Franco-Flemish Orlande de Lassus (Orlando di Lasso), spent most of his working life in Munich, Germany, at the Court of the Duke of Bavaria. Although by the end of the century the English surpassed the rest of the European world in the theatre, they continued to be undistinguished in the visual arts, as they had been throughout the century.

Format and Content:

As to my choice of the events listed: politics and religion were, of course, necessary, as was geography in this dynamic time of discovery and exploration. Mention of the introduction of new ideas or substances also seemed essential, since these changed people's way of living and looking at the world in a century of dramatic growth and change. Indeed, because of this enormous influx of new ideas and substances, the 16th century deserves to be considered the gateway to the modern world. In selecting individual books and works of art, rather than attempting to list every significant painting or publication I chose a representative cross section, so as to place the creators in the context of the century.

I have included a "bullet" format chronology of Firsts and Unusual Events for quick reference. For greater detail, the reader can refer either to the individual year in the year-by-year chronology, or to the Topical References by Year. I felt an extensive listing of references by year was necessary to give quick access to individual names, events and substances, especially for readers unsure of the year for an event, a group which includes most of us. The Topical References by Year contains a brief description of most of the people listed, as well as their dates, while the year-by-year chronology contains detail about their activities.

Some of the publications, developments or discoveries were given different dates in various sources. Occasionally, this is because the next or "new" year began on March 25 rather than on January 1. In the last fifth of the century it might be because only Catholic Europe adopted the revised Gregorian Calendar in 1582. Thus, when the first Spanish Armada sailed for England in 1588, the two countries were 10 days apart in dating. When confronted by conflicting dates, while I knew that only one could be right, I could not always determine which, and have indicated this. When an event's exact year was approximate or unknown in all the sources, I chose a likely year and indicated that this was an approximation. I elected to list life span dates only in the Topical References by Year, along with a brief description of the person, while places of publication for printed works appear in the body of the chronology.

1500-1509

1500

GEOGRAPHY

♦ Pedro Alvars de Cabral sails 45 days as commander of Portugal's second Indies Fleet of 13 ships and 1,200 men, becoming the first explorer to reach Brazil. Sighting a large hill, he lands at present-day Porto Seguro. Cabral finds brazil-wood, source of a valuable red dye, which gives the country its eventual name. Cabral names it "The Land of the True Cross," later amended to "True Cross" (Veracruz). He goes on to Mozambique, on the southeastern coast of Africa, and is the first to provide clear information about it in Europe. Continuing on to Calicut on the Malabar (south-west) coast of India, he establishes the first commercial treaty between Portugal and India.

♦ Diego Diaz of Portugal discovers Madagascar.

♦ Gaspar and Miguel de Corte Real of Spain explore the east coast of Greenland and Labrador, which they call the "North Cape of Asia." (to 1502).

♦ Juan de la Cosa of Spain, who accompanied Columbus on his second voyage in 1493, draws a portolan map of the New World. It shows Columbus's discoveries, also John Cabot's voyage to the coasts of Nova Scotia, Newfoundland and New England, which are marked as English possessions.

POLITICS

♦ King Louis XII of France conquers the Duchy of Milan, Italy.

♦ Lodovico Sforza, Duke of Milan recovers Milan from the French, only to lose it two months later, when he is captured and imprisoned in France until his death in 1508.

♦ Treaty of Granada: King Louis XII of France and King Ferdinand II of Aragon and Sicily agree to divide the Kingdom of Naples, which includes all Italy south of the city of Naples. King Ferdinand II of Aragon and Sicily is the husband of Queen Isabella of Castile. He is also King Ferdinand V of Castile and later King Ferdinand III of Naples. As King Ferdinand I, he is the first monarch of all Spain.

♦ The Diet of Augsburg establishes a Council of Regency for administering the Holy Roman Empire and divides Germany into six "circles" or regions.

♦ Dom Miguel of Portugal, heir to the thrones of Spain and Portugal, dies, leaving Juana of Castile and her husband Philip "the Handsome" of Habsburg as heirs to the throne of Spain.

♦ King Ferdinand of Aragon, husband of Queen Isabella of Castile, suppresses a Moorish revolt in Granada.

♦ The Muslim Turks take the port of Modon in the Ionian Sea away from the Republic of Venice.

♦ Ivan III, Grand Duke of Moscovy and ruler of Russia, takes the border town of Chernigov from Poland.

♦ Lucretia Borgia's third husband, Alfonso of Aragon, Duke of Bisceglie, is murdered, probably by her brother Caesare. Lucretia is the daughter of Rodrigo Borgia, Pope Alexander VI. Lucretia's first two marriages were annulled, and some sources disregard the first marriage entirely.

RELIGION

♦ Pope Alexander VI proclaims a Year of Jubilee, and imposes a tithe to fund a proposed crusade against the Muslim Turks.

LITERATURE AND THE ARTS

♦ Desiderius Erasmus of Rotterdam: *Adagia* (Adages); Paris; a collection of ancient Latin proverbs with lengthy comments and opinions by Erasmus; 2nd printing in 1508. This was his best selling work during his lifetime.

♦ The first edition of *Till Eulenspiegel* is published in Lubeck, Germany.

♦ Michelangelo Buonarotti completes his sculpture of the "Pieta" in Rome. Begun in 1497, it was commissioned by Cardinal Jean Villiers of France.

♦ Albrecht Dürer paints one of several self portraits, in this one clad in furs, and "The Nativity"; Nuremberg, Germany.

♦ Sandro Botticelli paints "Mystic Nativity."

♦ Raphael does a pastel drawing of Isabella d'Este, wife of Francesco Gonzaga, Marquis of Mantua. It is probably the study for a lost oil painting.

♦ Hieronymus Bosch: while none of his paintings is dated, during the next decade he probably painted "The Garden of Earthly Delights," "The Temptation of St. Anthony" and "Ship of Fools." Later, Bosch's paintings are eagerly collected by King Philip II of Spain.

♦ Flemish composer Josquin Despres goes to France. Evidence suggests he was there until 1503, and did some work for King Louis XII.

♦ Hans Folz of Nuremberg reforms the songs of the Mastersingers. From this time on, worldly subjects are permissable.

SOCIETY, EDUCATION

♦ First regular postal service is established, running between Vienna and Brussels, under the aegis of the Holy Roman Empire.

♦ First black lead pencils are used in England.

♦ First recorded Caesarian operation is performed on a living woman by Swiss pig gelder Jakob Nüfer.

- Italian version of the *trompe* (forcing air by the suction of a water chute) replaces use of the bellows in the forging of iron.
- The first annual horserace meetings are held at Chester, England.
- Silver guilders are introduced as coinage in Germany. They continue in use in Austria until 1892.
- The first cat is bred in North America, the beginning of the American Short Hair breed.
- Thomas Linacre is appointed tutor to Prince Arthur, eldest son of King Henry VII of England.
- The University of Valencia is founded in Spain.
- The first commercial colleges are founded in Venice.

1501

GEOGRAPHY

- Amerigo Vespucci embarks on his second voyage of discovery for Spain in May, exploring the coast of Brazil (through 1505).
- First voyage of the Anglo-Portuguese Syndicate to North America.
- Rodrigo de Bastides of Spain, together with Juan de la Cosa, explores the Caribbean coast, including the Gulf of Darien and Panama (to 1502).

POLITICS

- France and Spain occupy the Kingdom of Naples.
- The French enter Rome.
- Pope Alexander VI declares that King Louis XII of France is also King of the Kingdom of Naples.
- Ivan III, Grand Duke of Muscovy and ruler of Russia, invades Lithuania.
- Prince Arthur, eldest son of King Henry VII of England, marries Princess Catherine of Aragon, youngest daughter of King Ferdinand and Queen Isabella of Spain.

- Shah Ismail, Sheikh of Ardabil, conquers Persia and founds the Safavid dynasty (in power until 1736).
- Basel and Schaffhausen cantons are admitted as members of the Swiss Confederation.
- Leonardo Loredan becomes Doge of the Republic of Venice (to 1521).
- Lucretia Borgia marries Alfonso d'Este, Duke of Ferrara, her fourth husband.

RELIGION

- Pope Alexander VI issues a Papal Bull ordering the burning of any books that deny the Catholic Church's authority.
- Jews are expelled from Naples. They are allowed to return in 1509.
- King Ferdinand of Aragon declares that Granada is a Christian kingdom, after quelling a rebellion by the Moors.
- Pope Alexander VI issues a Papal bull (*Eximiae devotionis*) granting to the crown of Castile (Spain) all tithes levied in the Americas.
- King Henry VII of England declines the Pope's invitation to lead a crusade against the Turks.
- Pope Alexander VI sends Polydore Vergil to England as deputy-collector of "Peter's pence." Vergil remains in England for about 21 years, where he writes many books on English history.

LITERATURE AND THE ARTS

- Ottaviano dei Petrucchi:*Harmonice musices odhecaton* A; Venice. This is the first printing of polyphonic vocal music from movable type. A compilation of works by various composers, it contained 96 pieces.
- Fra Filippo Lippi paints "St. Catherine."

SOCIETY, EDUCATION

♦ First consignment of far eastern spices is shipped from Lisbon to the Portuguese factory in Antwerp for distribution to western Europe.

♦ Aldus Manutius first uses italic type at his Aldine Press in Venice, Italy.

♦ HRE Maximilian I founds the University of Wittenberg, Germany.

1502

GEOGRAPHY

♦ Christopher Columbus leaves in May on his fourth and last voyage of discovery for Spain. He is the first explorer to reach Nicaragua, also visiting Honduras and Panama. He founds a short-lived colony at Belen, near the present Costa Rica border (until 1504).

♦ Vasco da Gama of Portugal, leading Portugal's third Indies fleet of 14 ships, reaches Mozambique, Sofala, and Cochin, India, and bombards Calicut on the Malabar (southwest) coast, founding a colony at Cochin. Da Gama cuts off the ears, noses, and hands of 800 Moors and sends them ashore to the local ruler, suggesting he make curry of them.

♦ Joao de Nova of Portugal discovers St. Helena Island in the South Atlantic Ocean. This becomes an important watering place for ships on long voyages.

♦ Second voyage of the Anglo-Portuguese Syndicate, commanded by Miguel Corte-Real of Portugal, reaches Newfoundland and possibly the Gulf of St. Lawrence, claiming the entire coast of present-day Canada for Portugal.

POLITICS

♦ France and Spain go to war in Italy over the partition of Naples. Beginning in July, the war continues until 1503.

- Arthur, Prince of Wales and heir to the English throne, dies in April, supposedly from a mysterious illness called the "sweating sickness."
- Arthur's younger brother Henry becomes Prince of Wales and heir to the English throne.
- King Henry VII of England refuses the request of Queen Isabella of Castile and King Ferdinand of Aragon to refund Princess Catherine's dowry.
- Peasants revolt in the bishopric of Speyer, Germany.
- Venetians seize Santa Maura from the Turks.
- Sarai, the capital of the Golden Horde (the Mongols on the Qipcaq steppe of Asia) is destroyed by armies under Ivan III, Grand Duke of Moscovy and ruler of Russia.

RELIGION

- All Muslims in Castile and Leon, Spain, are directed by Queen Isabella and King Ferdinand to choose between Christianity and exile.

LITERATURE AND THE ARTS

- Albrecht Dürer paints a watercolor of "The Hare," the most famous watercolor painting of the century..
- Giovanni Bellini paints "The Baptism of Christ."
- Sandro Botticelli paints "The Last Communion of St. Jerome."
- Lucas Cranach paints "The Crucifixion" in Vienna.
- Josquin Despres: *First Book of Masses*, printed by Ottaviano dei Petrucchi; Venice.
- Leonardo da Vinci is appointed chief engineer in the service of Caesare Borgia. Borgia, illegitimate son of Pope Alexander VI, is Duke of Romagna and Valentinois, Captain General of the Papal army, and onetime Cardinal.
- Aldine Press, Venice, publishes the first printed edition of Thucydides' *The Peloponnesian War*.

SOCIETY, EDUCATION

♦ Peter Henlein of Nuremberg, Germany constructs the first watch, called the "Nuremberg Egg."

♦ A Portuguese ship exports 2,000 ounces of gold, in the form of jewels and other objects, made by the Akan people in Ghana, Africa, who are noted for the beauty of their workmanship. Throughout the Portuguese occupation, 12 to 15 ships each carry that much back to Portugal every year, where it is melted down for its content.

♦ Margaret, Countess of Richmond and Derby, mother of King Henry VII, founds professorships of divinity at Oxford and Cambridge Universities, England.

1503

GEOGRAPHY

♦ Zanzibar becomes a Portuguese colony.

♦ Casa de la Contratacion (House of Commerce) is founded in Seville, Spain, to train and license navigators, and deal with affairs relating to West Indies trade.

POLITICS

♦ France is defeated by Spain at the Battles of Cerignola and Garig in April.

♦ Gonzalo de Cordova defeats the French army and enters Naples in May.

♦ Margaret Tudor, daughter of King Henry VII of England, marries King James IV of Scotland. She is the grandmother of Mary Queen of Scots, and the source of Mary's claim to the English throne.

♦ Pope Alexander VI and his son Caesare Borgia fall ill at a supper party, and it is thought that they were poisoned. The Pope contracts a fever and dies. Caesare recovers, but his dominion begins to fall apart.

♦ Pope Julius II, successor to Caesare's dead father Pope

Alexander VI, has Caesare Borgia arrested. Forced to surrender his castles, Borgia flees to Naples. Arrested there, he is imprisoned in Spain for two years, escaping in Nov. 1506 and fleeing to his brother-in-law, the King of Navarre.

♦ Ivan III, Grand Duke of Muscovy and ruler of Russia, dies and is succeeded by his son Vasili (Basil) III.

♦ Russia gains Lithuania and Polish border territories in war with Poland.

♦ Venice abandons Lepanto and signs a treaty with the Turks.

♦ War of Succession between Bavaria and the Palatinate.

♦ Henry Tudor, English Prince of Wales, is betrothed to Catherine of Aragon, his brother Arthur's widow.

RELIGION

♦ Pope Alexander VI dies of fever in Rome on August 18, but it may have been partially the result of poisoning.

♦ Pope Pius III (Cardinal Francesco Todeschini-Piccolomini) is elected Pope, dying on October 12.

♦ Pope Julius II (Giuliano della Rovere, the nephew of Pope Sixtus IV) is elected Pope on November 1.

♦ First English translation of Thomas à Kempis's treatise *On the Following* or *Imitation of Christ);* London. These admonitions for leading a spiritual life, written in mid 15th century, have continued in use from then until the present, by Christians of all sects.

LITERATURE AND THE ARTS

♦ Leonardo da Vinci begins to paint a portrait of "Mona Lisa," the Neapolitan wife of Zanobi del Giocondo (hence the portrait's familiar name "La Gioconda"); until apx.1505, in Florence, Italy.

SOCIETY, EDUCATION

♦ Pedro di Navarro of Spain uses explosive mines during the siege of Naples.

♦ Portuguese send African slaves to South America.
♦ Canterbury Cathedral is completed in England (begun in 1070).
♦ Nicolaus Copernicus becomes a doctor of canon law at Ferrara, Italy.

1504

POLITICS

♦ Queen Isabella of Castile dies, leaving King Ferdinand of Aragon a widower. Her daughter Juana is heir to Castile. Her grandson Archduke Charles of Hebsburg will become King Charles I of Spain in 1516, and in 1520 Holy Roman Emperor Charles V, founder of the Habsburg dynasty.
♦ Treaty of Lyons : King Louis XII of France cedes Naples to King Ferdinand of Aragon. Naples is now under Spanish control.
♦ Basil (Vasili) III, Grand Duke of Muscovy, is named "Sovereign of All Russia."
♦ Rupert, son of the Elector Palatine, is defeated in the Bavarian War by Albert of Bavaria.

RELIGION

♦ Desiderius Erasmus of Rotterdam: *Enchiridian Militis Christiani* (Handbook of the Christian Soldier). He explains the nature of Christianity for the general reader.

LITERATURE AND THE ARTS

♦ Michelangelo Buonarotti completes his giant statue of "David" in Florence, Italy (begun in 1501).
♦ Albrecht Dürer engraves "Adam and Eve"; paints "Adoration of the Magi."
♦ Lucas Cranach the Elder draws "Rest of the Virgin during the Flight into Egypt."
♦ Raphael paints "The Marriage of the Virgin."

- Giorgione paints "The Madonna" at Castelfranco Cathedral, Italy.
- Hieronymus Bosch receives a commission from Philip "the Handsome" of Habsburg, husband of Juana of Castile, to paint "The Last Judgment."

SOCIETY, EDUCATION

- King Henry VII of England places guilds and trade companies under the supervision of the Crown.
- Venice sends ambassadors to the Sultan of Turkey, proposing the construction of a Suez Canal.
- Postal service between Vienna and Brussels, begun in 1500 under the aegis of the Holy Roman Empire, is extended to Madrid.
- Pope Julius II issues a bull establishing the University of Santiago de Campostela in Spain.
- University of Seville, Spain, is founded.

1505

GEOGRAPHY

- Amerigo Vespucci, at the end of his second voyage, having sailed for 2,000 miles south along the coast of Brazil to a point beyond the Rio de la Plata (Argentina), concludes that South America is an independent continent, not part of India. Upon his return, he is appointed the first Pilot Major of the Casa de la Contratacion (to 1512). German mapmaker Martin Waldseemuller suggests that the new continent be named after him.
- Amerigo Vespucci publishes the pamphlet *Mundus Novus* in Lisbon, describing South America as a "new world."
- The Portuguese establish trading posts and factories on the Malabar (southwestern) coast of India.
- Francisco de Almeida is appointed first Viceroy of Portugal's territories in India, leaving Portugal with 21 ships for the Malabar (southwestern) coast of India.

POLITICS

♦ Treaty of Blois : King Ferdinand of Aragon, widower of Isabella of Castile, contracts to marry Germaine de Foix, niece of King Louis XII of France. King Louis resigns his rights in Naples to Germaine, but if Ferdinand dies without issue France will recover those portions assigned to Spain by the Treaty of Granada of 1500. Archduke Charles of Habsburg, future Holy Roman Emperor, is betrothed to Claude, infant daughter of King Louis XII of France. The engagement is broken off in 1506.

♦ Treaty of Salamanca: King Ferdinand of Aragon undertakes to rule Castile jointly with his daughter Juana of Castile and her husband Philip "the Handsome" of Habsburg.

♦ Maximilian of Habsburg, Emperor of Germany and King of the Romans, begins the reformation of the Holy Roman Empire, which he interprets as a universal Habsburg monarchy.

♦ Henry, English Prince of Wales, denounces his marriage contract with Catherine of Aragon, his brother Arthur's widow.

♦ Emperor Hongzhi, 10th Emperor of the Ming Dynasty in China, dies. The eunuch Liu Chin is all-powerful in the government.

LITERATURE AND THE ARTS

♦ Raphael paints "The Madonna of the Grand Duke."
♦ Lorenzo Lotto paints "The Maiden's Dream."
♦ Albrecht Dürer goes to Italy for the second time, remaining there until 1507.

SOCIETY, EDUCATION

♦ Martin Luther enters the Augustinian monastery at Erfurt.
♦ Albrecht Dürer travels from Germany to Venice in a total time of 14 days.
♦ Pope Julius II calls Michelangelo to Rome.

- Scipione del Ferro solves a form of cubic equation.
- Jakob Wimpfeling: *Epitoma rerum Germanicae*; the first general history of Germany; based on various original sources.
- John Colet is appointed Dean of St. Paul's Cathedral, London.
- Christ's College of Cambridge University, England, is founded by Margaret, Countess of Richmond and Derby.

1506

GEOGRAPHY

- Giovanni Contarini makes the first map of the Americas to be printed, showing the West Indies separated by only 20 degrees from Zipangu (Japan), with South America as "Terra Sancte Crucis"; Florence; engraved by Francesco Rosselli.
- Pope Julius II issues a bull, *Ea quae*, that prohibits any attempt to revive the Line of Demarcation established in Pope Alexander VI's bull of 1493, *Inter Caetera*, that divided the New World discoveries between Spain and Portugal along an imaginary boundary line from north to south a hundred leagues west of the Azores and Cape Verde Islands, providing that the land and sea beyond the line should be a Spanish sphere. *Ea quae* is the third of four bulls from Pope Alexander VI. The fourth, *Dudum siquidem*, had estended the previous grant to include "all islands and mainlands whatever, found or to be found . . . in sailing or travelling towards the west and south, whether they be in regions occidental or meridional and oriental and of India."
- Tritao da Cunha of Portugal discovers the island named after him.

POLITICS

- Philip "the Handsome" and Juana of Castile, sailing from the Netherlands to Castile to claim their inherited throne, are driven by storms to land in England, where they are entertained by King Henry VII at Windsor Castle in January.

♦ Treaty of Windsor in February: Philip "the Handsome" betrothes his sister Margaret of Austria, to King Henry VII. Philip agrees to undertake the extradition of the Yorkist pretender to the English throne, Edmund, Earl of Suffolk. Henry agrees to guard the Netherlands during Philip's absence in Spain, and to aid him, if needed, in conquering Castile.

♦ King Ferdinand of Aragon marries Germaine de Foix.

♦ Pope Julius II, at the head of an army, leaves Rome to conquer Perugia, later deposing the Duke of Bologna and taking Bologna.

♦ Philip "the Handsome" of Habsburg dies in September. Because his widow Juana of Castile is considered insane, a Council of Regency is nominated, led by Cardinal Jimenez.

♦ Edmund, Earl of Suffolk, extradited to England as per the Treaty of Windsor, is imprisoned in the Tower of London.

♦ Sigismund I ("the Old") becomes King of Poland. He was Grand Prince of Lithuania.

♦ Popular movement against the nobility in Genoa. The people appoint a Doge.

♦ Zhengde (Cheng Tih) becomes the 11th Emperor of the Ming Dynasty in China (to 1521).

RELIGION

♦ Pope Julius II lays the cornerstone for the new St. Peter's Basilica in Rome.

♦ First pogrom in Lisbon: 2,000 "converted" Jews are killed.

LITERATURE AND THE ARTS

♦ The Laocoön statue group (sculplted in 2 B.C.) is unearthed in Rome.

♦ Donato Bramante begins to build the new St. Peter's Basilica in Rome.

SCOCIETY, EDUCATION

♦ Jakob Fugger, Augsburg merchant, imports spices from the East Indies to Europe by sea, instead of using the land route.

♦ Niccolo Machiavelli creates a militia in Florence, the first national army in Italy.

♦ Syphilis, of the virulent and potentially fatal type, reaches China.

♦ Johann Reuchlin: *De Rudimentis Hebraicis* ; Pforzheim, Germany; Hebrew dictionary and grammar. A Christian humanist second only to Erasmus, he later fights against the suppression of Jewish books (in 1509).

♦ University of Frankfurt an der Oder is founded in Germany.

1507

GEOGRAPHY

♦ Martin Waldseemuller of Germany produces a map of the world (*Cosmographiae introductio*). The first use of the name "America," after Amerigo Vespucci, for the New World, his map shows South America as separate from Asia.

♦ Francanzano de Montalboddo: *Paesi novemente retrovati* (Newly Discovered Countries); the first great source book of the New World discoveries; Vicenza; six Italian editions, six French, and two German.

♦ Alvise Cadamosto: *La Prima Navigazione per l'Oceano alle terre de' Negri della Bassa Ethiopia*; an account of his exploration of The Gambia, on the west coast of Africa.

POLITICS

♦ Diet of Constance recognizes the unity of the Holy Roman Empire and founds the Imperial Chamber; imperial taxation and armed levies are made permanent.

♦ Margaret of Austria becomes Regent of the Netherlands

during the minority of the Archduke Charles of Habsburg (later the Holy Roman Emperor).

- King Henry VII of England reneges on his match with Margaret of Austria, and begins secret attempts to marry the widowed Juana of Castile.
- A marriage treaty is signed agreeing that the Archduke Charles of Habsburg will marry Princess Mary Tudor, daughter of King Henry VII of England.
- Caesare Borgia is killed in battle. The archtype of the Italian Renaissance "condottiere," he was the probable model for Machiavelli's *Il Principe* (The Prince).

RELIGION

- Pope Julius II proclaims that indulgences (remission of punishment for the souls of the dead in Purgatory) will be given to those who contribute money for the rebuilding St, Peter's Basilica in Rome. This is the "selling" of indulgences that Martin Luther protests in 1517.
- Martin Luther is ordained as a member of the Augustinian order.

LITERATURE AND THE ARTS

- Albrecht Dürer paints "Adam and Eve."
- Raphael paints "Holy family with a Palm."
- Lorenzo Lotto paints "Madonna and Child and Four Saints."

SOCIETY, EDUCATION

- Palazzo Strozzi is completed in Florence (begun in 1489).
- King Henry VII of England appoints Polydore Vergil as Historiographer Royal.
- Orlando Galla of Venice improves the manufacture of glass mirrors.
- Second epidemic of the "sweating sickness" in England, the first occuring in 1485. A mysterious, extremely fast-moving, often fatal (sometimes within a few hours) disease, it infected both rich and poor.

1508

GEOGRAPHY

♦ Ptolemy's *Geographia* is is published in Rome by Bernardus Venetus de Vitalibus, the first edition of the *Geographia* to include European voyages of exploration to the New World.

♦ The Spanish begin to keep a chart book record of their geographic discoveries, calling it the *Padron Real*. It is kept at the Casa de la Contratacion (House of Commerce) in Seville.

♦ Diego Lopes de Sequeira of Portugal explores Madagascar.

POLITICS

♦ Maximilian of Habsburg, Emperor of Germany, and King of the Romans since 1486, assumes the title of Holy Roman Emperor Maximilian I without being crowned.

♦ Pope Julius II confirms that Maximilian I has automatically become the Holy Roman Emperor.

♦ League of Cambrai : Margaret of Austria (Regent of the Netherlands), the Cardinal of Rouen and King Ferdinand of Aragon join forces with HRE Maximilian I and King Louis XII of France against Venice.

♦ HRE Maximilian I makes Augsburg financier Jakob Fugger a hereditary Knight of the Holy Roman Empire.

RELIGION

♦ Pope Julius II grants to the crown of Castile (Spain) the right to make all ecclesiastical appointments in its possessions in the Americas.

LITERATURE AND THE ARTS

♦ Michelangelo Buonarotti begins to paint the ceiling of the Sistine Chapel in Rome at the request of Pope Julius II (until 1512).

♦ Luca Signorelli paints "The Coronation of the Virgin" for the Filippini Chapel of the Church of St. Francis in Arcenia, Italy.

- The Elector of Saxony, Frederick the Wise, gives a signature motto to his court painter Lucas Cranach the Elder: a winged serpent with a ring in its mouth, that Cranach uses as signature on all his paintings from then on; Wittenberg, Germany.
- Raphael enters the service of Pope Julius II.
- *The Maying or Disport of Chaucer* is the first book printed in Scotland.

SOCIETY, EDUCATION

- Regular courses in Greek begin at the University of Paris, taught by Girolamo Aleandro.
- Guillaume Budé: *Annotationes in Pandectas* (Annotations on the Pandects) criticizes medieval interpretations of Roman law, urging scholars to study Roman law directly, with philology a necessary preparation for doing so.
- The University of Alcalá, Spain, is founded by the Archbishop of Toledo, Francisco Ximenes de Cisneros.

1509

GEOGRAPHY

- Battle of Diu establishes Portuguese control of the seas off western India: Francisco de Almeida , first Portuguese governor-general of the Malabar coast area, defeats a combined Gujerati and Egyptian fleet.
- Alfonso d'Alboquerque is appointed governor-general of the Malabar coast area as successor to Francisco d'Almeida . During his tenure, he strengthens existing bases and founds new ones.
- First European manual of navigation and nautical almanac is printed in Portugal: *Regimento do astrolabio e do quadrante*. It had been in circulation as a manuscript since the 1480's.

POLITICS

- Henry Tudor, King Henry VII of England, dies and is succeeded by his son, Henry, who becomes King Henry VIII (to 1547).

♦ King Henry VIII of England marries Catherine of Aragon, his brother Arthur's widow, and they are crowned together.

♦ Pope Julius II joins the League of Cambrai alliance.

♦ France declares war on Venice. Venice offers to deliver Faenza and Rimini to the papacy in order to divide the League of Cambrai , but the Pope refuses and excommunicates Venice.

♦ France defeats Italy at battle of Agnadello, and becomes master of northern Italy in May, but Venice regains control of Padua in July.

♦ Jakob Fugger of Augsburg lends 170,000 ducats to HRE Maximilian I to finance his war against Venice.

RELIGION

♦ Persecution of Jews in Germany: the converted Jew, Johann Pfefferkorn, receives authority from HRE Maximilian I to confiscate and destroy all Jewish books, especially the Talmud; the Christian humanist Johoann Reuchlin opposes the action.

♦ John Fisher: *The Seven Penitential Psalms*; London, Wynkyn de Worde.

LITERATURE AND THE ARTS

♦ Alexander Barclay translates Sebastian Brant's 1494 satire *Narrenschiff* (Ship of Fools) into English; London, Richard Pynson.

♦ Raphael Sanzio is hired by Pope Julius II to paint the rooms (*camare*) of the Vatican.

♦ Gerard David paints "The Madonna and Child with Saints and Musical Angels," that includes liknesses of himself and his wife.

♦ William Cornysh is appointed Master of the Children (director of the children's choir) of the English Chapel Royal.

SOCIETY, EDUCATION

♦ An earthquake destroys Constantinople.

- An artisan makes the first wallpaper (tapestries with glue-coated backs) for use at the master's lodging of Christ College, Cambridge University, England.

- Bartolome de Las Casas, Catholic Bishop of Chiapas, Mexico, recommends that every Spanish colonist should bring some Negro slaves with him to the new world, in order to prevent harsh treatment of the Mexican natives.

- Francesco Guicciardini writes *Historia Fiorentina*; Florentine history from 1378 to 1509. This remained unpublished until 1859.

- Basenose College, Oxford, and St. John's College, Cambridge, are founded in England.

- John Colet, Dean of St. Paul's Cathedral in London, endows St. Paul's School (to 1512). Greek, Latin and a good Christian education are to be given to 153 scholars.

- Erasmus of Rotterdam becomes a professor of Greek and divinity at Cambridge University, England (to 1514).

1510-1519

1510

GEOGRAPHY

- The Portuguese acquire Goa, a large and prosperous city on an island off the Malabar coast of western India.
- The Spanish esplore the North American east coast as far north as Charleston, S.C.
- The Spanish settle on the island of Puerto Rico in the West Indies.
- Ludovico de Varthema: *Itinerario*—relating his travels (1502-07) to the East via the Red Sea and his return around the Cape of Good Hope. He is the first Christian to enter Mecca and leave to tell about it. The book is an immediate success, with many editions.

POLITICS

- Pope Julius II absolves the Venetian Republic from the excommunication of 1509, and withdraws from the League of Cambrai.
- Pope Julius II and the Venetian Republic form the Holy League to drive King Louis XII of France out of Italy .
- Pedro Navarro takes Tripoli and Algiers for Spain, but is killed in an ambush in North Africa.
- Hamburg, Germany, becomes a Free City of the Holy Roman Empire.

◆ The Principality of Moscow annexes the town of Pskov from Poland.

◆ Shah Ismail of Persia drives the Usbeks from Khorasan.

RELIGION

◆ Martin Luther visits Rome as a delegate of the Augustinian order.

LITERATURE AND THE ARTS

◆ Lucas Cranach the Elder begins a woodcut series of "Christ and the Twelve Apostles" (to 1515).

SOCIETY, EDUCATION

◆ Leonardo da Vinci designs a horizontal water wheel (based on the principle of the water turbine).

◆ A French upholsterer makes the first "air bed," an inflatable mattress he calls the "wind bed."

◆ The London Company of Mercers is appointed trustees of St. Paul's School, the first example of non-clerical management in education.

◆ A New Sumptuary Law is passed in England, regulating the dress to be worn by the different classes so they can be immediately distinguished at first sight. There are specific directives about which colors, fabrics, types of furs, etc., may be worn by which class.

1511

GEOGRAPHY

◆ The Portuguese, under Alfonso d'Alboquerque, conquer Malacca in the Indonesian archipelago, placing the western terminus of Chinese trade in Portuguese hands. They also discover the spice-producing island of Amboyna.

◆ Diego de Velasquez de Cuellar occupies Cuba for Spain.

◆ Vasco Nunez de Balboa founds a Spanish colony at Darien, Panama.

- The Spanish establish the Council of the Indies to coordinate the administration of the colonies in the Americas.
- Ptolemy's *Geographiae* is published in Venice, containing 28 maps. The text is edited and corrected by Bernardus Sylvanus of Eboli, the first to question and amend Ptolemy's works. This is the first use of cordiform projection.

POLITICS

- HRE Maximilian I and King Henry VIII of England join the Holy League against France.

LITERATURE AND THE ARTS

- Mathias Grunewald begins to paint the Isenheim altar triptych (nine paintings; completed in 1516); Maintz, Germany. Grunewald is the *Mathis der Maler* (Mathias the Painter) of Paul Hindemith's twentieth century opera of that name.
- Albrecht Dürer paints "The Adoration of the Trinity."
- Arnolt Schlick: *Spiegel der Orgelmacher und Organisten*; Speyer, Germany. This is the first work published in German on organ building and playing, for which HRE Maximilian I grants Schlick 10 years of copyright protection.

SOCIETY, EDUCATION

- An edition of Vegetius' treatise *De Re Militari* (On Military Matters) is published. First written in the 4th century, it was used extensively in Medieval and Renaissance Europe, and contains an engraving depicting an underwater diver using a breathing tube.
- King Henry VIII of England begins to reform the Royal Navy.

1512

GEOGRAPHY

- Sebastian Cabot makes a map of Gascony and Guienne for King Henry VIII of England.

POLITICS

- ◆ The Swiss join the Holy League, and drive the French out of Milan.
- ◆ The French defeat Spanish and papal forces at Ravenna, Italy. The hero of the battle is Pierre du Terrail, Chevalier de Bayard "le chevalier sans peur et sans reproche" (the knight without fear and without reproach).
- ◆ England and France go to war, a revival of the Hundred Years War (to 1513). King Henry VIII of England spends four months in the field, returning home in triumph.
- ◆ Russia and Poland go to war (until 1522).
- ◆ Selim I becomes Sultan of Turkey (to 1520), after forcing his father, Bayezid II, to abdicate.

RELIGION

- ◆ The Fifth Council of the Lateran is convened on May 5 in Rome by Pope Leo X, at the Basilica of St. John Lateran. It condemns all who believe the individual soul is mortal, and pronounces that the immortality of the soul is church dogma which must be accepted by the faithful (to March 16, 1517).
- ◆ All Jewish goldsmiths and merchants are expelled from Timbuktu and Gao, Africa, by Mohammed Askia.

LITERATURE AND THE ARTS

- ◆ Michelangelo Buonarotti completes painting the frescos on the Sistine Chapel ceiling in Rome, after four years of work.
- ◆ Leonardo da Vinci moves to Rome.
- ◆ Raphael paints a portrait of Pope Julius II.
- ◆ Josquin Despres: *Second book of Masses*; Venice; Petrucci.
- ◆ Arnolt Schlick: *Tabulaturen etlicher lobgesang* ; Maintz, Germany. These are the first German printed organ tabulatures, and include some of Schlick's own compositions. It was published as a practical companion to his *Spiegel der Orgelmacher und Organisten* of 1511.

- Florentine sculptor Pietro Torrigiano arrives in England to design and build a tomb for King Henry VII and his Queen (to 1517).

- The first use of the word *masque* to denote a poetic form of drama appears in an entry for 1512 in Edward Halle's *Chronicle* (first published in 1542, entitled *Union of the Noble Families of Lancastre and Yorke*). He describes the first masque known to have been performed at the court of King Henry VIII: "on the day of Epiphany at night the King, with eleven others, were disguised after the manner of Italy called a Mask, a thing not seen before in England."

SOCIETY, EDUCATION

- The English Parliament passes a law forbidding the games of tennis, bowls and skittles. The owners of any premises where they are played will be punished.

- The English Parliament passes a law requring every man over 17 and under 60, except priests and high court judges, to keep a longbow and four arrows in his house.

- The English Parliament forbids anyone to practice as either a physician or surgeon within seven miles of the city of London without a licence from the Bishop of London or the Dean of St. Pauls (that can be obtained only after examination by four doctors of physic); or outside the London area without a license from the diocesan bishop.

- Most of Westminster Palace, one of King Henry VIII's royal residences, is destroyed by fire. It is never rebuilt as a residence. Westminster Hall escapes destruction.

- The English Royal Navy builds double-deck ships of 1,000 tons with 70 guns.

- English troops mutiny in Spain because of lack of beer. Sent by King Henry VIII to northern Spain to assist King Ferdinand of Aragon in taking the kingdom of Navarre away from the French, the soldiers were told that no beer was available, only wine or cider. Lacking their daily ration of beer, they rebelled, and their commander, the Marquess of Dorset was forced to bring them home.

1513

GEOGRAPHY

◆ Vasco Nunez de Balboa of Spain crosses the Isthmus of Panama at Darien and discovers the Pacific Ocean. It was, however, named the "Pacific" Ocean by Fernando Magellan; Balboa calls it the "South Sea."

◆ Juan Ponce de Leon, governor of the Spanish Colony at Puerto Rico, lands in Florida on Easter Sunday, naming the land "Pascua Florida."

◆ A Portuguese expedition under Jorge Alvarez reachs Canton, China, the first recorded visit of European vessels to Chinese waters in more than 150 years.

◆ Francisco Serrao of Portugal explores Java, Timor, and reaches the Moluccas ("the Spice Islands").

◆ Martin Waldseemuller, German cartographer, publishes what is in effect **the first atlas**, an edition of Ptolemy's *Geographia*, in Strasbourg. It shows greater detail of the new discoveries and includes two up-to-date maps of Africa, illustrating all known coastal places.

POLITICS

◆ The Battle of Flodden Field between England and Scotland is fought. King James IV of Scotland is killed.

◆ James IV's infant son James becomes King James V of Scotland, with his mother Margaret Tudor as Regent.

◆ The Battle of Novara is fought. The French are driven out of Italy.

◆ The French attack, but fail to take, the strategic city of Fuenterrabia in northern Spain.

◆ King Henry VIII of England meets HRE Maximilian I at Therouanne, France (near St. Omer).

- HRE Maximilian I tells King Henry VIII of England that he may eventually resign his empire to him, and may adopt him as a son and grant him the Duchy of Milan. None of this ever comes to pass.
- Treaty of Mechlin : HRE Maximilian I, King Henry VIII of England, Pope Leo X, and King Ferdinand of Aragon agree to invade France.
- Christian II becomes the last King of United Scandinavia (Denmark, Sweden and Norway). In 1513, he is crowned King of Denmark and Norway. In 1515, he is crowned King of Sweden.

RELIGION

- Pope Julius II dies in February. He initiated the tradition of Papal patronage of the arts, a tradition that continued into the 17th century.
- Pope Leo X (Giovanni de' Medici, son of Lorenzo the Magnificent) is crowned. He is the first of two Medici popes, the second being his cousin Giulio, who reigned as Clement VII from 1523.
- Jews are allowed to return to Florence (banished in 1494).

LITERATURE AND THE ARTS

- Niccolò Machiavelli writes *Il Principe* (The Prince); published in 1532. The Prince's character is based on Caesare Borgia, son of Pope Alexander VI. Machiavelli publishes the comedy, *La Mandragola*.
- Michelangelo sculpts the statue of *Moses*; Rome.
- Albrecht Dürer engraves "Knight, Death and the Devil" (apx. date).
- William Cornysh takes the Chapel Royal singers to France in the retinue of King Henry VIII of England.
- Andrea Antico is awarded the first privilege to print music in the Papal States by Pope Leo X.

♦ Pope Leo X begins to establish a sculpture gallery at the Vatican.

♦ The Aldine Press, Venice, publishes an edition of Plato.

SOCIETY, EDUCATION

♦ Raphael draws up plans for the excavation of the buildings of ancient Rome.

♦ A Greek printing press is established in Rome.

♦ Alfonso d'Alboquerque , Portuguese governor-general on the Malabar (southwestern) coast of India, sends a performing elephant to Pope Leo X.

♦ King Manoel I of Portugal offers the Pope a lifesize sugar effigy of himself, depicted as surrounded by 12 cardinals and 300 candles, one and a half metres high.

1514

GEOGRAPHY

♦ Santiago, founded by Diego de Valasquez de Cuellar, becomes the capital of Cuba.

♦ Pope Leo X issues the bull *Praecelsae devotionis*, giving his blessing to discoveries and conquests by the Portuguese, and granting Portugal all lands which might be seized from heathen peoples in Africa, India and any other region that might be reached by sailing east.

POLITICS

♦ Turkey and Persia go to war.

♦ Anne of Brittany, Queen of France, dies.

♦ Princess Mary Tudor, sister of King Henry VIII of England, marries King Louis XII of France.

♦ King Louis XII's daughter Claude marries his nephew François, Duke of Angoulême (later King François I of France).

♦ Margaret Tudor, Regent of Scotland, marries Archibald Douglas, Earl of Angus.

- HRE Maximilian I and King Ferdinand I of Spain sign a truce with King Louis XII of France.
- A peasants' revolt in Hungary, led by George Dozsa, is suppressed by John Zapolya.
- Basil (Vasili) III, ruler of Russia, takes the town of Smolensk from Poland.
- Polish-Lithuanian armies crush the Russians at Orsza.
- Sultan Selim I of Turkey defeats Shah Ismail of Persia at Tchadiran, and enters Tabriz.

RELIGION

- The House of Fugger, merchant bankers of Augsburg, obtains the right to sell papal indulgences in Germany.
- Thomas Wolsey is named Archbishop of York in England, and begins construction of the palace of Hampton Court.
- The University of Alcala de Henares, Spain, begins to publish a "Polyglot Bible" (Latin, Greek, Hebrew, and Aramaic), known as *The Complutensian Bible*; to 1517.
- Pope Leo X issues a Bull calling for reforms of the cardinalate and papal administration.

LITERATURE AND THE ARTS

- Raphael paints a portrait of Baldassare Castiglione, author of *The Courtier*
- Michelangelo works on the Chapel at Castel St. Angelo, Rome.

SOCIETY, EDUCATION

- King Louis XII of France grants the guild of vinegar-makers the privilege of distilling it to make brandy.
- The Corporation of Trinity House is founded in London to provide navigational help on the Thames River.
- Silver mines are opened in western Yunnan, China.
- The Cathedral of Salamanca, Spain, is begun (completed in 1733).
- Pineapples are first imported to Europe.

1515

GEOGRAPHY

♦ The Portuguese capture the island of Hormuz, giving them effective control of the Strait of Hormuz, and thus the entire Persian Gulf.

POLITICS

♦ King Louis XII of France dies in January.

♦ François de Valois, Duke of Angoulême, becomes King of France as François I.

♦ Mary Tudor, widow of King Louis XII of France, secretly marries Charles Brandon, Duke of Suffolk, in February. Her brother, King Henry VIII of England, pardons them after the Duke makes over to him Mary's dowry from her marriage to Louis, and pays a fine of £ 24,000. They are publicly married in May.

♦ The English and French sign a peace treaty.

♦ The French defeat the Swiss and regain Milan at the Battle of Marignano. Pierre de Terrail, the Chevalier de Bayard, wins the brilliant victory for King François I, who, in order to honor him, allows himself to be knighted by the Chevalier.

♦ The French and Swiss sign the Treaty of Geneva.

♦ Treaty of Vienna between HRE Maximilian I, King Sigismund I of Poland, and King Vladislav of Hungary concerning mutual royal succession of the Habsburg and Jagellon families.

♦ HRE Maximilian I cedes Verona, Italy, to the Venetians.

♦ Archduke Charles Habsburg of Austria becomes Governor of the Netherlands.

♦ King Christian II of Denmark and Norway overthrows Sten Sture, Regent of Sweden, and becomes King of Sweden as well. He is crowned in 1520, thus becoming King of United Scandinavia.

- The Kingdom of Navarre comes under the crown of Castile (Spain).
- Frederick the Wise, Elector of Saxony joins the Elector Palatine, the Duke of Wurttemberg and the Margrave of Baden in their union opposing the Swabian League.
- The Scottish Parliament names the Duke of Albany, nephew of King James III, as Lord Protector of Scotland. Margaret Tudor, Queen Regent, flees to England.
- Turks under Sultan Selim I defeat the Persians at the battle of Chaldiran in Armenia, afterwards marching on to Tabriz and annexing the upper portion of the Tigris-Euphrates valley (Kurdistan).

RELIGION

- The Lateran Council's decree *De impressione librorum* forbids printing of books without permission of the church authorities.
- Thomas Wolsey, Archbishop of York, is made Lord Chancellor of England and becomes a Cardinal.

LITERATURE AND THE ARTS

- Desiderius Erasmus: *Moriae Encomium* (The Praise of Folly); Paris; dedicated to Sir Thomas More.
- Lodovico Ariosto, court poet for Duke Alfonso d'Este in Ferrara: *Orlando Furioso*. This is an epic poem about the hero Roland, intended as a continuation of Boiardo's unfinished 15th century narrative poem *Orlando Innamorato*, about the Charlemagne romances. Dedication: "For the Delight and Recreation of the Lords, and persons of gentle soul, and for the Ladies . . ."
- English morality play *Everyman*, based on the 1495 Dutch morality play *Eickerlijk* by Pieter Dorland van Diest; R. Pynson, London.
- Raphael is appointed architect-in-chief of St. Peter's Basilica, Rome, and does tapestry cartoons for the Sistine Chapel (to 1516).

- Titian paints "Sacred and Profane Love"; Venice.
- Correggio paints "The Madonna of St. Francis."
- Hans Holbein the Younger moves to Basel, Switzerland, settling there in 1520. Here, he does many woodcuts and drawings for stained glass, as well as portraits, including one of Erasmus.
- Hampton Court Palace is completed for Cardinal Wolsey in England.

SOCIETY, EDUCATION

- The first use of the "Iron Maiden" torture device is recorded in Nuremberg, Germany.
- The first nationalized factories, for the manufacture of weapons and tapestries, are established in France.

1516

GEOGRAPHY

- Juan Diaz de Solis, Pilot Major of Spain, searching for a passage to the Pacific Ocean, explores the estuary of the Rio de la Plata in present-day Argentina. He is killed there.
- The Portuguese reach China. Raphael Perestrello has been sent there by the Indian Viceroy, Alboquerque.

POLITICS

- Ferdinand of Aragon, King of Spain, dies in January.
- Charles of Habsburg, grandson of Ferdinand of Aragon and Isabella of Castile, son of Philip "the Handsome"of Habsburg, and Juana "la loca"(the mad) of Castile is crowned King Charles I of Spain. In 1520, he becomes Holy Roman Emperor Charles V. This is the foundation of the Habsburg dynasty in Spain. Cardinal Jimenez de Disneros is appointed Regent.
- Peace Treaty of Noyon between France and Spain, in August: the French relinquish their claim to the Kingdom of Naples and Milan remains under French control.

♦ Peace of Brussels : HRE Maximilian I accedes to the Peace of Noyon , overturning his treaty with England, waiving his claims to Italy for 200,000 ducats, and handing control of Verona to Venice.

♦ Treaty of Freiburg : France and the Swiss agree to permanent peace. This treaty remains in force until 1789.

♦ Sultan Selim I of Turkey defeats the Egyptians at the battle of Marj-dabik, near Aleppo, and annexes Syria.

RELIGION

♦ The Dominican monk Johann Tetzel sells indulgences in Germany.

♦ Jews are expelled from Genoa, Italy. They are allowed to return in 1517.

♦ The Concordat of Bologna between Pope Leo X and King François I of France stipulates that France will have internal independence in ecclesiastical appointments, and that appeals to Rome from France will be restricted.

♦ Erasmus of Rotterdam publishes a New Testament with both Greek and Latin texts; Basel, Switzerland.

LITERATURE AND THE ARTS

♦ Sir Thomas More: *Utopia* (published in Latin); Louvain. A second edition appears in Paris in 1517 and in Basle in 1518. In 1519, editions are published in Florence, Vienna, and Venice. It is translated into English in 1551.

♦ Dosso Dossi , court painter for Duke Alfonso d'Este of Ferrara, paints "Melissa," depicting the good witch of Lodovico Ariosto's *Orlando Furioso*.

♦ Raphael paints "The Sistine Madonna" in Rome.

♦ Mathias Grunewald completes the Isenheim Altarpiece.

♦ King François I of France invites Leonardo da Vinci to stay in France, installing him at the Castle of Cloux, near Amboise, with a retainer of seven hundred crowns a year. Leonardo remains here until his death.

SOCIETY, EDUCATION

- ♦ Indigo blue dye comes to Europe.
- ♦ Franz von Taxis is named postmaster-general of the Netherlands. The imperial mail service is extended to Rome and Naples.

1517

GEOGRAPHY

- ♦ Portuguese found a factory in Colombo, Ceylon. They visit China with nine ships under Ferdinand de Andrada.
- ♦ Francisco Hernandez de Cordova of Spain discovers the Yucatan peninsula in Mexico.

POLITICS

- ♦ Ottoman Turks under Sultan Selim I capture Cairo, Egypt, bringing the Mameluke Empire to an end. Arabia, Syria and Egypt are added to the Ottoman Empire.

RELIGION

- ♦ **Martin Luther writes 95 theses protesting the sale of indulgences by the Catholic Church** (an indulgence is the remission of punishment for sins) in Wittenberg, Germany. There is no evidence that he posted the theses on a church door, but they were publicly circulated. **The Protestant Reformation begins.**
- ♦ Pope Leo X closes the Lateran Council in Rome, declaring that all reforms of the Church have been accomplished.
- ♦ Johann Reuchlin: *De arte cabbalistica*—the author's own mystical ideas grounded in the Jewish Kabbalah.

LITERATURE AND THE ARTS

- ♦ Andrea del Sarto paints "The Madonna of the Harpies."
- ♦ Quentin Matsys: portrait of Erasmus.
- ♦ Andrea Antico: *Frottole intabulate da sonare organi libro*

primo; Rome; the first printed publication of Italian keyboard music notated in keyboard tablature.

SOCIETY, EDUCATION

♦ "Evil May Day" riots in London; 2,000 rioters protest the presence of foreigners in London, assaulting them and looting their shops. Sixty rioters are hanged on Cardinal Wolsey's orders.

♦ A virulunt third epidemic of the "sweating sickness" appears in England, spreading across the English Channel to Calais and Antwerp.

♦ A Royal Commission on enclosure of common lands is appointed in England.

♦ The wheel-lock musket is invented by a gunsmith in Nuremberg, Germany.

♦ The Cathedral of Seville, Spain, is completed (begun in 1402).

♦ Father Diego Daza, Archbishop of Seville, Grand Inquisitor of the Faith, and Confessor of the Royal Court, establishes the Dominican Colegio de San Tomas in Seville, Spain.

♦ Corpus Christi College, Oxford University, is founded by Richard Fox, Bishop of Winchester in England.

♦ College de Trois Langues (College of Three Languages) is established in Louvain, now Belgium.

1518

GEOGRAPHY

♦ Juan de Grijalva of Spain explores the Yucatan coast of Mexico.

♦ The Barbary States of Algiers and Tunis are founded.

POLITICS

♦ The Treaty of London creates an organization to promote collective security among the European powers. It is signed in October by England, France, HRE Maximilian I, Spain, and the Pope. It was devised by England's Cardinal Wolsey. Two days after the signing, a proxy marriage celebration is held for Princess Mary Tudor, daughter of King Henry VIII of England, and the Dauphin of France.

LITERATURE AND THE ARTS

♦ Raphael paints a portrait of Pope Leo X accompanied by two Cardinals.

♦ Albrecht Dürer paints a portrait of Jakob Fugger, the Augsburg merchant banker.

♦ Lodovico Ariosto, court poet for the Duke d'Este in Ferarra, arranges regular dramatic performances in the theatre at court.

SOCIETY, EDUCATION

♦ The Royal College of Physicians is founded in London by Thomas Linacre.

♦ Pynson Publishers of London use Roman type face for one of their books.

♦ The Flemish merchant Lorens de Gominot receives a license (*asiento*) from King Charles I of Spain to import 4,000 African slaves to the Spanish American colonies for a period of eight years.

♦ King François I of France orders two daggers with watches (horloges) set into their gold-covered (gilded) pommels, for his personal use.

♦ East Asian porcelain is imported to Europe.

♦ Leonardo da Vinci, resident in France as a guest of King François I, draws up plans for a grand canal linking the Seine and Soane rivers.

♦ Johannis Trithemius: *Polygraphia*; Oppenheim, Germany; treatise on cyphers. It is published in French in 1561. Cyphers and codes were used extensively throughout the century.

1519

GEOGRAPHY

♦ Fernando Magellan, Portuguese navigator employed by Spain, leaves in September with five ships on his voyage of exploration, seeking a water passage to the Molucca spice islands. **Completed in 1522, this is the first circumnavigation of the globe.** In October, he discovers the Strait of Magellan at the tip of South America. After five weeks of storms in the strait, he comes to an ocean where he voyages in good weather and calm seas, naming the ocean "Pacific." Voyaging further in the Southern Hemisphere, he identifies earth's two closest galactic neighbors (160,000 light years away), that are later named the Large and Small Magellanic Clouds in his honor. Magellan carries trade goods supplied by the Fuggers of Augsburg.

♦ The Spanish found a colony at Panama.

♦ Domenico Alvarez de Pineda of Spain explores the Gulf of Mexico, from Florida to the city of Vera Cruz in Mexico.

♦ Hernan Cortes of Spain, with 11 ships and 700 soldiers, sets out from Cuba and lands on the coast of Mexico, bringing Arabian horses to North America. In November, he enters Tenochtitlan (now Mexico City) and is received by Montezuma, the Aztec ruler.

♦ Portuguese traders reach Burma.

POLITICS

♦ HRE Maximilian I dies in January.

♦ King Henry VIII of England attempts to gain the Pope's support as a candidate in the election for the next Holy Roman Emperor, as successor to Maximilian I. Henry had at first supported the candidacy of King François I of France.

♦ Charles of Habsburg, King Charles I of Spain, grandson of HRE Maximilian I, is elected Holy Roman Emperor Charles V in June, reigning until 1556. He is opposed in the election by King François I of France, who is favored by Pope Leo X. A substantial amount of the 850,000 ducats used by Charles to finance his election is provided by the Fugger merchant banking house of Augsburg, Germany.

RELIGION

♦ The Protestant Reformation begins in Switzerland, led by Ulrich Zwingli.

♦ Martin Luther has a disputation in public with Johann Eck in Leipzig, Germany.

LITERATURE AND THE ARTS

♦ Albrecht Dürer draws a portrait of HRE Maximilian I.

SOCIETY, EDUCATION

♦ A settlement for paupers is established in Augsburg, Germany.

♦ St. George's Chapel at Windsor Castle , England, is completed (begun 1473).

♦ HRE Charles V orders that all worked gold objects from the New World are to be be melted down and valued for the "Royal Fifth" (the King's share).

♦ King François I of France begins construction of the Chateau of Chambord in the Loire Valley. Construction is interrupted a number of times, and finally broken off at the death of King Henri II in 1559, to be resumed in the 17th century. The original concept and design for the chateau are thought to be by Leonardo da Vinci, resident in France from 1517.

1520-1529

1520

GEOGRAPHY

- Fernando Magellan reaches the Pacific Ocean in November, and sails west toward the Philippine Islands, reaching them 110 days later.
- Portuguese traders settle in China.
- The Portuguese send a mission to Ethiopia (to 1526).

POLITICS

- "Field of the Cloth of Gold": King Henry VIII of England meets with King François I of France in June, near Calais, France, in a field between Guisnes and Ardres. England and France sign a treaty confirming the proposed marriage between the English princess Mary Tudor and the French dauphin, and for ending French interferance in Scottish affairs. Neither aim is achieved. The costumes and pavilions of both courts are so sumptuous that contemporaries describe it as the eighth wonder of the world.
- Charles V is formally crowned Holy Roman Emperor at Aachen (Aix-la-Chapelle) by Pope Leo X in October, having defeated François I of France in the election.
- Secret treaty between King Henry VIII of England and HRE Charles V.

791-MOSH

- Suleiman I (the "Magnificent") becomes Sultan of Turkey (to 1566). Turkish power is at its height.
- King Christian II of United Scandinavia defeats the Swedes at Lake Asunden, and is crowned King of Sweden in Stockholm. Four days later, in spite of his grant of amnesty, he massacres Eric Vasa and leading Swedish bishops and nobles in the "Swedish Bloodbath."
- Revolt of the "Comuneros" in northern Spain, as a protest against Habsburg rule. Towns throughout Castile protest King Charles's (also HRE Charles V) treatment of them (to 1521).

RELIGION

- Pope Leo X excommunicates Martin Luther in the bull *Exsurge*, and declares him to be a heretic. Luther publicly burns the bull.
- Martin Luther writes *Address to the most Serene and Mighty Imperial Majesty and to the Christian Noblilty of the German Nation*, urging German princes and nobles to nationalize the Church.
- The beginning of the Protestant Anabaptist religious movement in Germany is led by Thomas Munzer.

LITERATURE AND THE ARTS

- The Royal Library of France is founded by King François I at the Palace of Fontainbleau, with Guillaume Budé, scholar and humanist, as Royal Librarian.
- Lucas van Leyden does an etching and engraving of HRE Maximilian I, in commemoration of his death in 1519.
- Michelangelo designs the Medici Chapel in Florence (to 1534), with tombs for Lorenzo and Giuliano de' Medici.
- Giulio Romano completes Raphael's painting of "The Transfiguration" at the Vatican in Rome.
- Albrecht Altdorfer paints one of the earliest landscapes without figures, "Landscape with a Footbridge" (apx date).

♦ Titian paints "Bacchus and Ariadne."

♦ Heinrich Niehoff begins building organs in Amsterdam. Together with his son, grandson, and pupils, he builds a number of large organs in Flanders and northern Germany throughout the century.

♦ William Cornysh supervises the English Chapel Royal's musical ceremonies for the "Field of the Cloth of Gold," including the staging of pageants.

SOCIETY, EDUCATION

♦ The Chinese of the Ming Dynasty make their first use of cannon bought from the Portuguese.

♦ Chocolate is brought from Mexico to Spain, and is sold in slab form.

♦ Gaspard Koller invents rifling on fire-arms.

♦ King Henry VIII of England orders the building of bowling lanes at Westminster Palace, London, most of which was destroyed by fire in 1512.

♦ Aztec gold objects and jewels from Mexico are put on display at HRE Charles V's court in Brussels. Artist Albrecht Dürer, son of a goldsmith, expresses amazement at their remarkable quality of design and workmanship.

1521

GEOGRAPHY

♦ Fernando Magellan and 40 of his crew are killed by natives in the islands later called the Philippines, during his expedition circumnavigating the globe.

♦ Hernan Cortes of Spain conquers the Aztecs in Mexico at their city of Tenochtitlan, the site of present-day Mexico City, after an eight-week siege. This is the end of the Aztec empire. At this time, the native population of the region is about eleven million. Twenty years later it is 6 1/2 million, and by the end of the century it is reduced to 2 1/2 million.

♦ Francisco de Gordillo of Spain explores the American Atlantic coast as far north as South Carolina.

POLITICS

♦ France and Spain go to war over rival claims to Italy (until 1529).

♦ The French capture the city of Fuenterrabia in northern Spain (recovered by Spain in 1524).

♦ Spanish "Comuneros" rebels are defeated and the leaders of the anti-Habsburg movement are executed.

♦ HRE Charles V grants his brother, Archduke Ferdinand of Habsburg, the Habsburg possessions in Lower Austria, Carinthia, Styria and Carinola.

♦ Archduke Ferdinand of Habsburg marries Anna, daughter of King Ladislaus of Hungary and Bohemia, bringing both these kingdoms under the rule of Austria.

♦ Mary of Austria marries Louis, King of Hungary.

♦ John III "the Pious" becomes King of Portugal (to 1557) upon the death of his father, King Manuel I.

♦ The Turks under Sultan Suleiman I the Magnificent take the city of Belgrade.

♦ The Papal States declare bankruptcy.

RELIGION

♦ The First Diet of Worms is convened in Germany by HRE Charles V. Protestant leader Martin Luther defends his doctrines before Charles and the Papal Nuncio. Luther is banned from the Holy Roman Empire and his books are ordered destroyed. Imprisoned in the Wartburg, he begins a German translation of the Bible.

♦ Pope Leo X issues a bull naming King Henry VIII of England "Defender of the Faith" for his book written in opposition to Martin Luther (*Assertio septem sacramentorum*

(Defense of the Seven Sacraments). This title is still used by British sovereigns.

♦ John Fisher, Bishop of Rochester and Chancellor of Cambridge University: *Sermon*; London; an argument in opposition to the Lutheran schism.

♦ Pope Leo X dies in December.

LITERATURE AND THE ARTS

♦ Niccolò Machiavelli: *Libro dell' arte della guerra* (The Art of War); Florence; written for his patron Lorenzo de' Medici.

♦ Lucas Cranach the Elder does a woodcut portrait of Martin Luther disguised as "Junker Jorg" (Lord George) for a secret visit to Wittenberg after the Diet of Worms.

SOCIETY, EDUCATION

♦ The manufacture of silk is introduced to France.

♦ Peasants on the island of Majorca revolt and massacre the nobility.

♦ John Major: *Historia Majoris Britanniae* (A History of GreaterBritain); Paris. Among Major's pupils was Protestant leader John Knox.

1522

GEOGRAPHY

♦ One ship out of the five that sailed in 1519 with Magellan's expedition completes the **first circumnavigation of the globe**, arriving in Spain in September under the command of Sebastian del Cano. Thirty-five out of the original 280 crew members survive the three year voyage. The circumnavigation establishes the diameter of the earth at 25,000 miles, as the ancient Greek mathematician and geographer Eratosthenes had predicted.

♦ Sebastian del Cano, while completing Magellan's circumnavigation of the globe, discovers New Amsterdam Island.

♦ Spanish forces conquer Guatemala.

- HRE Charles V appoints Hernan Cortes Governor of New Spain (Mexico).
- Pascual de Andagoya of Spain leads a land expedition from Panama to discover Peru (Biru).
- Francisco Montano of Spain climbs Mount Popocatepetl, Mexico
- Portuguese ships reach Brunei, North West Borneo.
- Giovanni da Verrazano captures two treasure ships sent by Hernan Cortez from Mexico to Spain, turning the treasure over to King François I of France, who decides that the Americas are worth his attention.

POLITICS

- HRE Charles V defeats the French at the Battle of Biocca, driving them out of Milan. Later, he also drives them out of Genoa.
- England declares war against France and Scotland.
- Treaty of Brussels : HRE Charles V grants his brother, Archduke Ferdinand of Austria, the Habsburg possessions in southwestern Germany and the Tirol.
- HRE Charles V goes to England, where he signs the Treaty of Windsor with King Henry VIII, in which they agree to invade France in May 1524. He also visits with his aunt, Queen Catherine of Aragon.
- English forces ravage Normany and Picardy in France.
- King Henry VIII of England refuses to continue the truce with Scotland as long as the Duke of Albany remains north of the border.
- The War of the German Knights under Ulrich von Hutten and Franz von Sickingen is fought against the bishoprics. Von Sickingen lays siege to Trier.
- The Turks under Sultan Suleiman I take the Island of Rhodes from the Knights of St. John, who relocate to Malta in 1530, thereafter calling themselves the Knights of Malta.

- HRE Charles V, who is also King Charles I of Spain, returns to Spain, remaining there until 1527.
- Lübeck declares war on Denmark, and ravages Bornholm.
- Danish nobles revolt against King Christian II of United Scandinavia (Denmark, Sweden and Norway), alleging his misrule.
- Jiajing (Chia Ching) becomes the 12th Emperor the of the Ming Dynasty in China (to 1567).

RELIGION

- Adrian of Utrecht, Regent of Spain, is elected Pope Adrian VI as successor to Pope Leo X.
- Martin Luther returns to Wittenburg. He condemns fanatics and iconoclasts, and introduces a liturgy in German, with communion in both kinds for the laity. He also finishes translating the New Testament into German (the Old Testament is completed in 1534). Wittenberg printer Hans Lufft produces 100,000 copies of it during the next 40 years.
- Protestant leader Ulrich Zwingli condemns fasting and the celibacy of priests in Zurich, Switzerland.

SOCIETY, EDUCATION

- Hamburg, Germany: a physician is executed for dressing as a woman so he can observe childbirth.
- Albrecht Dürer designs a flying machine for use in war.
- Spanish philosopher and humanist, Juan Luis Vives, is brought to England to be tutor to Princess Mary Tudor, daughter of King Henry VIII and Queen Catherine of Aragon. He is imprisoned in 1527 for opposing King Henry's divorce from Catherine of Aragon.
- While visiting in England, HRE Charles V and King Henry VIII play tennis together at Baynards Castle in London as partners in a doubles match against the Prince of Orange and the Marquis of Brandenburg. The match ends in a draw.

1523

GEOGRAPHY

♦ The Spanish found the town of Villa de la Vega (now known as "Spanish Town") on the island of Jamaica in the West Indies. This is the capitol of Jamaica from 1523 to 1872.

♦ The Portuguese are expelled from China.

POLITICS

♦ Gustavus Vasa is elected King of Sweden, as Gustavus I, after leading a successful revolt against King Christian II of United Scandinavia. This marks the end of the Kalmar Union among the three Scandinavian kingdoms.

♦ Danes depose King Christian II, electing his uncle, the Duke of Schleswig Holstein, as King Frederick I (to 1533).

♦ Sir Thomas More is elected Speaker of the English House of Commons.

RELIGION

♦ Pope Adrian VI dies.

♦ Pope Clement VII (Guilio de' Medici, the illegitimate son of the younger brother of Lorenzo the Magnificent) is crowned.

♦ The first Lutheran martyrs are burned at the stake in Brussels.

LITERATURE AND THE ARTS

♦ Hans Sachs: *Die Wittenbergisch Nachtigal* (The Wittenberg Nightingale); Nurnberg, Germany; an allegorical tale praising Martin Luther's reforms. Sachs, a master in the Nurnberg Singschule from 1517 was the most prolific German dramatist/poet of the 16th century, and a principal character in Richard Wagner's 1868 opera*Die Meistersinger von Nurnberg.*

♦ Titian paints "Bacchus and Ariadne" for Duke Alfonso d'Este in Ferrara (some sources give the date as 1520).

- Hans Holbein the Younger paints a portrait of Erasmus of Rotterdam, and does illustrations for "The Dance of Death."
- Dosso Dossi paints "Jupiter, Mercury and Virtue" at the court of Duke Alfonso d'Este in Ferrara, where he is court painter.
- Giulio Romano paints "The Stoning of St. Stephen."

SOCIETY, EDUCATION

- A plague epidemic occurs in Paris during the summer.
- The first maritime insurance policies are issued at Florence, Italy.
- Anthony Fitzherbert: *Book of Husbandry*; London; the first manual of agricultural practice.

1524

GEOGRAPHY

- Giovanni da Verrazano, a Florentine navigator sailing for France, explores the eastern coast of North America. Landing at North Carolina, he discovers New York Bay, Manhattan Island and the Hudson River, and continues north as far as Newfoundland. His written account for King François I is the first description of the northeast coast of America.
- Esteban Gomez of Spain sails along the North American coast from Nova Scotia to Florida (to 1525).
- The Spanish found Guatemala City.
- Vasco da Gama of Portugal is appointed Viceroy to India
- The Spanish Council of the Indies becomes a formal element in the government of Castile, to coordinate the administration of Spanish colonies in the Americas.
- Peter Apian: *Cosmographicus liber*; the first text book of general theoretical geography.

POLITICS

- James V is declared fit to govern as King of Scotland. His first Queen is Madeleine, the daughter of King François I of

France. She dies in 1537, six months after their wedding. His second marriage is in 1538 to Marie, daughter of the French Duke of Guise.

- The French are driven out of Italy. Pierre du Terrail, the Chevalier de Bayard is mortally wounded in battle. According to tradition, he dies reciting the *Miserere.*
- The Treaty of Malmö: Denmark confirms the independence of Sweden under the Vasa King, Gustavus I.
- Shah Ismail of Persia dies and is succeeded by his son Tahmasp I.
- The Peasants' Revolt begins in Southern Germany (to 1525). Rebels demand the abolition of enclosures and feudal services.

RELIGION

- Pope Clement VII issues a papal bull confirming Pope Leo X's bull of 1521, granting the title Defender of the Faith to King Henry VIII of England.
- The Protestant leader Huldrych Zwingli abolishes the Catholic Mass in Zurich, Switzerland.
- Juan Luis Vives: *De institutione foeminae Christianae* (Education of the Christian Woman); Antwerp; in Latin; dedicated to Queen Catherine of Aragon, wife of King Henry VIII of England. It was translated into Spanish in 1529, and later into English, French, German, Italian, and Dutch. Vives thinks a woman's role should be restricted to the home, and not overlap that of men.

LITERATURE AND THE ARTS

- Lucas Cranach the Elder paints "The Judgment of Paris."
- Italian artist Giulio Romano does 16 drawings explicitly depicting various postures of sexual intercourse. They are engraved by Marcantonio Raimondi, printed by Baviera Carocci di Parma, and begin to circulate in the higher eschelons of Roman society. Pope Clement VII, outraged, orders them destroyed, with distribution of them punish-

able by death. Later, these will be used as illustrations for *Sonetti Lussuriosi* (Lustful Sonnets) by Pietro Aretino, generally known as *I Modi* . Giulio Romano is the only artist mentioned by name in the plays of William Shakespeare (as sculptor of the statue of Hermione in *The Winter's Tale* , at 5.2.94-9). After this trouble in Rome, Giulio goes to work for the Marchese of Gonzaga at his court in Mantua (Gonzaga becomes a duke in 1530), remaining there until Gonzaga's death in 1540, when he moves on to Bologna.

♦ Parmigianino paints "Self Portrait in a Convex Mirror"; Parma.

♦ Wynkyn de Worde prints Wakefield's *Oratio,* in which Italic type is used for the first time in English typography; London.

SOCIETY, EDUCATION

♦ Turkeys from South America are eaten for the first time at the English court.

1525

GEOGRAPHY

♦ Roderigo de Bastides of Spain founds Santa Marta, the first settlement of the future New Granada in the West Indies.

POLITICS

♦ King François I of France is captured in battle by HRE Charles V at the Battle of Pavia between the French and the victorious Germans and Spanish. He is imprisoned for 11 months in Spain. As a result of this victory, HRE Charles V becomes effective master of Italy.

♦ The English Cardinal Thomas Wolsey is forced to abandon the "Amicable Loan," a tax without Parliamentary sanction that he had levied on all goods worth £ 50 a year, in order to meet the expenses of a proposed invasion of France. Following this, Wolsey seeks a truce with France.

- A peace treaty between England and France is signed. France agrees to pay an annual pension of 100,000 crowns to King Henry VIII of England.
- Albert of Brandenburg, Grand Master of the Teutonic Knights, surrenders the lands owned by his order to Poland, forming the secular duchy of Brandenburg, with himself as duke under Polish suzerainty.
- ThePeasants' Revolt in southern Germany is suppressed, and its leader, Protestant Anabaptist movement founder Thomas Munzer, is executed.
- King Henry VIII of England gives his illegitimate son by Mary Boleyn, Henry Fitzroy, the title Duke of Richmond.
- The Mughal (Mongol) Emperor Babar "the Tiger" invades the Punjab in northeastern India.

RELIGION

- Matteo Bassi founds the Catholic Capuchin Order of monks.
- Protestant leader Martin Luther marries former nun Katherine von Bora.
- Louise of Savoy, Queen Mother of France, requires the Parlement of Paris to appoint a commission for the trial of Lutheran Protestants. A French translation of the New Testament is burned.
- The Imperial Diet is summoned to Augsburg, Germany, for a discussion of the religious situation. The meeting produces no decisions or plans.
- Zacharie Ferreri prepares a revised hymnal at the request of Pope Leo X.
- William Tyndale begins to translate the Bible into English. Printed by Peter Schoeffer at Worms, Germany, it is then smuggled into England.
- The first part of William Tyndale's translation of the "New Testament" from the Greek is printed in Cologne, Germany, by Peter Quentell. This also is smuggled into England, and

is thought to be the first Protestant tract in English to be circulated there.

LITERATURE AND THE ARTS

♦ Pietro Aretino: *La Cortegiana* (The Courtesan); Venice; a play depicting the corruption and wastefulness of the Roman court. Popular lampooner Aretino is considered the first journalist and publicist of the modern world.

♦ Albrecht Dürer: *Underweysung der Messung* (Manual of Measurement); Nuremberg. A teaching tool for artists who want to master the science of perspective, it contains descriptions of 2 apparatuses for tracing an object in perspective, and instructions for rendering various solids.

SOCIETY, EDUCATION

♦ The English Cardinal Thomas Wolsey completes the construction of York Palace in the City of Westminster (now part of London). It is renamed Whitehall Palace in 1530. Wolsey also gives his Hampton Court Palace to King Henry VIII.

♦ Muskets are first used by the Spanish infantry at the Battle of Pavia.

♦ Hops are introduced to England from Artois, France.

♦ Niccolò Machiavelli presents his *Istorie Fiorentine* (The History of Florence) to Pope Clement VII.

♦ The Chinese government orders the destruction of all oceangoing ships and the arrest of their owners.

♦ English Cardinal Thomas Wolsey endows Cardinal College, Oxford , on the site of St. Frideswide's Monastery. In 1546, it is refounded as Christ Church College by King Henry VIII.

1526

GEOGRAPHY

♦ Sebastian Cabot, Pilot Major for HRE Charles V, sets sail on an expedition sponsored by Spanish merchants to the Moluccas spice islands in the East Indies.

- Lucas Vasquez de Ayllon founds a settlement called San Miguel in what is presently the Carolinas. It is soon abandoned.
- Portuguese ships visit New Guinea.
- Gonzalo Fernandez de Oviedo y Valdes: *Sumario de la natural y general istoria de las Indias* (Summary of the Natural and General History of the Indies); Toledo; Spain.

POLITICS

- Treaty of Madrid between HRE Charles V and King François I of France, who is imprisoned in Spain. In return for his release, François agrees to give up claims to Milan, Genoa, Naples, Flanders, Artois, Burgundy and Navarre; to marry Charles's sister, Eleonore, the widowed Queen of Portugal; and to provide troops to assist Charles against Rome or the Turks. He surrenders his sons François and Henri as hostages to the Spanish. Once back in France, François claims duress and renounces the treaty, and the Pope absolves him from any obligation to abide by it.
- League of Cognac: an alliance of King François I of France and Pope Clement VII, together withVenice, Florence, and Francesco Sforza of Milan, against HRE Charles V. Asti and Genoa are to be restored to France; Milan is to go to Sforza as a French fief, et al.
- Elector John of Saxony and Philip, Landgrave of Hesse, sign the League of Gotha, forming an association of Protestant princes.
- HRE Charles V marries Princess Isabella of Portugal .
- The Turks under Sultan Suleiman I defeat and kill King Louis II of Bohemia and Hungary at the Battle of Mohacs , in the south of Hungary, also capturing the Hungarian city of Buda. A seven-year truce is signed between the Turks and John Zapolya, who is chosen by Suleiman to be King of Hungary. The western and northern sections of Hungary are taken over by Austria. The French urge the Sultan to attack Germany.

- John Zapolya is crowned King of Hungary.
- Ferdinand of Habsburg, ruler of Austria and younger brother of HRE Charles V, succeeds to the Bohemian throne. This marks the birth of the Austro-Hungarian state.
- Succession to the Hungarian throne is disputed between the Ottoman Empire and Ferdinand of Austria (until 1528).
- Mughal (Mongol) Empire is founded in India, after Babar ("the tiger," first Mughal emperor, a descendant of Tamerlane) defeats the last Delhi Sultan, Ibrahim Lodi, at the Battle of Panipat, and takes possession of Agra after defeating the Rajah of Gwalior.

RELIGION

- HRE Charles V forbids religious innovations in the empire, but offers the Protestant princes his services in persuading the Pope to summon a general council of the church.
- Authorities in Zurich, Switzerland, make the rebaptizing of adults and attendance at Anabaptist meetings punishable by drowning.
- Martin Luther writes the *German Mass and Order of Service.*
- William Tyndale's complete translation of the "New Testament" from the Greek is printed in Worms, Germany; the first printed "New Testament" in English.

LITERATURE AND THE ARTS

- Hans Holbein the Younger visits England for the first time (to 1529), beginning his portraits of notable English men and women.
- English composer John Taverner is appointed instructor of the choristers of the choir of Cardinal College, Oxford , England. Cardinal College was founded by Cardinal Wolsey, and later renamed Christ Church College.

SOCIETY, EDUCATION

- Peasants revolt in Austria, and are suppressed with great cruelty
- The card game piquet is first played.
- Babar, first Mughal emperor of India, acquires the Koh-i-noor ("mountain of light') and Agra diamonds. The Koh-i-noor is now a 108.95 carat oval white brilliant-cut stone set in the crown of the British Queen Mother. The Agra is a pale pink cushion-cut stone of about 41 carats, currently owned by a Hong Kong corporation.

1527

GEOGRAPHY

- Sebastian Cabot, employed by HRE Charles V to look for a water passage to the Pacific Ocean, explores the coast of Brazil and the Rio de la Plata (River Plate) as far as the Apipe rapids in the Parana.
- Panfilo de Narvaez of Spain explores the northern shore of the Gulf of Mexico west of Florida. His expedition is wrecked in a storm, and Alvar Nunez Cabeza de Vaca is thrown ashore in Texas, not returning to Mexico City until 1536. During the course of their efforts to return to Mexico, he and his men build five boats.
- Sebastian Cabot builds the fortifications of Santo Espiritu in Paraguay.

POLITICS

- The **Sack of Rome** occurs in May, by HRE Charles V's German and Spanish mercenary troops, At least 4000 inhabitants are killed, and many art treasures are looted. Pope Clement VII is captured and imprisoned at Castel Sant' Angelo.
- The Medici family is expelled from Florence, and the Florentine Republic is reestablished. In 1530, after Pope

Clement VII signs a treaty with HRE Charles V, the Imperial troops take Florence, and restore the rule of the Medici.

♦ The Habsburg administration in Austria is reorganized. Ferdinand of Austria is crowned King of Bohemia in Prague, and is recognized as sole King of Hungary.

♦ Ratification of a treaty of perpetual peace between King François I of France and King Henry VIII of England takes place in August.

RELIGION

♦ The Protestant Reformation comes to Sweden. King Gustavus Vasa confiscates Catholic Church lands.

♦ Jews are banished from Florence, Italy (allowed to return in 1531).

♦ John Fisher, Bishop of Rochester, pronounces against Henry VIII's proposed divorce from Queen Catherine of Aragon.

♦ A Baptist sect is founded in Zurich, Switzerland.

♦ The first Protestant University is founded at Marburg, Germany, by Philip, Elector of Hesse.

LITERATURE AND THE ARTS

♦ Pietro Aretino: *I Modi* (The Ways); 16 erotic sonnets to be used with the 1524 drawings by Giulio Romano, engraved by Marcantonio Raimondi; Rome. Aretino is wounded in the sack of Rome, and dies shortly thereafter.

♦ Hans Holbein the Younger paints "Sir Thomas More and His Family" in London, and "Lady with a Squirell."

♦ Lucas Cranach the Elder paints "Jealousy" in Augsburg , Germany.

♦ Adrian Willaert founds a singing school in Venice, after being appointed *maestro di cappella* (master of the chapel) for St. Mark's Basilica, one of the most highly paid and prestigious cathedral posts in Europe.

♦ Pierre Attaignant prints *Chansons nouvelles* (new songs) in Paris, the first edition of these secular Parisian songs.

SOCIETY, EDUCATION

◆ Paracelsus is appointed municipal physician and University Professor in Basel, Switzerland. Throwing Avicenna's *Canon* and Galen's works into a bonfire, he announces that his courses in medicine will be based on his own experience with patients. He lectures in the German vernacular rather than Latin. In his Neoplatonic philosophy, the life of man is inseparable from that of the universe.

1528

GEOGRAPHY

◆ Augsburg merchant bankers Welser receive the privilege of colonizing Venezuela from HRE Charles V.
◆ The first printed "rutter" (a book of sailing directions) is published in English. An expanded edition is published in 1541, and continues in use as late as the 1580's, along with another translated from the Dutch.

POLITICS

◆ England and France declare war on the Holy Roman Empire.
◆ The French are expelled from Naples and Genoa. Genoa becomes a republic under the protection of HRE Charles V.
◆ King John Zapolya of Hungary makes a treaty with Sultan Suleiman I of Turkey, recognizing the Sultan's suzerainty.
◆ English merchants doing business in Spain and the Netherlands are arrested, causing a commercial crisis.
◆ Beginning of the wars between Dayan Khan, leader of the Mongols, and the Chinese.

RELIGION

◆ King Henry VIII of England sends Stephen Gardiner and Edward Fox to Rome in an effort to persuade Pope Clement VII to hasten proceedings in the King's suit for divorce. The Pope, reluctant to offend Queen Catherine's nephew HRE Charles V, does not take any action.

- The Protestant reformation begins to take root in Scotland.
- Austrian Portestant Anabaptist leader Balthasar Hubmair is burned at the stake for heresy in Vienna.
- The Catholic religious Order of the Capuchins is organized, as a branch of the Observants, with the aim of enforcing the strict monastic rule instituted by St. Francis of Assisi.

LITERATURE AND THE ARTS

- Baldassare Castiglione *Il Cortegiano* (known in English as *The Book of the Courtier*), Venice; a manual for courtiers in dialogue form, set in the court of Urbino; in Italian.
- Sebastian Franck: *Von dem graulichen Laster der Trunckenheit so in disen letsten Zeite* (The Vice of Drinking).
- Erasmus of Rotterdam: *De recta latini graecique sermonis pronuntiatione* popularly known as *Ciceronianus* ; Basel and Paris; a satire on Latin scholarship.

SOCIETY, EDUCATION

- The fourth epidemic of the "sweating sickness" breaks out in England. It spreads throughout England, but does not spread to Scotland or Wales. It is a very severe epidemic, with high mortality in London. King Henry VIII moves frequently to avoid contamination. It also breaks out on the continent, killing 1,000 in Hamburg, Germany, within a few weeks of its appearance in England, and causing many deaths in northern and eastern Europe. It does not appear in France, Italy, or the southern countries, and does not recur in England until the last epidemic in 1551.
- A serious outbreak of the plague occurs in England.
- Weavers in Kent, England, riot against Cardinal Wolsey's decision to relocate the English staple town for wool from Antwerp to Calais.
- Cardinal Wolsey dissolves 22 religious houses having fewer that seven members, in order to obtain funds to found colleges at Ipswich and Oxford.

- Diego de Siloe begins to build the Cathedral in Granada, Spain.
- Paracelsus: *Die kleine Chirurgia* (The Little Surgery)—first manual of surgery; Basel, Switzerland.

1529

GEOGRAPHY

- Diego Ribero, a Portuguese working for HRE Charles V, draws a world map showing the east coasts of the Americas, reflecting the discoveries of Columbus, Cabot and Giovanni da Verrazano, among others. This is believed to duplicate information contained in the Spanish "Padron General," (now lost), the official record of Spanish discoveries.
- Treaty of Zaragoza: HRE Charles V pledges all his rights in the Moluccas to Portugal for 350,000 ducats, with a line of demarcation fixed at seventeen degrees east of the islands.

POLITICS

- Turks take the city of Buda in Hungary, and attack Austria, laying unsuccessful siege to Vienna; in 1683, the Turks attack Vienna again, still unsuccessfully
- Peace of Cambrai between France and HRE Charles V ("Ladies' Peace") is joined by England; HRE Charles V gives up all claims to Burgundy.
- King François I of France renounces all French claims in Italy.
- Treaty of Barcelona between Pope Clement VII and HRE Charles V.

RELIGION

- King Henry VIII of England dismisses the Lord Chancellor, Cardinal Thomas Wolsey, for failing to obtain the Pope's consent to his divorce from Queen Catherine of Aragon.
- Sir Thomas More is appointed Lord Chancellor of England. He is the first layman to hold this position.

- King Henry VIII summons the "Reformation" Parliament and begins to cut English ties with the Church of Rome. The House of Commons attacks mortuary dues and other clerical abuses.
- Martin Luther and Ulrich Zwingli hold a disputation on the sacrament of the Eucharist ("holy communion") at Marburg, Germany.
- The short catechism with a preface by Martin Luther, known as "Luther's Catechism" is published and adopted in the churches of southern Germany.
- Second Diet of Speyer opens in Germany. The Lutheran minority ("Protestants") protests against the decisions of the Catholic majority. The Diet imposes censorship on newspaper-type publications.
- Father Bernardino de Sahagun starts a Catholic Franciscan mission in Mexico.

LITERATURE AND THE ARTS

- Albrecht Altdorfer paints "The Battle of Issus," an enormous panoramic scene depicting Alexander the Great's victory over Darius, King of the Persians.
- Parmigianino paints an allegorical portrait of HRE Charles V.
- Lorenzo Lotto paints "Christ and the Woman taken in Adultery."
- Jean Clouet becomes court painter to King François I of France.
- Martin Agricola: *Musica instrumentalis deutsch* (German Musical Instruments)—a treatise on musical instruments; enlarged in 1545; Wittenberg, Germany

SOCIETY, EDUCATION

- Women appear on stage in Italy for the first time.
- Michelangelo designs fortifications for the city of Florence, Italy.

- Michel de Nostredame ("Nostradamus") becomes a Doctor of Medicine in France.
- A new English regulation requires an inventory of possessions be drawn up at the death of every man or woman.
- King Henry VIII of England is released from his debts by a statute enacted by the "Reformation" Parliament.
- King François I founds the College of France, initially an academy for the study of Greek and Hebrew
- The Library of Hamburg , Germany, is founded.
- HRE Charles V begins to build the Canal of Aragon, Spain.

1530-1539

1530

GEOGRAPHY

♦ Francisco Pizarro and Diego de Almagro of Spain leave Panama for the conquest of Peru, accompanied by 180 men, 27 horses and two cannon.

♦ Peter Martyr Anglerius (Pietro Martire d'Anghiera): first complete edition of *De Orbe Novo* (On the New World), in Latin; Alcala de Henares, Spain; the earliest book on discoveries in the New World.

POLITICS

♦ Pope Clement VII crowns HRE Charles V as King of Italy and Holy Roman Emperor, in February in Bologna. This is the last papal coronation of a Holy Roman Emperor. Charles convinces the Pope to oppose King Henry VIII of England's divorce from Catherine of Aragon, who is Charles's aunt.

♦ Diet of Augsburg is convened in June in the hope of persuading the German states, which are torn by religious strife, to stand together against the Ottoman Turkish threat. HRE Charles V attends

♦ **The Confession of Augsburg** is signed at the Diet of Augsburg by the Protestant Princes, who form the Schmalkaldic League against HRE Charles V and his Catholic allies. This is considered the most important

Protestant statement of belief during the Reformation, and was based on articles previously drawn up by Martin Luther. In effect, it is the official creed of the Lutheran Church.

♦ Babar, Mughal Emperor of India, dies in Delhi and is succeeded by his son Humayun.

♦ The English Cardinal Thomas Wolsey is arrested as a traitor and dies while travelling to London for trial.

♦ King François I of France marries his second wife, Queen Eleonore of Portugal , widow of King Manuel I and sister of HRE Charles V, in fulfillment of the 1526 Treaty of Madrid

RELIGION

♦ The Catholic Crusader Knights of St. John, formerly established on the island of Rhodes, are reestablished on the island of Malta by HRE Charles V, becoming known thereafter as the Knights of Malta.

♦ Pope Clement VII issues a bull in March forbidding all ecclesiastical judges and lawyers from speaking or writing on the question of King Henry VIII of England's marriage, and suspends prodeedings in the case until September.

♦ William Tyndale's English translation of the first five books of the "Old Testament" from the Hebrew (the *Pentateuch*) is printed at Antwerp.

LITERATURE AND THE ARTS

♦ Titian paints a portrait of Cardinal Ippolito de' Medici and "Woman in a Fur."

♦ Antonio Allegri da Correggio paints "Adoration of the Shepherds" and "Leda and the Swan."

♦ Agnolo Bronzino sculpts a bust of Guidobaldo di Montefeltro.

♦ Lucas Cranach the Elder paints a pair of paintings of Adam and Eve and "Judith with the Head of Holofernes"; Wittenberg, Saxony.

SOCIETY, EDUCATION

♦ King François I of France declares that eight of his jewels are the property of the crown. These are **the first designated "crown jewels" of Europe.**

♦ Claude Garamond is created "imprimeur du roi" (King's printer) by King François I of France. A type-face bearing his name is still in use. He designed a Greek type for François I, that was used as a pattern until the 19th century.

♦ The Venice Arsenal completes construction of the first galleon capable of sailing on the high seas (begun in 1526).

♦ King Henry VIII relocates the English court to Whitehall Palace, originally owned by Cardinal Wolsey and called York Palace.

♦ A criminal code and police regulations are established for the Holy Roman Empire.

♦ English merchants trading with Spain organize themselves into a company.

♦ Reinerus Gemma, Frisius ("Frisius" indicates he was a native of Friesland) suggests that longitude can be found by means of a difference of times.

♦ Raimund and Anton Fugger of Augsburg, sons of Augsburg merchant banker Georg Fuger, are given the imperial dignity of counts of Kirchberg and Weissenhorn by HRE Charles V.

♦ Erasmus of Rotterdam: *De civilitate morum puerilium* ; Basel, Switzerland; English translation in 1532 by Robert Whittinton as *A lytell booke of good maners for chyldren.* It sets forth the highest standard of manners for children. There were a total of 5 English editions by 1555.

♦ Otto Brunfels: *Herbarum vivae eicones ad natura imitationem summa cum diligentia et artificio effigiatae* (Living Portraits of Plants); Strasbourg, Germany; an illustrated compendium of plants native to Europe.

1531

GEOGRAPHY

◆ Portugal begins to colonize Brazil. Nicolas Villegagnon visits the site of the future city of Rio de Janeiro.

◆ Diego de Ordaz of Portugal explores the Orinoco River.

POLITICS

◆ Ferdinand of Habsburg, King of Hungary, Austria and Bohemia is elected King of the Romans.

◆ Ferdinand of Habsburg and King John Zapolya of Hungary sign a truce.

◆ King François I of France signs an alliance with John Zapolya of Hungary.

◆ HRE Charles V appoints his sister, Margaret of Hungary, as Regent of the Netherlands (to 1552). She issues a decree establishing councils for justice, finance and foreign affairs.

◆ The Protestant Schmalkaldic League is joined by the Duke of Brunswick, the city of Lübeck, and Catholic Bavaria. The League holds two conferences to plan military action against HRE Charles V. Most of the north German cities and principalities support the League.

◆ King Christian II of Denmark, in exile in the Netherlands since 1523, attempts to invade Norway, with the aid of HRE Charles V. His attempt to remove his successor, King Frederick I, ends when he is defeated in 1532, and he is imprisoned for the rest of his life.

◆ Pope Clement VII gives permission for his neice, Catherine de' Medici, to marry Henri, Duke of Orleans (the future King Henri II of France). A secret clause in the agreement pledges Papal support for King François I's efforts to recover Milan and Genoa from HRE Charles V.

RELIGION

◆ Pope Clement VII forbids King Henry VIII to re-marry until his case is decided.

- King Henry VIII of England is recognized as the supreme head of the church in England. An Act of Supremacy follows to support this in 1533.
- "The English Queen Catherine of Aragon is established in a separate household, and King Henry VIII does not see her again.
- Civil war in Switzerland between the Catholic Forest Cantons and Protestant Zurich. The Catholic Forest Cantons are victorious. Protestant reformer Ulrich Zwingli is killed at the Battle of Kappel. The war is ended by the Peace of Kappel, giving each canton and district the right to worship as it chooses. Protestant Zurich is forced to comply.
- Pope Clement VII founds the Catholic Inquisition in Portugal.
- **Our Lady of Guadalupe appears to Juan Diego**, a Mexican peasant. He has this vision of the Blessed Virgin Mary on Tepeyec hill, formerly the home of the Aztec goddess Tonantzin. The inside of Diego's cloak is miraculously imprinted with the Virgin's image and filled with fresh roses.
- Marguerite d'Angoulême (Queen of Navarre, sister of King François I of France, and grandmother of King Henri IV of France) writes *Le Miroir de l'ame Pecheresse* ("The Mirror of a Sinful Soul"). A Catholic who is sympathetic to the Protestant reforms of Martin Luther, she says the devotional poems deal with "the discord being in human kind by the contrariness of spirit and flesh and its peace throught spiritual life." It is translated into English in 1544 by Princess Elizabeth Tudor of England, then age 11, who later reigns as Queen Elizabeth I.

LITERATURE AND THE ARTS

- Titian paints "The Magdalen."
- Parmigianino paints "Cupid Carving His Bow."
- Andrea Alciato: *Emblematum Liber*, Augsburg; the first of the

emblem books; reprinted Paris, 1534; Lyon, 1544; Antwerp, 1584; Padua, 1621. It is later known as *Emblematum libellus*, and eventually as *Emblemata* . An emblem was a kind of personal logo or identification used by royalty and nobility, consisting of a symbolic picture accompanied by a descriptive verse. Alciato's work influenced Henry Peacham's *Minerva Britanna* of 1612.

SOCIETY, EDUCATION

♦ The Antwerp Stock Exchange is founded.

♦ A "great comet" (later named "**Halley's Comet**") appears in the skies, arousing a wave of public fear and superstitious speculation throughout Europe.

♦ Sir Thomas Elyot: *The Boke Named the Governour*, London; education for statesmen, to be read by those who wish to equip their sons for government service.

♦ Beatus Rhenanus: *Rerum Germanicarus libri tres*—a history of Germany in three volumes, the first of its kind.

♦ Robert Estienne: *Thesaurus linguae Latinae*—the first Latin-French dictionary; Paris.

♦ Juan Luis Vives: *De Tradendis Disciplinis* ; Bruges; advocates the serious study of cooking, building, navigation, agriculture and clothmaking. Vives warns the scholar against despising the manual worker.

♦ Erasmus of Rotterdam publishes the first scholarly edition of Aristotle's works; in Latin; Basel, Switzerland.

♦ The University of Granada is founded in Spain by HRE Charles V.

1532

GEOGRAPHY

♦ Francisco Pizarro and Diego de Almagro of Spain capture the Inca King Atahualpa at his capitol, Cajamarca, as part of their conquest of Peru.

POLITICS

- King François I of France and King Henry VIII of England hold a meeting in Calais to sign the Treaty of Boulogne , forming an alliance together. Henry is accompanied by Anne Boleyn, to whom he has given the title Marquess of Pembroke. François gives Anne a large diamond.
- HRE Charles V invades Italy.
- HRE Charles V and Pope Clement VII hold a conference at Bologna to plan a defensive league among the Pope, Milan, Ferrara, Mantua, Genoa, Lucca and Siena. The Republic of Venice refuses to join.
- The Electors of Trier and the Palitinate, and Philip, Landgrave of Hesse, withdraw from the Protestant Schmalkaldic League.
- Sultan Suleiman I of Turkey invades Hungary, and advances toward Vienna.
- John Frederick becomes Elector of Saxony on the death of his father, John.
- The Mongols under Dayan Khan are defeated for the first time by the Chinese.

RELIGION

- Sir Thomas More resigns as Lord Chancellor of England, since, as a Catholic, he cannot support King Henry VIII's divorce from Queen Catherine of Aragon.
- Thomas Cranmer is named Archbishop of Canterbury in England. He is consecrated in March 1533.
- The English clergy agree to obey King Henry VIII, in a formal act of submission.
- Pope Clement VII issues a brief, warning King Henry VIII of England to put an end to his relationship with Anne Boleyn, under pain of excommunication.
- A Turkish invasion forces HRE Charles V to agree to the Peace of Narumberg with German Protestants, in which he secretly pledges religious toleration.

LITERATURE AND THE ARTS

- ◆ Niccolò Machiavelli: *Il Principe* (The Prince) is published posthumously in Rome. It was written in 1513.
- ◆ The first collected edition of the works of Geoffrey Chaucer is issued in London by W. Thynne. It also contains a number of incorrect attributions.
- ◆ Lucas Cranach the Elder paints "The Payment."
- ◆ Giulio Romano paints a fresco "Sala de Giganti" at the Palazzo di Te, Mantua.
- ◆ Hans Holbein the Younger, German painter, returns to London permanently and begins to paint "The Merchants of the Steelyard" (completed in1536).
- ◆ King Henry VIII of England founds the Gentlemen and Choristers of the Chapel Royal, at St. James's Palace, London.

SOCIETY, EDUCATION

- ◆ The "Flanders Galleys" (begun in 1314) sail for the last time. This was an annual convoy of Italian galleys bearing luxury goods from the far east to England, the Low Countries and the north.
- ◆ Sugar cane is first cultivated in Brazil.
- ◆ The Diet of Ratisbon approves the "Caroline Code," containing material from Roman, German and Christian sources, as a reform of German criminal law.

1533

GEOGRAPHY

- ◆ Francisco Pizarro of Spain captures the Inca capitol at Cuzco, and completes his conquest of Peru. He kills the Inca King, Atahualpa, who had been his prisoner.
- ◆ Hernan Cortez attempts to found a colony in Lower California (to 1535).
- ◆ The Spanish conquer the Yucutan peninsula of Mexico.

- Pedro de Heredia of Spain founds the city of Cartagena in South America.
- The King of Portugal creates hereditary captaincies in Brazil.

POLITICS

- King Henry VIII of England marries Anne Boleyn privately in January.
- Thomas Cranmer, Archbishop of Canterbury, declares that the marriage of King Henry VIII and Catherine of Aragon is null and void, and that between Henry and Anne Boleyn is lawful
- Anne Boleyn is crowned Queen of England in June
- Pope Clement VII excommunicates Henry VIII in July
- A daughter, Elizabeth, is born to Henry VIII and Anne Boleyn in September
- Peace between Sultan Suleiman I of Turkey and Ferdinand of Habsburg, King of Austria.
- King Frederick I of Denmark and Norway dies.
- Prince Christian, son of King Frederick I, becomes King Christian III of Denmark and Norway.
- Catherine de' Medici marries the French Dauphin, Henri de Valois. Her Uncle, Pope Clement VII gives her the finest pearl necklace in Europe—six long strands of white pearls, together with twenty-five enormous pear-shaped black pearl drops.
- Ivan IV (later Tsar Ivan "the Terrible") becomes Grand Duke of Muscovy at the age of three, after the death of his father, Vasily (Basil) III, Grand Duke of Muscovy and ruler of all Russia.

LITERATURE AND THE ARTS

- Hans Holbein the Younger paints "The Ambassadors" (The Ambassador Jean de Dinteville with Georges de Selve).
- Lorenzo Lotto paints "Portrait of a Lady."
- Titian is appointed court painter to HRE Charles V.

SOCIETY, EDUCATION

♦ First of the Inca treasure of gold and emeralds captured by Francisco Pizarro reaches Seville, Spain, in December.

♦ The Spanish first encounter the potato, of which the Incas cultivate hundreds of varieties, during the conquest of Peru.

♦ A scourer of drains and sinks for Henry VIII's royal palaces is appointed. He makes a circuit among the palaces of Windsor, Whitehall, Hampton Court, Richmond, Greenwich and Eltham.

♦ John Leland, Chaplain to King Henry VIII of England, is appointed "King's Antiquary," empowered to search for and collect records and books from cathedral libraries, abbeys, priories and colleges.

♦ *Allerhand Farben und mancherley weyse Dunten zu bereyten*—a manual for the production of paints and inks, is published in Augsburg, Germany.

♦ Nicholas Udall: *Floures for Latine Spekynge selected and gathered oute of Terence;* London; a compilation and translation of works by the Latin comedy writer. Udall became headmaster of Eton school in c.1534.

1534

GEOGRAPHY

♦ Jacques Cartier of France, with two ships and 61 men, makes his first voyage to North America. Leaving in April and sighting the coast of Labrador in May, he explores the St. Lawrence River (named for the saint whose day it was when it was first seen), establishing a basis for French claims to Canada. He makes three voyages, to 1542.

POLITICS

♦ King François I of France signs a secret treaty with the German Protestant princes.

- Henry VIII makes peace with his nephew, King James V of Scotland
- The Turks capture Tunis, Baghdad and Mesopotamia.
- The Irish, led by George Oge, Earl of Kildare , rebel against the English occupation. After suppression by the English, the Earl, his son, and most of his close relatives are executed.
- Christian III is crowned King of Denmark and Norway.

RELIGION

- King Henry VIII is declared the supreme head of the church in England by the Act of Supremacy, and the succession to the crown is through his children by Anne Boleyn. This is **the final break between England and Rome.**
- Pope Clement VII dies in September.
- Pope Paul III (Alessandro Farnese) is crowned in September, and appoints a number of reforming cardinals.
- **Ignatius Loyola founds the Society of Jesus** (known is the Jesuits) in Spain, in partnership with Francis Xavier. The original aim of the society is pilgrimage to the Holy Land.
- Protestant reformer Martin Luther completes translating the Bible into German, with his translation of the Old Testament.
- Protestant William Tyndale issues a revised version of his English Bible in Antwerp.
- Protestant Anabaptists under the leadership of John of Leiden establish a "communistic state" at Munster, Germany.
- Elizabeth Barton, "The Nun of Kent,"charged with treason, is executed for opposing the matrimonial policy of King Henry VIII of England.

LITERATURE AND THE ARTS

- François Rabelais:*Gargantua* and Part II of *Pantagruel* ; Paris.
- John Heywood: *A Play of Love* interlude; London

- Titian paints a portrait of HRE Charles V.
- Michelangelo moves from Florence to Rome, after completing the tomb of the Medici family in Florence.
- Benvenuto Cellini designs two gold medals with the likeness of his patron, Pope Clement VII.

SOCIETY, EDUCATION

- Moscow: St. Basil's Cathedral is erected.
- The English Parliament (at the sixth session of the "Reformation" Parliament) passes a law that limits farmers to owning 2,000 sheep, in an effort to prevent further enclosures of common land and the loss of arable land.
- Francesco Guicciardini begins to write a *History of Italy* (to 1540) in Florence. He sets a new standard for scrupulous accuracy, verification of sources, and impartiality of tone.
- Polydore Vergil : *Historiae Anglicae Libri XXVI*; Basel, Switzerland; a history of England in 26 volumes. A 27th book was added to the third edition of 1555.

1535

GEOGRAPHY

- Jacques Cartier of France, on his second voyage to North America, navigates the St. Lawrence River, and visits the future sites of Quebec and Montreal (to 1536).
- The Spaniards explore Chile (to 1537).
- Antonio de Mendoza is appointed the first Viceroy of New Spain (Mexico). He serves with distinction and makes it the best administered of all Spain's colonies.
- The city of Lima, Peru, is founded.
- Gonzalo Fernandez de Oviedo y Valdes: *La historia general de las Indias* (The General History of the Indies); Seville, Spain.

POLITICS

- France and Turkey sign an offensive/defensive alliance, aimed at HRE Charles V, as well as a commercial treaty.

- HRE Charles V enters Sicily.
- Francesco Maria Sforza, Duke of Milan, dies in November. Milan comes under direct Spanish control, since Sforza's death extinguishes the ducal family's male line.
- HRE Charles V enters Naples.
- HRE Charles V conquers Tunis and frees 20,000 Christian slaves
- Diet of Schmalkalden: English envoys ask the Protestant German princes to form an alliance with England.

RELIGION

- King Henry VIII of England assumes the title "Supreme Head of the Church" and the English clergy renounce their allegiance to the Pope.
- Sir Thomas More is convicted of treason and beheaded for failing to take the oath of succession required by the Act of Supremacy. More is canonized by the Roman Catholic Church in 1935.
- Cardinal John Fisher is beheaded as punishment for refusing to recognize Henry VIII as head of the church in England. He also is canonized in 1935.
- The Protestant Anabaptist commune at Munster, Germany, is conquered by the Hessian army. Their leader, John of Leiden, is tortured to death. Munster returns to Catholicism.
- The Edict of Coucy , issued by King François I of France, suspends heresy persecutions for six months to give heretics time to recant. It remains in force until 1537.
- William Tyndale is arrested in Brussels, at the instigation of agents sent by King Henry VIII of England. He is imprisoned there.
- A group of Catholic Carthusian monks are publicly executed in London. Their charterhouse (monastery building) becomes the property of the crown. Catholic Europe is outraged.

♦ Angela Merici founds the Catholic Order of Ursulines at Brescia, Italy, for the education of girls and care of the sick and needy.

LITERATURE AND THE ARTS

♦ Hans Holbein the Younger paints a portrait of King Henry VIII of England.

♦ Parmigiano paints "Madonna dal Collo Longo" (Madonna with the Long Neck); Parma, Italy.

SOCIETY, EDUCATION

♦ Niccolò Tartaglia works out a general solution for mathematical "equations of the third degree."

♦ English Parliament passes a Statute of Uses curbing the power of landowners to devise their lands by testament (leave land to heirs in their wills).

♦ Marino Sanudo's *Diarii* is is completed (begun c1496); a record of the history and daily life of Venice, using official documents as sources.

♦ Venice: *La tariffa delle puttane di Venegia* (The Price List of the Whores of Venice), a satiric catalogue listing 110 courtesans and 25 procuresses is published in Venice, without naming either author or publisher. Information provided includes names, addresses, specialties and prices. Another catalogue is issued in 1565.

1536

GEOGRAPHY

♦ Hernan Cortes , exploring under the flag of Spain, reaches Southern California.

♦ The Spanish found the settlement of Asuncion on the Paraguay River, the first permanent settlement in the interior of South America.

♦ Pedro de Mendoza of Spain founds a settlement on the site

of the present-day city of Buenos Aires in South America, and sends expeditions in search of an inland route to Peru.

♦ Alvar Nunez Cabeza de Vaca of Spain reaches the present state of Arizona.

POLITICS

♦ France conquers Savoy and Piedmont, and occupies Turin. King François I hopes to gain the duchy of Milan for his third son.

♦ King François I of France and Sultan Suleiman I of Turkey sign a new alliance.

♦ Queen Anne Boleyn, King Henry VIII of England's second wife, is beheaded in London, having been convicted of treason for alleged adultery. At her requet, a swordsman is brought from France to behead her. Usually, beheading was by axe, and only persons of higher rank were entitled to be beheaded. Others were hanged, drawn and quartered.

♦ King Henry VIII marries Jane Seymour , his third wife.

♦ The eighth and last session of the English "Reformation" Parliament convenes.

♦ King James V of Scotland visits France.

♦ Wales is incorporated with England, by act of the English Parliament.

RELIGION

♦ An English Act of Parliament declares that the authority of the Pope is void in England.

♦ Monasteries in England are suppressed under the direction of Thomas Cromwell, Earl of Essex and Lord Privy Seal (continuing to 1539). In the process, 376 religious houses are dissolved, and their enormous wealth becomes the property of the English crown.

♦ Protestant William Tyndale, translator of the English Bible, is first strangled and then burned at the stake in Antwerp, after being imprisoned there for 16 months.

- Pope Paul III's bull for the reform of many papal offices is read in the papal consistory.
- The "Pilgrimage of Grace," a Catholic uprising in the north of England led by Robert Aske of Doncaster, is suppressed. As many as 30,000 rebelled in Lincolnshire and Lancashire. The cities of York and Hull surrendered to the rebels.
- The English prelate Reginald Pole is created a cardinal.
- John Calvin arrives to lead the Protestants in Geneva in July. He publishes *Institutio Christianae religionis* (Institutes of the Christian Religion) in Basel, espousing a religious point of view further from Catholicism than Luther's: " . . . it is evident that man never arrives at true self-knowledge before he has looked into the face of God and then come away to look at himself. " Calvin dedicates the work to King François I of France, persecutor of Protestants.
- The Protestant reformation comes to Denmark and Norway.

LITERATURE AND THE ARTS

- Hans Holbein the Younger is appointed painter to King Henry VIII of England, and paints a large mural at Whitehall Palace depicting Henry VIII and Queen Jane Seymour , together with Henry's parents, King Henry VII and Queen Elizabeth of York. The mural is destroyed when the palace burns in 1698.
- Michelangelo is commissioned by Pope Paul III to turn Capitoline Hill in Rome (the Campidoglio) into a piazza with imposing civic buildings. He begins work on the "Last Judgment" in the Sistine Chapel.

SOCIETY, EDUCATION

- An English Act of Parliament amends laws on vagrancy and poor relief, a first move toward subsidy for the poor.

1537

GEOGRAPHY

♦ The Portuguese obtain Macao as a trading post, establishing a permanent settlement there in 1557.

♦ Francisco de Orellana of Spain makes a permanent settlement at Guayaquil, in present-day Ecuador.

♦ Pedro Nuñes: *Tratado da sphera com a theorica do Sol e da luna*; Lisbon; a navigational treatise, one of the best and most original of the century. Nuñes realizes that the course of a ship cutting meridians at a constant angle (the lexodrome) is a spiral, not a curve.

POLITICS

♦ The French invade Italy. A truce is arranged by Pope Paul III.

♦ English Queen Jane Seymour dies after the Caesarean section delivery of her son Edward at Hampton Court Palace on October 12.

♦ King Henry VIII of England creates the Council of the North as a permanent body to govern the northern counties, after the suppression of "The Pilgrimage of Grace" rebellion.

♦ The Turks beseige the strategically important island of Corfu on the west coast of Greece, but fail to take it.

♦ King James V of Scotland marries Princess Madeleine, daughter of King François I of France, in January. She dies six months later.

♦ Alessandro de' Medici is assassinated in Florence. His brother Cosimo de' Medici succeeds him as Duke of Florence.

RELIGION

♦ German Lutherans decline an invitation from Pope Paul III to attend a general council.

♦ Robert Aske, leader of the north England religious rebellion"The Pilgrimage of Grace" is sentenced to death despite King Henry VIII's promise of a pardon, and is executed in York. Many other leaders of the Pilgrimage are executed as well.

♦ John Calvin founds his system of government for Church and State in Geneva, Switzerland—"the perfect school of Christ."

♦ King Christian III of Denmark and Norway issues *Ordinance for the Danish Church*, with the approval of Martin Luther.

LITERATURE AND THE ARTS

♦ **The complete works of Marcus Rullius Cicero (***Opera omnia***) are published** in Venice, in Latin, by Aldine Press, with notes by Pietro Victorius. This is one of the most important works of classical scholarship of the entire century.

♦ Hans Holbein the younger paints a portrait of Queen Jane Seymour .

♦ Sansovino (Jacopo Tatti), state architect of Venice, designs a facade for the logietta of the Doge's Palace, and a Library creating new relations between the Campanile and the Piazza and Piazzetta.

♦ Pierre Attaignant is appointed *imprimeur et libraire du Roy en musique* (printer and bookseller in music for the King) by King François I of France. Attaignant invented and introduced a new method of printing music in which the staff-segments and notes were combined, so that both could be printed in a single impression, a much faster and less expensive method for printing music.

♦ The first conservatories of music are founded in Italy: in Naples, for boys; and in Venice for girls.

SOCIETY, EDUCATION

♦ The **first copyright library** is established by law, in Paris. Printers are required to supply copies of the works they publish.

- King François I of France divides the privilege of making brandy between the vinegar-makers and the victuallers.
- A plague epidemic breaks out in the London area.
- Gerardus Mercator publishes the first map of Flanders.
- Niccolò Fontana (called "Tartaglia"): *La Nova Scientia*; Venice. He explains the trajectory of bullets, developing the science of ballistics.
- University of Lisbon is transferred to Coimbra, Portugal.

1538

GEOGRAPHY

- Bogota, Colombia, is founded by Gonzalo Jimenez de Quesada of Spain.
- Francisco Pizarro's former partner in the conquest of Peru, Diego de Almagro, is strangled by order of Pizarro.
- **Gerardus Mercator uses the names "America" and "North America" for the first time in his maps.**

POLITICS

- The Truce of Nice between France and Spain is arranged through the mediation of King François I's wife, Queen Eleonore. François and HRE Charles V agree to a ten-year truce, and discuss repression of Protestant heresies.
- The Catholic League of Nuremberg is formed as a counterpart to the Protestant Schmalkaldic League. Signers include HRE Charles V, King Ferdinand of Austria, Duke George of Saxony, the Elector of Bavaria, and the Bishops of Maintz and Salzburg.
- King Henry VIII of England negotiates for an alliance with the German Protestant princes.
- King James V of Scotland marries Marie of Guise, daughter of the French Duke of Guise, the most powerful man in France next to King François I.
- King Ferdinand of Austria and King John Zapolya of

Hungary sign the Peace of Groswardein , by which the childless Zapolya agrees that Ferdinand will acquire the whole of Hungary upon Zapolya's death.

RELIGION

♦ Pope Paul III issues a bull excommunicating and deposing Henry VIII of England as King, and excusing his subjects from allegiance to him.

♦ The exiled English Catholic Cardinal Reginald Pole urges France and Spain to undertake a crusade against Henry VIII, "the most cruel and abominable tyrant."

♦ King François I of France issues an edict, at the Parlement of Toulouse, calling for the persecution of French Protestants.

♦ Protestant reformer John Calvin, expelled from Geneva, settles in Strasbourg, Germany.

♦ A wave of iconoclasm sweeps southern England. Sacred relics, images and shrines in churches and abbeys are destroyed, notably the shrine of St. Thomas à Becket in Canterbury.

LITERATURE AND THE ARTS

♦ Vittoria Colonna: *RimeSpirituali* (Spiritual Verses); published three more times to 1544; Parma, Italy. Colonna later moved to Rome, where she was a close friend of Michelangelo, and closely associated with members of the reform party at the papal court.

♦ Titian paints "The Urbino Venus."

♦ Andrea Palladio builds the Villa Godi in Lonedo, Italy.

SOCIETY, EDUCATION

♦ King Henry VIII of England begins construction of the Palace of Nonsuch, not completed until after his death. It was demolished by King Charles II in 1670, and excavated by archaeologists in 1959-60.

♦ King François I of France orders the first set of flat dinner service plates from an Antwerp goldsmith.

- A professorship of oriental languages is established at the College de France, Paris.
- Sir Thomas Elyot: *The dictionary of syr thomas Eliot*; London; the first English dictionary.

1539

GEOGRAPHY

- Hernan de Soto of Spain arrives at Tampa Bay, Florida , with 600 men, to begin a search for gold. Continuing his march westward, in what is present-day Alabama de Soto defeats Chief Tuscaloosa and kills several thousand Native Americans during the nine hour battle of Mauvilla.
- Spain annexes Cuba.
- The Inca army of the leader Charcas surrenders to the Spanish. The royal Inca chief Manco Inca takes refuge at Vilcabamba. Spanish control of Peru becomes complete.
- Domenico de Goes: *Commentarius rerum gestatum in India citra Gangeum*; Lisbon; a history of Portuguese India.

POLITICS

- Treaty of Toledo is signed by King François I of France and HRE Charles V, in which they bind themselves to make no new alliance with England without mutual consent. Further marriages are arranged between the royal houses of Habsburg and Valois.
- The Truce of Frankfurt is signed by HRE Charles V and the German Protestant princes. The princes had demanded a permanent religious settlement, but Charles agrees to six months only.
- King Henry VIII of England signs a marriage treaty to marry Anne of Cleves, older sister of William Duke of Cleves, in order to foster an alliance between England and the Protestant princes of Germany.
- The city of Ghent rebels against HRE Charles V's Netherlands

Regent, Mary of Hungary, and asks other cities in the area to join with them, unsuccessfully.

RELIGION
♦ The English Parliament enacts the Six Articles of Religion "abolishing diversity of (religious) opinions" in England, and repealing the Ten Articles enacted in 1536.
♦ The Elector of Brandenburg becomes a Protestant, and the Duchy of Saxony is inherited by a Lutheran. Thus, all the north German states are now Protestant.
♦ King Henry VIII of England founds six new bishoprics.

LITERATURE AND THE ARTS
♦ Richard Taverner translates Erasmus's *Adagia* into English; London.
♦ Hans Holbein the Younger paints a miniature portrait of Princess Anne of Cleves for King Henry VIII of England, who is looking to her as a possible fourth wife. Partly on the basis of the portrait, Henry decides to marry her.
♦ Titian paints a portrait of King François I of France, sight unseen, based on a medal designed by Benvenuto Cellini.
♦ Persian weavers begin knotting two enormous "medallion" carpets (having large circular medallions at the center), continuing through 1540. Now among the most famous of Safavid carpets extant, they are thought to have been used first at a shrine in the city of Ardabil, from which their present name is derived. One is at the Victoria and Albert Museum in London, the other at the Los Angeles County Museum of Art.

SOCIETY, EDUCATION
♦ The first Christmas tree is erected at Strasbourg Cathedral, Germany.
♦ King François I decrees that Paris French is the French to be spoken throughout France.
♦ A public lottery is held in France.

1540-1549

1540

GEOGRAPHY

♦ Francisco Vasquez de Coronado of Spain leads an expedition sent by the Governor of Mexico to the Rio Grande area (now part of the southwestern United States) in search of the legendary, supposedly fabulously rich "Seven Cities of Cibola." He explores as far as one of the Zuni villages near the present Arizona-New Mexico state line, and is disappointed to find no gold there. He introduces horses and sheep to the natives of the area.

♦ Garcia Lopez de Cardenas, a member of Coronado's expedition, is led by Native American guides to the South Rim of the Grand Canyon of Arizona.

♦ Hernando de Alarcon sails up the Sea of Cortez to the mouth of the Colorado River, ascending beyond the confluence of the Gila River. He is the first European to explore a great river of the American West.

POLITICS

♦ King Henry VIII of England marries Anne of Cleves, his fourth wife, following negotiations by Thomas Cromwell, Earl of Essex.

♦ King Henry VIII has his marriage with Anne of Cleves

101

annulled, and marries his niece, Catherine Howard , his fifth wife.

♦ Thomas Cromwell is executed on a charge of high treason in London.

♦ HRE Charles V executes the leaders of the Ghent rebellion.

♦ HRE Charles V gives the Duchy of Milan to his son Philip (later King Philip II of Spain).

♦ King John Zapolya of Hungary dies, and is succeeded by his infant son John Sigismund, in defiance of the treaty of 1538, that gave the succession to Archduke Ferdinand of Austria.

♦ Archduke Ferdinand of Austria attacks Hungary, laying siege to Buda, and Sultan Suleiman I of Turkey intervenes.

♦ Philip, Landgrave of Hesse, contracts a bigamous marriage, discrediting the Lutheran cause in Germany.

♦ The English Parliament suppresses the Military Order of St. John of Jerusalem (crusader knights).

♦ A treaty between the Republic of Venice and Turkey is signed in Constantinople. Venice surrenders territories and agrees to pay an annual indemnity to Turkey.

♦ Afghan rebel Sher Shah becomes Emperor of Delhi, India.

RELIGION

♦ The De Soto expedition performs the first Christian baptism of Native Americans, at Ocmulgee River near present-day Macon, Georgia.

♦ Portuguese Catholics destroy the Hindu temples in Goa.

♦ King François I of France issues the Edict of Fontainbleau , establishing a new procedure for the trial of heretics.

♦ Protestant reformer John Calvin: *Commentarii in epistalam Pauli ad Romanos* (Commentaries on St. Paul's Epistle to the Romans); Strasbourg, Germany.

♦ Pope Paul III issues the bull *Regimini militantis ecclesiae*, confirming the Society of Jesus (the Jesuit Order).

♦ The Fathers of the Oratory, a religious order for men, is formed in Rome.

LITERATURE AND THE ARTS

♦ Titian paints "The Young Englishman."

♦ King François I of France brings the Italian sculptor and jewel-maker Benvenuto Cellini to France. Cellini remains in the King's service until 1545, with an annual salary of seven hundred crowns.

♦ Five members of the Bassano family of musicians from Venice come to work for King Henry VIII of England as members of "The King's Music," the group of professional instrumentalists that provides music at the English court. The first Bassano family member arrived at Court in about 1531, and Bassano family members remained in the royal employ until the time of King Charles II.

SOCIETY, EDUCATION

♦ Chester, England: authorities ban the annual Shrove Tuesday football game, saying it is too violent.

♦ The Japanese begin to renew piracy on the coast of China.

♦ The hottest summer within living memory in London.

♦ King Henry VIII of England founds the Regius Professorships of divinity, Greek, Hebrew, civil law and physics at Oxford and Cambridge Universities.

♦ Robert Estienne ("Stephanus") is appointed printer to King François I of France, for works in Latin, Greek and Hebrew.

♦ Nicholas Oursian builds a huge clock for Hampton Court Palace in England, showing the days of the week and the months, the hours, the time of high water at London Bridge, the phases of the moon, the signs of the zodiac, and the sun moving round the stationary earth.

♦ Rhaeticus (Georg Joachim von Lauchen): *Narratio prima de libris revolutionum Copernici* ; Danzig; the first and most effective defence of the Copernican astronomical system, that places the sun at the center of a solar system, around which the earth and other planets revolve.

1541

GEOGRAPHY

♦ Hernan de Soto of Spain discovers the Mississippi River and crosses it, continuing to explore westward.

♦ Francisco Pizarro is assasinated at his palace in Lima, Peru, by supporters of his former partner in exploration and conquest, Diego de Almagro (whom he had murdered in 1538).

♦ Pedro de Valdivia of Spain founds the city of Santiago, Chile.

♦ Jacques Cartier of France, on his third voyage, establishes a short-lived settlement in the lower St. Lawrence basin of Canada (to 1543).

♦ Francisco Vasquez de Coronado of Spain continues his explorations of the American southwest, leading an expedition from New Mexico across the buffalo-filled plains of present-day Texas, Oklamona and Eastern Kansas in a quest for the supposedly rich Gran Quivira region.

♦ Gerardus Mercator: *Sphere terrestre* (terrestrial globe); Louvain; 41 cm in diameter. Mercator was neither the inventor nor the first user of this projection, but he was the first to apply it in a nautical chart for use by seamen.

POLITICS

♦ Queen Catherine Howard of England, fifth wife of King Henry VIII, is imprisoned in the Tower of London, accused of immoral conduct.

♦ King François I of France reaches an accord with Sultan Suleiman I of Turkey, and later signs a treaties with the Duke of Cleves, claimant to Gelderland, and Denmark.

♦ The Scots attack Northumberland and the English border country.

- King Henry VIII makes a royal progress to the north of England
- Philip, Landgrave of Hesse, reaches an accord with HRE Charles V, recognizing Charles's brother, Archduke Ferdinand of Austria, as successor to Charles as Holy Roman Emperor, and promising to abandon his allies in France and Cleves.
- Sultan Suleiman I of Turkey attacks Hungary, ostensibly in support of Archduke Ferdinand of Austria's claim to the crown. Suleiman takes the city of Buda and gains control of the country. Hungary remains a Turkish province until 1668.
- Treaty of Gyalu : King John Zapolya's widow cedes Hungary to Archduke Ferdinand of Austria.
- HRE Charles V's attempt to take Algiers fails, largely because of storms, and the Turks retain control of the Mediterranean.

RELIGION

- John Knox goes to Scotland to preach the Protestant Reformation.
- Protestant reformer John Calvin returns to Geneva, Switzerland, from Strasbourg, Germany. He begins efforts to establish "The City of God."
- The Diet of Ratisbon meets (April-July) in the presence of HRE Charles V, who attempts to reconcile rival creeds in Gremany. Charles admits Protestants to the Imperial Chamber and renews the Catholic League of 1538.
- Jews are expelled from Naples.
- Ignatius Loyola is elected General of the Catholic Society of Jesus (Jesuits).
- King Henry VIII of England assumes the titles of King of Ireland, and Head of the Irish Church. Previously, he was called the "Lord" of Ireland

SOCIETY, EDUCATION

- ◆ A large earthquake occurs in Santiago, Guatemala.

1542

GEOGRAPHY

- ◆ Juan Rodriguez Cabrillo of Spain explores Upper and Lower California. Leaving Navidad, Mexico, on June 27, he arrives at Ballast Point, San Diego, on September 28.
- ◆ Francisco de Orellana of Spain, who had served with Francisco Pizarro, discovers the Amazon River and sails its entire length as far as the Atlantic Ocean. His reports claim that some of the local tribes are led by women, which leads to naming the river for the women warriors of Greek legend.
- ◆ Hernan de Soto dies of fever on the banks of the Mississippi River, and his body is consigned to the waters for burial.
- ◆ Antonio de Mota of Portugal enters Japan, as the first European visitor. This is the first Japanese contact with firearms.
- ◆ Jesuit missionary Francis Xavier arrives in Goa on the western coast of India.

POLITICS

- ◆ The Battle of Solway Moss is fought between England and Scotland, in which the English are victorious. Twelve hundred Scots are killed versus only seven individual Englishmen. King James V of Scotland dies three weeks later, after suffering a complete breakdown.
- ◆ Mary Stuart, the one-week-old daughter of King James V, becomes Queen of Scotland, with her French mother, Marie of Guise, as Regent. Mary remains Queen of Scotland until she is deposed in 1567.
- ◆ Queen Catherine Howard of England is executed. She was Henry VIII's fifth wife.

- War breaks out between France and the HRE Charles V. François I of France is angered that the Duchy of Milan had been given to Charles's son Philip.
- Joachim of Brandenburg attacks Turkey.
- HRE Charles V's campaign against the Turks in Hungary fails
- The Chinese are defeated by Altan Khan, de facto ruler of the Mongols.

RELIGION

- Pope Paul III calls a general church council for 1545 at Trent (Trento, Italy), that will convene in 1545, after some delays.
- Pope Paul III establishes the Inquisition in Rome.
- Protestant reformer John Calvin publishes a new catechism and liturgy in Geneva, Switzerland.
- The Parlement of Paris orders the suppression of John Calvin's *Institutes* (of 1526).
- Martin Luther consecrates a Bishop of the Lutheran Church.
- Father Juan de Padilla, a Spanish Franciscan missionary with Coronado's expedition, is murdered by the Kansas tribe of Native Americans, in Kansas, the first missionary killed in what is now the United States.

LITERATURE AND THE ARTS

- Sylvestro di Ganassi dal Fontego: *Regola rubertino*, in 2 volumes: Venice; a treatise on playing the viola da gamba. This is the most complete discussion of 16th century perfoming practice.

SOCIETY, EDUCATION

- Thomas Elyot: *Bibliotheca Eliotis, Eliotis librarie* ; London; an enlargement of his dictionary of 1538.
- Magdalen College of Cambridge University is founded in England.

1543

GEOGRAPHY

◆ Juan Rodriguez Cabrillo writes an account of his voyages of discovery in Upper and Lower California, the oldest written record of human activity on the west coast of the United States. He includes material on Native American societies, local flora and fauna. It is first published in 1886.

◆ Portuguese traders arrive in Japan, and introduce firearms.

POLITICS

◆ King Henry VIII of England marries Catherine Parr , his sixth wife.

◆ Treaty of Greenwich between England and Scotland is signed in July, to secure peace and provide for the betrothal of Mary Queen of Scots to Prince Edward Tudor. It is repudiated by the Scottish Parliament in December.

◆ Prince Philip of Habsburg (later King Philip II of Spain), son of HRE Charles V, marries the Infanta Maria of Portugal, his first wife (d. 1546)

◆ France invades Luxembourg.

◆ Combined French and Turkish fleets capture Nice.

◆ An alliance is formed between King Henry VIII of England and HRE Charles V against Scotland and France

RELIGION

◆ Pope Paul III issues the *Index Librorum Prohibitorum*, a list of books that Catholics may not read. It is issued again in 1557, 1559, and 1564.

◆ English law forbids anyone to read the English Bible aloud to another person, and anyone under the rank of a gentleman to read it privately to himself.

◆ Spanish Catholic Inquisition burns its first Protestant martyrs.

◆ Portuguese Catholic Inquisition burns its first heretic.

LITERATURE AND THE ARTS

♦ Sir Thomas More: *Richard the Third*; posthumously published in London; an important step in the development of English prose.

♦ Titian paints "Ecce Homo" and portraits of the Farnese family, including Pope Paul III.

♦ Hans Holbein the Younger dies of the plague in London. Earlier in the year he had painted a self-portrait.

♦ Benvenuto Cellini designs a magnificent large gold and enamel saltcellar for King François I of France, one of the wonders of 16th century goldwork.

SOCIETY, EDUCATION

♦ Merchants of Seville, Spain, form the "Consulado"—a merchant guild for the protection of their trading monopoly.

♦ Spanish navigator and mechanician Blasco da Garray submits the design for a steamboat to HRE Charles V.

♦ The city of Pisa, Italy, lays out the first botanical garden in Europe.

♦ Nicholaus Copernicus: *De revolutionibus orbium coelestium* (On the Revolutions of the Heavenly Spheres); Nuremberg, Germany. He argues that the earth and the planets revolve around the sun, phrasing it as speculative hypothesis rather than fact.

♦ Andreas Vesalius: *De humani Corporis fabrica* (On the Fabric of the Human Body); Padua; Italy. It is based on his dissections of the human body: "the most important . . . branch of the art of medicine . . . is based above all on the investigation of nature," and contains beautiful, detailed drawings by Jan Stephan van Calcar. Vesalius soon replaces the ancient Greek physician Galen as the standard for medical knowledge.

1544

GEOGRAPHY

◆ Lourenco Marques and Antonio Calderia of Portugal explore the rivers in the region of Delagoa bay, East Africa.

◆ Silver is discovered at Potosi, Peru, in South America (now Bolivia), one of the richest silver mines in history.

◆ Sebastian Cabot of Spain: *Declaratio chartae novae navigateriae domini almirantis*; Antwerp; an engraved map of the known world. Cabot gives credit to the Greek astronomer Ptolemy and "modern discoveries" by the Spanish and Portuguese.

POLITICS

◆ King Henry VIII of England and HRE Charles V invade France. Henry VIII, leading his troops in the field, captures Boulogne after a three-month siege.

◆ The Peace of Crépy is signed between France and HRE Charles V, who has not consulted his ally, King Henry VIII of England.

◆ English troops burn every structure except the castle in Edinburgh, Scotland.

◆ The English Parliament recognizes the royal succession of Princesses Mary and Elizabeth, after Prince Edward

◆ Sweden is proclaimed an hereditary kingdom with the right to Kingship descending through the male line of the Vasas, at the Diet of Vesteras.

◆ Denmark repudiates its alliance with France.

◆ Sweden makes an alliance with France, to counter Denmark's alliance with HRE Charles V.

◆ Ivan IV, Grand Duke of Muscovy and ruler of all Russia, takes the government into his own hands at the age of fourteen.

RELIGION

◆ Gerardus Mercator, Flemish cartographer, is imprisoned for heresy, but released for lack of evidence.

SOCIETY, EDUCATION

♦ Seville, Spain: a total of 154 shipments of treasure from the Americas are received throughout the year.

♦ St. Bartholomew's Hospital, London, is re-founded.

♦ The University of Konigsberg is founded by Albert I, Duke of Prussia.

1545

POLITICS

♦ The Truce of Adrianople is signed between HRE Charles V, King Ferdinand of Austria and Sultan Suleiman I of Turkey.

♦ French troops land on the English Isle of Wight, and attempt to retake Boulogne in France.

♦ Pope Paul III makes his son, Pier Luigi Farnese, the Duke of Parma, without permission from HRE Charles V.

RELIGION

♦ The **Roman Catholic Church's Council of Trent is convened** in the Cathedral of Trento, Italy, by Pope Paul III on December 13. Under Jesuit guidance, it intends to reform the Catholic Church (the "**Counter Reformation**"). Thirty-one high church dignitaries attend the first session, among them Papal Legates Cardinal Giovanni Maria del Monte (later Pope Julius III) and Cardinal Marcello Cervini (later Pope Marcellus II), as well as the English Cardinal Reginald Pole. Italian Cardinal Carlo Borromeo is chiefly responsible for its the council's overall success during its eighteen years of meetings, and has the principal part in drawing up the Roman Catechism. The council meets in three sessions: March 1545-winter 1547; May 1551-May 1552; April 1561-July 1563.

♦ Diet of Worms opens: Protestant princes express dissatisfaction with terms established by the Council of Trent, and demand a permanent religious settlement for Germany. HRE Charles V refuses their demands.

♦ King François I of France orders another massacre of Protestants in April (by June 3000 are killed).
♦ The German Palitinate becomes Protestant.
♦ Jesuit Father Francis Xavier visits Malacca. He writes from there to King John of Portugal, urging him to establish the Inquisition in Goa in order to repress Judaism.

LITERATURE AND THE ARTS

♦ Agnolo Bronzino ("Il Bronzino") paints Eleanora of Toledo, wife of Cosimo de' Medici.
♦ Titian paints portraits of Pietro Arretino and Venetian Doge Andrea Gritti.
♦ William Scrots of the Netherlands, formerly court painter to the Regent of the Netherlands, is appointed court painter to King Henry VIII of England with annual wages of 62 pounds, 10 shillings.

SOCIETY, EDUCATION

♦ French printer Claude Garamond designs his antique typography. "Garamond" still is used as the name of a printing font.
♦ The "Mary Rose," the finest new ship in the English Navy, sinks in the harbour of Portsmouth immediately after launching, as King Henry VIII watches.
♦ A botanical garden is opened by the University of Padua, Italy.
♦ King Henry VIII of England refounds Wolsey College of Oxford University as Christ College.
♦ Giralomo Cardano: *Artis Magnae sive de regalis Algebrae liber unus* ; Nuremberg, Germany; a comprehensive treatise on algebra in which the formulae for solving cubic and quartic equations were published for the first time. Cardano was accused of plagiarism from Niccolò Tartaglia, who had solved equations of the third degree in 1535.
♦ Conrad Gessner: *Bibliotheca universalis* ; Zurich, Switzerland; a catalogue in four volumes, in Greek, Latin and Hebrew, of

all past writers with the titles of their works; publication completed in 1555. It was the first of its kind, and the cornerstone for all subsequent bibliographical work.

1546

GEOGRAPHY
♦ A serious Mayan uprising in Mexico is put down by the Spanish.

POLITICS
♦ Peace of Ardres ends England's war with France and Scotland. Boulogne is to remain in English hands for eight years, and then be returned to France for a payment of two million crowns.
♦ Bohemian troops invade Saxony.
♦ The Turks occupy Moldavia

RELIGION
♦ Following Martin Luther's death, the German Protestant Schmalkaldic League prepares for civil war in Germany.
♦ The Protestant princes at Ratisbon denounce the Catholic Council of Trent.
♦ Etienne Dolet, French scholar and printer of scholarly books, is charged with publishing heretical works (Protestant versions of the scriptures, in French). At first pardonned by King François I, he is rearrested, convicted, hanged and burnt at the Place Maubert in Paris.
♦ Ann Askew, a Protestant, is tortured and burned at the stake for heresy in Smithfield, England.

LITERATURE AND THE ARTS
♦ Michelangelo designs the dome and undertakes the completion of St. Peter's Basilica, Rome.
♦ Pierre Lescot begins construction of the Louvre Palace in Paris.

♦ Titian paints a portrait of Pope Paul III and his nephews.

♦ Lavina Teerlinc is hired by King Henry VIII of England to be court miniturist and also appointed to the Queen's Privy Chamber with an an annual salary of £ 40. Teerlinc is the daughter of the noted illuminator Simon Benninck of the Ghent-Bruges School.

♦ The first book in Welsh is printed: *Yny Lhyuyr hwnn.*

SOCIETY, EDUCATION

♦ The fortune of the Fugger merchant banking family of Augsburg is valued at four million gulden.

♦ Gerardus Mercator states his opinion that the earth has a magnetic pole.

♦ Georg Agricola: *De natura fossilium*; Basel, Switzerland; treatise on fossils, considered the first mineralogy textbook. This is a section of the larger work, *De ortu & causis subterraneorum lib.v.*.

♦ King Henry VIII of England founds Trinity College at Cambridge University, England.

1547

POLITICS

♦ Battle of Muhlberg: HRE Charles V defeats the Protestant Schmalkaldic League.

♦ King François I of France dies.

♦ Henri de Valois, his son, is crowned King Henri II of France, and his wife, Catherine de' Medici, is crowned Queen of France.

♦ The Crown of Brittany is united with the Crown of France.

♦ King Henry VIII of England dies.

♦ Edward Tudor, age 11, Henry's son by Queen Jane Seymour, becomes King Edward VI of England after his father's death, with Edward Seymour, Duke of Somerset, as Lord Protector.

♦ Hungary and Turkey sign a five-year truce. Sultan Suleiman

I restores most of western Hungary to Archduke Ferdinand of Austria, and pays him annual tribute for his eastern share.

♦ The cities of Augsburg and Strasbourg submit to HRE Charles V.

♦ The French capture St. Andrew's Castle in Scotland.

♦ Ivan IV, Grand Duke of Muscovy, is crowned as the first Tsar of Russia. Known to history as Ivan "the Terrible," he is crowned in Moscow by the Bishop (Metropolitan) of Moscow in January. In February he marries a member of a family that later takes the name Romanov.

♦ The Crown of Bohemia is proclaimed hereditary in the House of Habsburg.

RELIGION

♦ Portuguese Catholic Holy Office prepares its first index of prohibited books.

♦ The Council of Trent is transferred to Bologna, Italy.

♦ La Chambre Ardente (the burning chamber) is created in Paris as a criminal court for the trial of heretics, as persecution of Protestants in France becomes more severe.

♦ Cosimo de' Medici advises HRE Charles V to undertake a complete reform of the Catholic Church through the Council of Trent.

SOCIETY, EDUCATION

♦ King Henry VIII of England contracts with the Fuggers of Augsburg to purchase the most famous jewel in Europe, called the "Three Brethren" because it is set with three enormous "balas" rubies (red spinels). Henry dies before receiving it. His son, King Edward VI, takes delivery of it. Queen Elizabeth I wears it in some portraits. It disappears forever during the reign of King Charles I.

♦ Edward Seymour, Duke of Somerset and Lord Protector for King Edward VII, begins to build Somerset House in the Strand, London.

- French replaces Latin as the official language of France.
- An English statute authorizes punishing convicted vagrants by slavery.
- Moscow is destroyed by fire.
- Peter Martyr lectures in theology at Oxford University, England.
- Andrew Boorde: *The Breviary of Health*; London; five more printings to 1598; a medical compendium including first aid procedures. "I do not wryte these bokes for lerned men, but for symple and unlerned men that they may have some knowledge to ease them selfe in their dyseyses and infirmities . . ."

1548

GEOGRAPHY

- Rich silver veins in Zacatecas and Guanajuato, Mexico, are first mined by the Spanish.
- Gonzalo Pizarro, son of Francisco Pizarro, is defeated at the Battle of Xaquixaguana, Peru, by Pedro de la Gasca, after which he is executed.

POLITICS

- HRE Charles V annexes 17 provinces of the Netherlands, beginning 80 years of war between Spain and the Netherlands.
- The Turks occupy Tabriz, Persia.
- King Sigismund I of Poland dies and is succeeded by his son Sigismund II Augustus.
- Maximilian, eldest son of HRE Ferdinand I and Anna of Bohemia and Hungary, becomes King of Bohemia.
- English Lord Protector, the Duke of Somerset, explores the possibility of a union of England and Scotland.
- Mary Queen of Scots, at age 5, is betrothed to the French Dauphin and goes to live at the French court, leaving her

mother Queen Marie of Guise (widow of King James V) in Scotland as Regent.

RELIGION

♦ Jesuit Father Ignatius Loyola: *Spiritual Exercises* (written in 1521)
♦ Church of England Archbishop Thomas Cranmer: *Catheachismus, that is to say, a shorte instruction into christian religion*; London
♦ First edition of the Book of Common Prayer is published in London
♦ A royal edict forbids the performance of "mystères" (a type of play about religious subjects) in Paris.
♦ Princess Elizabeth Tudor's translation of Marguerite of Angoulême's "The Mirror of a Sinful Soul" is published in Germany as *A Godly Medytacyon of the Christen Sowle*.

LITERATURE AND THE ARTS

♦ Titian paints "Charles V at the Battle of Muhlberg," creating the prototype for equestrian state portraits.
♦ Tintoretto paints "The Miracle of St. Mark."

SOCIETY, EDUCATION

♦ Hôtel de Bourgogne, the first roofed theatre, is opened in Paris.
♦ A pepper plant indigenous to Guinea is first grown in England.
♦ Sir Thomas Gresham founds seven professorships in London.
♦ Sebastian Cabot is made Inspector of the Royal Navy by King Edward VI of England.
♦ The University of Messina is founded in Italy.

1549

GEOGRAPHY

♦ Thome de Souza of Portugal founds Sao Salvador.

♦ The Audiencia of New Granada is created, with Santa Fe (present-day Bogota, Colombia) as the provincial capital.

♦ Siegmund freiherr von Herberstein: *Rerum moscoviticarum commentarii* (Notes on Russia); Vienna; one of the earliest books on travel. Later editions are printed in Venice (1550), and Basel, Switzerland (1551).

POLITICS

♦ Maximilian, son of Archduke Ferdinand of Austria, is recognized as the next King of Bohemia.

♦ Thomas, Lord Seymour of Sudeley, brother of the Duke of Somerset, Lord Protector, is executed for treason in London. He had married Henry VIII's widow, Catherine Parr, and was suspected of attempting to seduce Henry's daughter Elizabeth while she lived in their house.

♦ The Duke of Somerset is removed as Lord Protector of King Edward VI of England, and is imprisoned in the Tower. He is succeeded by John Dudley, Earl of Warwick, later named Duke of Northumberland. Rebellions follow: in the north, to protest enclosure laws; in the west, advocating the restoration of the Catholic liturgy.

♦ HRE Charles V declares the seventeen provinces of the Netherlands independent of the Holy Roman Empire, forming a circle of their own. Charles remains in the Netherlands for the rest of the year.

♦ France declares war on England. They capture Ambleteuse and begin a siege of Boulogne, both British possessions on French soil.

♦ Tsar Ivan IV "the Terrible" calls the first national assembly in Russia.

RELIGION

♦ Pope Paul III dies.

♦ Act of Uniformity: introduction of a uniform Protestant church service in English, with the use of King Edward VI's

Book of Common Prayer . Only this book may be used in services. It was repealed in 1553 and restored in 1559 and 1662.

♦ Zurich, Switzerland: Consensus Tigurnus agreement between Protestant reformer John Calvin and rival Protestant sect, the Zwinglians, on the nature of Holy Communion.

♦ Jesuit Father Francis Xavier lands at Kagoshima, Japan, on his first mission to introduce Christianity (until 1551).

♦ Jesuit missionaries are sent to South America.

LITERATURE AND THE ARTS

♦ Joachim du Bellay: *L'Olive*; Paris; the first sonnet sequence in the French language, in the syle of Petrarch.

♦ Piero Ligorio designs the Villa d'Este at Tivoli, outside Rome.

♦ Andrea Palladio designs the Basilica at Vicenza, Italy.

SOCIETY, EDUCATION

♦ Joachim du Bellay: *La Deffense et illustration de la langue francaise*; Paris. This was the first statement of the theories espoused by the poetic group known as "La Pléiade," who rejected medieval traditions and patterned their works on the ancient Greeks and Romans. After Pierre de Ronsard, Bellay was the most important member of the group.

119

1550-1559

1550

POLITICS

- The Peace of Boulogne ends England's war against France and Scotland. England returns Boulogne to France upon payment of 400,000 crowns.
- Sir William Cecil is named principal Secretary of State for England.
- Mecklenburg, Prussia and Austria combine in the Defensive League against HRE Charles V. They approach France for an alliance.
- Gustavus Vasa, King of Sweden, founds the city of Helsinki, now the capital of Finland.
- A League of Native American Nations (called the Iroquois Confederacy) is established in the area now comprising New York State by Chief Haio hawt' ha (Hiawatha) and his Huron mentor. Mohawk, Cayuga, and Oneida tribes participate. Later, the Seneca and Onondaga tribes also join. The League is a cooperative union, with each tribe maintaining its independence.
- The Chinese Mongols beseige the city of Peking (Beijing) for a week.

RELIGION

◆ Pope Julius III (Cardinal Giovanni Maria del Monte) is crowned.

◆ John Marbeck: *The Booke of Common Praier Noted*; London; the first musical setting of services from the Church of England's 1549 Book of Common Prayer.

◆ Church of England Archbishop Thomas Cranmer: *A Defense of the True and Catholike Doctrine of the Sacrament* ; London.

LITERATURE AND THE ARTS

◆ Pierre de Ronsard: *Odes (Les quatre premiers livres des odes de Pierre de Ronsard)*; Paris.

◆ Olavus Petrie: *Tobia Commedia* ; Stockholm; the earliest Swedish stage play.

◆ Giovanni Grancesco Straparola: *Le piacevole notti* (The Delightful Nights); Venice; the first European collection of fairy tales.

◆ Lorenzo Lotto paints "A Nobleman in His Study."

◆ Michelangelo paints "Deposition from the Cross," that contains a self-portrait.

◆ Titian paints Prince Philip of Spain (later King Philip II) in armor.

◆ Loys Bourgeois: *Le droict chemin de musique* (The correct approach to music); Geneva. This contains the first explicit description of the French practice of performing evenly notated rhythms unevenly. ("notes inégales"), that continued until the late 18th century.

◆ Andrea Palladio designs the Palazzo Chiericati and the Villa Rotunda in Vicenza, Italy

SOCIETY, EDUCATION

◆ The first written reference to the English game of cricket appears in the wardrobe accounts of King Edward VI of England.

◆ The game of billiards is played for the first time in Italy.

1-MOSH

- Sealing wax is used for the first time.
- Cattle are introduced in South America.
- The city of Antwerp has 19 cane sugar refineries.
- Sir John Harington (the elder) translates Cicero's *De Amicita* as *The Booke of Freendeship*; London.
- Ortensio Lando: *Commentario delle piu notabili e mostruose cose d'Italia* (*Commentary on the most notable and monstrous things in Italy*); Venice; reprints to 1559. The book includes descriptions of all the food substances available throughout Italy.
- Rhaeticus (Georg Joachim von Lauchen): *Ephemeris ex fundamentis Corpernici*; Leipzig, Germany; second of his defences of the Copernican system. The first was in 1540.
- Paolo Giovio: *La prima{—la seconda} parte dell'historia del suo tempo* (*History of His Times*); Italy.
- Siegmund freiherr von Herberstein: *De natura fossilium*—a treatise on fossils.

1551

GEOGRAPHY

- Antonio de Mendoza, after serving as Viceroy of New Spain since 1536, is appointed Viceroy of Peru.
- Sebastian Cabot founds the company of Merchant Adventurers of London.

POLITICS

- A Habsburg family compact provides for Archduke Ferdinand to succeed to the imperial title and Habsburg lands on the death of HRE Charles V, with Charles's son Philip as Ferdinand's successor. The compact is abrogated in September 1555.
- Pope Julius III deprives Ottavio Farnese of the duchy of Parma.

- King Henri II of France begins campaigning in Italy against HRE Charles V.
- The Treaty of Kalsburg re-affirms Archduke Ferdinand's right to the crowns of Hungary and Transylvania. This is followed by an uprising in Transylvania in support of Archduke Ferdinand. Cardinal George Martinuzzi, the effective ruler, is assasinated.
- John Dudley, Earl of Warwick, is created Duke of Northumberland. His son Robert, Earl of Leicester from 1564, will be Queen Elizabeth I's chief favorite.
- Turkey and Hungary go to war (until 1562).
- The Turks fail to capture the island of Malta but take Tripoli.

RELIGION

- A group of Jesuit missionaries arrives in Japan.
- Jeruits found the Collegio Romano in Rome, as a papal university
- Jews are persecuted in Bavaria.
- Church of England Bishop Stephen Gardiner is deprived of the See of Winchester.
- The Muscovite State Church decrees that no Western religious art may be imported, and only icons in traditional style may be painted there.

LITERATURE AND THE ARTS

- English edition of Sir Thomas More's *Utopia*, translated from the Latin by Ralph Robinson; London.
- Giovanni Pierluigi da Palestrina is appointed Director of Music at St. Peter's Basilica, Rome.

SOCIETY, EDUCATION

- First licensing of alehouses and taverns in England and Wales.
- Girolomo Cardano visits London and casts the horoscope of King Edward VI.

- Fifth and last epidemic of a mysterious, fast-moving and usually fatal disease known as the "sweating sickness" in England, the first epidemic occuring in 1485, others following in 1507, 1517, and 1528. Among those killed by it presumably was Arthur, Prince of Wales, in 1502. Dr. John Caius writes a description of the symptoms and progress of the disease, that is now thought to have been caused by a virus, and to have reoccured in this century under another name (the honta virus).
- Printing is introduced in Ireland.
- The Chinese government makes it a crime to go to sea on a multimasted ship, even for purposes of trade.
- Martin Cortes: *Breve compendio de la sphera y de la arte de navegar* (Brief compendium of the scope and art of navigation); Seville, Spain. The most famous and most comprehensive manual of navigation of the entire century, it was translated into English in 1596.
- Pierre Bélon: *Histoire naturelle des estranges poissons marins* (Natural History of Unknown Ocean Fish); Paris; a treatise on fish.
- Conrad Gessner: *Historia animalium*; Zurich, Switzerland; the first part of his book on zoology.

1552

GEOGRAPHY

- Francisco Lopez de Gomara: *Historia general de las Indias*; Zaragosa, Spain; recollections of his work as private secretary to Hernan Cortez (to 1553).
- Bartholeme de Las Casas: *Thirty Most Just Propositions*; Collected Tracts. He advocates humane treatment of the native Americans in order to convert them to Christianity, and criticizes harsh treatment of the Indians by the Spanish encomenderos.
- Joao de Barros): *Asia (Decades of the Portuguese in Asia*, Vol I);

3rd volume printed in 1563; 4th volume, ed. by Lavanha, in 1615; a comprehensive history of the Portuguese in the East Indies.

POLITICS

♦ King Henri II of France and HRE Charles V go to war (until 1556).

♦ France seizes Toui, Metz and Verdun.

♦ Ivan IV (the "Terrible") of Russia begins the conquest of Kazan and Astrakhan, territory of the Mongols (to 1554), the first Russian conquest of Tatar territory. For the first time, the Volga becomes a Russian river.

RELIGION

♦ Second, revised edition of the Book of Common Prayer in England, written by Church of England Archbishop Thomas Cranmer; London.

♦ Jesuit Father Francis Xavier reaches St. John's Island (Chang chuen shan), off the mouth of the Canton River in China, but dies there of a fever without reaching the mainland.

♦ Treaty of Passau between the Elector of Saxony and King Ferdinand (for HRE Charles V) grants freedom of religion to the Lutherans.

LITERATURE AND THE ARTS

♦ Pierre de Ronsard: *Amours*, Vol. I; Paris.

♦ Etienne Jodelle: *Cleopatre captive*, the first classical tragedy in French, and *La Rencontre*, a comedy, are both performed before King Henri II of France in Rheims. Both plays are published in 1574 by Charles de la Motte, Paris.

♦ Titian paints a self-portrait

♦ Agnolo Bronzino (Il Bronzino) paints "Christ in Limbo." As a historical portraitist, he painted most of the Medicis, Dante, Boccacio and Petrarch.

♦ Philibert Delorme designs Chateau Anet. Construction lasts until 1559.

SOCIETY, EDUCATION

♦ St. Andrew's Golf Club, Scotland, is founded. Legend says that Mary Queen of Scots became the first woman golfer there.

♦ The privileges of the Hansa trading organization are curtailed in England.

♦ Bartolomeo Eustachio writes *Tabulae Anatomicae*; making known his discoveries of the eustachian tube of the ear and the eustachian valve of the heart; first published in 1754 .

♦ John Caius: *A boke, or counseill against the disease called the sweate, or sweatying sicknesse*; London; Richard Grafton. It contains suggestions for avoiding or curing the disease by a physician who had obsserved its progress first hand.

♦ Gilbert Walker Dice: *A Manifest Detection of the most vile and detestable use of-Dice-play*; London; detailed discussion of the methods and language of the dice hustler; approximate date and attribution.

♦ Sultan Suleiman "the Magnificent" begins to build a mosque for himself in Istanbul.

♦ Christ's Hospital, London, and 35 grammar schools are founded by King Edward VI in England.

♦ Collegium Germanicum (German College) is founded by the Jesuits in Rome.

1553

GEOGRAPHY

♦ The Muscovy Company is founded in London, with explorer Sebastian Cabot at its head. A principal objective is to find a northern route to the riches of the East Indies and Asia.

♦ Sir Hugh Willoughby of England, leading the first entirely English expedition of exploration under the aegis of the Muscovy Company, discovers Novaya Zemlya. He dies while wintering on the Kola Peninsula, in Russian Lapland.

♦ Richard Chancellor of England, separated from

Willoughby's expedition where he was "pilot-general," continues on to Russia via Archangel He concludes a treaty with the Russians giving freedom of trade to English ships.

POLITICS

♦ HRE Charles V withdraws from Metz and returns to Brussels, leaving Germany to govern itself. The Bishoprics of Metz, Toul and Verdun pass to the control of the French crown.

♦ HRE Charles V attempts, with no success, to restore imperial control to Siena, Italy, using forces from Naples.

♦ The League of Heidelberg is formed by Catholic and Protestant princes in Germany to preserve peace and prevent the election of Prince Philip of Spain as Holy Roman Emperor. This leads to war throughout Germany.

♦ HRE Charles V renounces his imperial crown, with the title of Holy Roman Emperor, in favor of his younger brother King Ferdinand I of Austria.

♦ HRE Charles V captures Terouanne from the French after a two-month siege.

♦ King Edward VI of England is persuaded by the Duke of Northumberland in June to name Lady Jane Grey as his heir. She is the eldest claimant to the throne from the Suffolk family, and a highly educated Protestant.

♦ King Edward VI of England dies in July.

♦ Lady Jane Grey is immediately proclaimed Queen of England by the Duke of Northumberland. She reigns for nine days (some sources say twelve) before being deposed.

♦ Mary Tudor, the Catholic daugher of King Henry VIII and Queen Catherine of Aragon, is proclaimed Queen of England in August.

♦ Lady Jane Grey and the Duke of Northumberland are tried for treason.

♦ Queen Mary of England signs a treaty in November, pledging to marry Prince Philip Habsburg of Spain (later King Philip II).

♦ A Turkish fleet, aided by the French, does much damage in the Mediterranean. This provokes a rebellian in Corsica that is suppresssed by the Genoese, with Spanish help.

♦ Sultan Suleiman I of Turkey makes peace with Persia.

RELIGION

♦ The powers of office for Roman Catholic bishops in England are restored.

♦ In Italy, all copies of the Jewish Talmud are ordered to be burned, and none are allowed to be published.

LITERATURE AND THE ARTS

♦ Hans Sachs, the Meistersinger: *Tragedia von der strengen Lieb Herr Tristrant* ; a version of the story of Tristran and Isolde, that probably originates in the 10th century.

♦ Nicholas Udall writes the comic play *Ralph Roister Doister;* London; published posthumously in 1567; inspired by the Roman comic writers Terence and Plautus.

♦ Diego Hurtado de Mendoza writes *Lazarillo de Tormes*, the first Spanish picaresque novel; his authorship is not entirely certain.

♦ William Baldwin writes *A Marvellous History intituled Beware the Cat.* Published in 1570 in London. This is the earliest original piece of long prose fiction in English, the first English "novel."

♦ Paolo Veronese paints the ceilings of the Doge's Palace in Venice.

♦ Antonio Moro goes to England, where he is knighted as Sir Anthony More by Queen Mary, and paints her portrait for Prince Philip of Spain, her prospective bridegroom.

♦ English composer Christopher Tye writes "The Acts of the Apostles," a musical setting dedicated to King Edward VI.

SOCIETY, EDUCATION

♦ The potato is first described by Pedro del Cieza de Leon in his *Chronicles of Peru.*

♦ The University of Lima is founded in Peru.

1554

GEOGRAPHY

♦ John Locke of England sails to Guinea, Africa.

♦ The city of Sao Paolo is founded in Brazil.

POLITICS

♦ Lady Jane Grey , briefly Queen of England after the death of King Edward VI, is executed.

♦ Protestant Church of England prelate Thomas Cranmer, Archbishop of Canterbury, is sent to the Tower of London. Charged with treason, he pleads guilty.

♦ Rebellion in England: Sir Thomas Wyatt marches on London.

♦ Princess Elizabeth Tudor (later Queen Elizabeth I) is imprisoned in the Tower of London, under suspicion of having conspired with the Protestant rebels. She is there from March through May.

♦ Queen Mary I of England marries Prince Philip of Spain (son of HRE Charles V, and later King Philip II of Spain) on 26 July. She allows him the "crown matrimonial," the right to be called King and to inherit the throne. Philip spends a total of 14 months in England before Mary's death in 1558. As a wedding present, he gives Mary the famous pearl pendant, "La Peregrina," which returns to Spain after her death. It is worn by many royal Spaniards, and was purchased in 1969 by actor Richard Burton for his wife, actress Elizabeth Taylor. Among Philip's entourage is the Spanish composer Antonio de Cabazon.

♦ The Turks conquer the coast of North Africa (completed 1556).

RELIGION

- Protestant reformer John Knox goes to Geneva, where he meets John Calvin.
- The English Parliament re-establishes Roman Catholicism as the state religion, and England is reconciled with Pope Julius III.

LITERATURE AND THE ARTS

- Antonio Moro (Sir Anthony More) is appointed court painter to Queen Mary I and King Philip of England.
- Andrea Palladio writes *L'antichita di Roma*, a guidebook to Roman antiquities.
- Giovanni Pierluigi da Palestrina: *First Book of Masses*, dedicated to Pope Julius III; Rome.

SOCIETY, EDUCATION

- From 1532 to 1554, 10,000 lbs of gold are produced by Japan. Much of it is acquired by Portugal.
- Girolamo Cardano produces pure alcohol.
- The first known autograph album is begun.
- Trinity College, Oxford University, is founded in England.
- Dilligen University is founded in Bavaria.

1555

GEOGRAPHY

- A French colony is founded on the Bay of Rio de Janiero, Brazil, as the first stage of "Atlantic France."

POLITICS

- Archduke Ferdinand of Habsburg opens the Diet of Augsburg.
- The Spanish regain Siena, in Italy, which surrenders after a famine. Prince Philip of Spain subsequently sells the city to Cosimo de' Medici.

- Prince Philip of Spain (King Philip of England) leaves England for the Netherlands in August.
- HRE Charles V resigns the government of the Netherlands, Milan and Naples to Prince Philip of Spain at a ceremony in Brussels.
- Japanese pirates attack Hangchow, China, and threaten the city of Nanking.

RELIGION

- The Religious Peace of Augsburg: HRE Charles V grants choice of religion to independent German cities. Lutheran states are to have equal rights with the Catholic.
- Pope Julius III dies in March.
- Cardinal Marcello Cervino is elected Pope Marcellus II, but dies three weeks afterward.
- Pope Paul IV (Cardinal Giovanni Pietro Caraffa) is crowned.
- Protestant reformer John Knox returns to Scotland from Geneva.
- John Rogers is burned at the stake in Smithfield, England, the first Protestant martyr under Queen Mary I. Rogers, formerly a Catholic priest, had helped William Tyndale to publish his English translation of the Bible.
- An anti-Calvinist uprising in Geneva is ruthlessly suppressed.

LITERATURE AND THE ARTS

- Louise Labé: *Oeuvres* (Works); Lyon, France. She exhorts women to make their mark on the age by writing: "The honour that knowledge will give will be entirely ours and it will not be taken from us by the thief's skill . . . or by the passage of time." In 1542, disguised as a knight, Labé fought at the siege of Perpignan.
- Nostradamus: *Les Propheties de Me. Michel Nostradamus*;; Lyon, France; this was books I-III, and the first part of Book IV of *Centuries*-, the first books of his prophecies, phrased in

rhyming quatrains. The rest of Book IV and Books V-VII may have been printed later in the year. All were in print by 1557.

♦ Antonio Moro paints a portrait of Queen Mary I of England, considered to be the best portrait of her.

♦ Orlande de Lassus: *Il primo libro di madrigali, 5vv* (First Book of Madrigals, for 5 voices); Venice, Italy.

SOCIETY, EDUCATION

♦ The English Muscovy Company is founded for the purpose of trade with Russia.

♦ Walter Rippon, a Dutchman living in London, builds a coach for the Earl of Rutland. This is the first coach made in England. In 1564, he builds one for Queen Elizabeth I.

♦ Tobacco is brought for the first time to Spain from America.

♦ Construction of Grey's Inn Hall is begun in London (to 1560).

♦ Zeno of Venice publishes a map of the northern seas.

♦ Conrad Gessner: *Mithridates de differentiis linguis* ; Zurich, Switzerland; an account of about 130 known languages, with the Lord's Prayer in 22 tongues.

♦ Alonso de Molina: *Aqui comienca un vocabulario en la lengua Castellana y Mexicana*; Mexico City; an Aztec/Spanish dictionary.

♦ Sir Thomas Pope founds Trinity College of Oxford University, England.

1556

GEOGRAPHY

♦ The Portuguese secure the right to establish a warehouse and settlement at Macao, downstream from Canton, China.

POLITICS

♦ HRE Charles V resigns his kingdoms of Spain and the Spanish Americas to his son, Prince Philip of Spain (Charles dies in

1558). The office of Holy Roman Emperor and control of the Habsburg lands had been pledged to his younger brother King Ferdinand I of Austria in 1553. Now Ferdinand becomes HRE.

♦ Prince Philip of Habsburg, son of HRE Charles V and King of England as husband of Queen Mary I of England, becomes King Philip II of Spain.

♦ King Henri II of France and King Philip II of Spain sign a truce.

♦ Pope Paul IV, claiming the right to select the Holy Roman Emperor, refuses to acknowledge Ferdinand of Habsburg, King Ferdinand I of Austria, as Holy Roman Emperor.

♦ Former Holy Roman Emperor Charles V leaves the Low Countries for Spain, to retire into the monastery of Yuste.

♦ The French, under François, Duke of Guise, invade Habsburg-controlled Italy.

♦ Pope Paul IV signs an armistice with Spain and calls for French aid.

♦ Humayun, Mughal Emperor of India, dies, and is succeeded by his son Akbar.

♦ French privateers sack the city of Havana, Cuba, a Spanish colony.

RELIGION

♦ Protestants are persecuted in England and about 300, including former Archbishop Thomas Cranmer, and Bishops Ridley and Latimer, are burned at the stake.

♦ Cardinal Reginald Pole is consecrated Archbishop of Canterbury, and assumes the position of Papal Legate in England.

♦ The Jesuit order (Society of Jesus) establishes itself in Prague.

LITERATURE AND THE ARTS

♦ Andrea Palladio and Daniello Barbaro publish a translation and commentary on Vitruvius' *Ten Books of Architecture*; Venice. Palladio does all the drawings.

♦ Orlande de Lassus: *Il primo libro di motetti, 5, 6vv* (The First Book of Motets for five and six voices); Antwerp.

SOCIETY, EDUCATION

♦ The Stationers' Company of London is granted a monopoly of printing in England.

♦ Sultan Suleiman I's Mosque in Constantinople is finished (from 1550).

♦ A powerful earthquake in Shansi, northwestern China, reportedly kills 830,000 people. This is the most damaging earthquake in recorded history.

♦ John Ponet, a refugee from Queen Mary I of England's persecution of Protestants, writes *A Shorte Treatise of Politicke Power*. He justifies and argues for the people's right to resist an evil ruler.

♦ Georgius Agricola: *De Re Metallica Libri XII*; Basel, Switzerland; a detailed record of 16th c. mining, ore-smelting and metal working. It contained 292 woodcuts from Agricola's own illustrations, that were used for 101 years in 7 editions. In 1912, it was translated into English by Herbert (later US President) and Mrs. Lou Hoover.

1557

GEOGRAPHY

♦ Hans Staden: *True History and Description of the Land of the Savage, Naked and Ugly Maneating Peoples of the New World of America*. Staden relates his experiences as a captive of the Tupinamba Indians of South America between 1542 and 1555.

POLITICS

♦ King Philip II of Spain, also King Philip of England, returns briefly to England, to procure England's support for Spain's war with France.

♦ France is defeated by Spain and England at the Battle of St. Quentin

♦ Scotland invades England.

♦ King John III of Portugal dies, and is succeeded by his grandson, who is called King Sebastian I.

♦ Pope Paul IV makes peace with King Philip II of Spain.

♦ The Livonian War (until 1582) involves Poland, Russia, Sweden and Denmark in a dispute over the succession to the Balkan territories.

RELIGION

♦ Pope Paul IV orders that all books detrimental to faith or morals are to be placed on the *Index Librorum Prohibitorum* (list of forbidden books). "Safe" books must carry the *imprimatur* (let it be printed) mark. Later editions of the *Index* are printed in 1564 and 1596.

♦ Protestant lords of Scotland revolt against Queen Marie of Guise, the French Catholic Regent, in December. They adopt a "Covenant" that binds them to labor for the triumph of the Gospel and to support a prayer book similar to that which was developed for the Protestant Church of England.

♦ The Cardinals of Lorraine, Bourbon and Chatillon are appointed Inquisitors-General in France.

LITERATURE AND THE ARTS

♦ *The Sack-Full of Newes* is the first English play to be censored.

♦ Jorg Wickram: *Der Goldfaden* (The Gold Thread); Strasbourg; one of the first German novels.

♦ Henry Howard, Earl of Surrey: posthumous publication of his blank verse English translation of Books I and IV of Virgil's *Aeneid*; London. Surrey was the first poet to use blank verse in English.

♦ Richard Tottel and Nicholas Grimald, compilers and publishers: *Tottel's Miscellany* (of Songs and Sonnets by Wyatt, Surrey and other aristocratic poets); London; one of the first English anthologies.

♦ Tintoretto paints "Susanna and the Elders."

SOCIETY, EDUCATION

♦ A serious influenza epidemic rages throughout Europe.

♦ National bankruptcy is declared in Spain, caused by the large influx of silver from the Americas.

♦ Robert Recorde: *Whetstone of Wit*; London; the first English treatise on algebra.

♦ The Accademia di San Luca is founded in Rome.

♦ Gonville College of Cambridge University, England, is re-founded as Gonville and Caius College.

1558

POLITICS

♦ England loses the port city of Calais to France. This was their last possession on French soil, that they had held for 211 years. French forces are commanded by François de Lorraine, the Duke of Guise. The English regard this as a national disaster, and oppose the succession of King Philip to the throne.

♦ King Ferdinand I of Austria, becomes Holy Roman Emperor officially, when his older brother Charles V's resignation is formally accepted.

♦ Mary Queen of Scots marries the French Dauphin, François de Valois. Queen Catherine de' Medici gives her the wonderful pearl necklace she had received from her Uncle, Pope Clement VII at the time of her marriage to Henri II in 1533.

♦ A Flemish army in the service of Spain, aided by an English fleet, defeats the French at Gravelines.

♦ Peace conference among England, France and Spain opens at Cambrai

♦ Queen Mary I of England dies on November 17.

- Elizabeth Tudor, Protestant daughter of King Henry VIII and Anne Boleyn, becomes Queen of England.
- Sir William Cecil is appointed chief Secretary of State for England.
- Russians penetrate central Asia in their war against the Mongols.
- Akbar, Mughal Emperor of India, conquers Gwalior.

RELIGION

- England repeals pro Catholic legislation.
- John Knox: *First Blast of the Trumpet Against the Monstrous Regiment of Women* ; Geneva. Knox argues that women are incompetent to rule.
- Large numbers of Protestant exiles return to England from Zurich and Geneva.

LITERATURE AND THE ARTS.

- Marguerite d'Angoulême, Queen of Navarre: posthumous publication of *Histoire des amants fontunez*, Paris. This was published in 1559 as *The Heptameron*, and contains 70 stories in the style of Boccacio's *Decameron*.
- Nostradamus: *Centuries*—the second book of his prophecies, phrased in rhyming quatrains.
- Benvenuto Cellini begins to write his autobiography (to 1566)
- Giorgio Vasari: *Vite de' piu eccellenti Pittori, Scultori e Architettori* (Lives of the Most Excellent Painters, Sculptors and Architects).

SOCIETY, EDUCATION

- Hamburg Stock Exchange is founded in Germany.
- France declares bankruptcy.
- Spanish law imposes the death penalty for importing foreign books without permission, and for unlicenced printing.
- Tobacco is grown in Spain.
- Portuguese introduce Europeans to the habit of taking snuff.
- Thomas Gresham formulates "Gresham's law," in his suggestions for reforming the English currency.

- Dr. John Dee is asked by Queen Elizabeth of England to name a propitious day for her coronation.
- The "La Peregrina" pearl pendant, a gift from King Philip of Spain to his bride, Queen Mary, is taken back to Spain; King Philip II leaves all the other jewels he had given to his wife with Queen Elizabeth I .
- Giovanni Battista (Giambatista) della Porta: *Magia naturalis* (Natural Magick) the first short version, four volumes; Naples; a wide-ranging discussion of scientific fact and marvel, from tempering steel to cookery, from counterfeiting gold to the production of new plants. At least 5 more Latin editions are published in the next 10 years. It was also published in Italian (1560), French (1565); and Dutch (1566); as well as Spanish and Arabic.
- Giovanni della Casa: *Il Galateo*; a treatise on manners, "Everyone should dress well, according to his age and his position in society . . . if he does not, it will be taken as a mark of contempt for other people."
- King Albert V of Bavaria founds the Bavarian Royal Library in Munich.

1559

POLITICS

- Treaty of Cateau-Cambresis ends the Habsburg-Valois wars between Spain and France; France gives up all conquests except Toul, Metz and Verdun; Spain now controls virtually all of Italy.
- Elizabeth Tudor is crowned Queen Elizabeth I of England on January 15. Total cost of the festivities is £16,741, excluding the coronation banquet.
- King Henri II of France dies of wounds accidentally received in a tournament.
- Mary Queen of Scots is crowned Queen of France, together with her husband King François II.

♦ King Philip II of Spain marries Princess Isabelle (Elisabeth) de Valois of France, his third wife.

♦ King Christian III of Denmark dies, and is succeeded by his son, who reules as King Frederick II

♦ Crown Prince Erik Vasa of Sweden seeks to marry Queen Elizabeth I of England, sending a delegation to the English court with his proposal.

RELIGION

♦ Pope Paul IV dies.

♦ Pope Pius IV (Giovanni Angelo de' Medici) is crowned.

♦ The English Act of Uniformity makes church attendance compulsory for Church of England services.

♦ Protestant reformer John Calvin establishes the Academy of Geneva, Switzerland.

♦ Protestant reformer John Knox preaches in Edinburgh in May, and the French Catholic Regent, Marie of Guise, is forced to flee the city.

♦ Spanish law requires that books considered detrimental to Catholic faith or morals be placed on the *Index librorum prohibitorum*. "Safe" books must carry an official *imprimatur* (let it be printed) mark.

♦ The Spanish government forbids Spanish students to attend most foreign universities, except for designated ones in Catholic countries (Rome, Bologna, Naples, etc.).

LITERATURE AND THE ARTS

♦ Marguerite d'Angoulême, Queen of Navarre: posthumous publication of *The Heptameron*; Paris; first published in 1558 as *Histoire des amants fortunez*, also in Paris; 70 stories in the style of Boccacio's *Decameron*.

♦ Jacques Amyot: *Les Vies des hommes illustres*; Paris; French translation of Plutarch's *The Lives of the Noble Grecians and Romans Compared*.

♦ William Baldwin: *A Mirror for Magistrates*; London; an enormously popular group of verse narratives, edited and principally authored by Baldwin.

- ◆ Titian paints "The Entombment of Christ."
- ◆ Pieter Brueghel the Elder paints "The Battle of Carnival"

SOCIETY, EDUCATION

- ◆ HRE Ferdinand I attempts to standardize the coinage of the Holy Roman Empire.
- ◆ King Henri II of France issues an edict making printing without authority punishable by death.
- ◆ Diane de Poitiers, Duchess of Valentinois, lifelong mistress of King Henri II, retires to her Chateau d'Anet immediately after his death, having first returned all of the King's jewels that were in her possession, as well as any personal jewels he had given her.
- ◆ The tulip is first mentioned in Western Europe, by Zurich physician and botanist Conrad Gesner, who observes it growing in Johann Heinrich Herwart's garden in Augsburg, Bavaria, and writes about its beauty. He calls it *tulipa turcarum*, because of its origin in Turkey and its resemblance to a turban. The tulip was known in northern Italy by the 1550's; arrived in Vienna by 1572; England by 1582; Frankfurt by 1593, and France by 1598.
- ◆ Queen Elizabeth I signs a proclamation against "excess in apparel," printed the next day. Other "sumptuary laws" follow in 1574, 1577, 1579, 1580 and 1597, none having any perceptible effect on people's dress.
- ◆ Michel de Nostradamus: *An Almanacke for the yeare of our Lorde God, 1559*—includes some prognostications as well as the weather and phases of the moon; London.
- ◆ The first known mention of tea in Europe, as *Chai Catai* (Tea of China) occurs in *Navigationi e Viaggi* (Voyages and Travels) by Giambattista Ramusio of Venice.
- ◆ William Baldwin: *Mirror for Magistrates*; London.
- ◆ The Geneva Academy is founded in Switzerland. It becomes a University in 1873.

1560-1569

1560

POLITICS

- The Treaty of Berwick between England and Scotland is signed in February. England agrees to come to Scotland's aid if it is attacked by France. The French are expelled from Scotland.
- Marie of Guise, Queen Regent of Scotland and mother of Mary Queen of Scots, dies in June.
- The Treaty of Edinburgh between England and France is signed in July. French troops are evacuated, and a Protestant Council of Regents is appointed. Queen Elizabeth I's right as Queen of England is recognized, and Mary Queen of Scots' claim to the English throne is annulled. In France, Mary refuses to ratify the treaty.
- King François II of France dies in December, leaving Mary Queen of Scots a widow. She makes plans to return to Scotland.
- Charles de Valois becomes King Charles IX of France, and Queen Mother Catherine de' Medici becomes Regent.
- King Gustavus Vasa (Gustavus I) of Sweden dies in September, and is succeeded by his son Eric, who rules until 1569 as King Erik XIV.
- Turkish galleys rout a Spanish fleet off Tripoli.

- Amy Robsart, wife of Queen Elizabeth I's favorite Sir Robert Dudley (later the Earl of Leicester) dies in a mysterious fall at their home in the country. Suspicion of foul play falls on Dudley, and thus his elegibility as a suitor to the Queen is damaged.
- Akbar, Mughal Emperor of India, conquers the Rajput kingdom and Lower Bengal, and establishes a new capital at Agra.
- Madrid becomes the capital of Spain.

RELIGION

- The Catholic Inquisition is established in the Portuguese East Indies.
- The estates of the realm of Scotland adopt John Knox's official confession of faith, the *Confessio Scotica*, and the Assembly of the Kirk (Church) accepts a book of discipline strongly influenced by Calvinism. This abolishes Papal jurisdiction over Scotland.
- Protestant immigrants are expelled from the imperial city of Aachen.
- The English language "Geneva Bible," using William Tyndale's translations of the Christian scriptures and the Book of Moses, is published in Geneva by reformers led by William Whittingham. The 1611 King James Bible uses most of Tyndale's wordings. This is the first English language Bible widely available in England.
- Pierre de Ronsard: *Les Discours*; Paris; poems about the French wars of religion.

LITERATURE AND THE ARTS

- Pierre de Ronsard: *Lex Oeuvres* ; Paris; a pocket-sized edition of his *Collected Works* ; 4 tomes in 3 volumes.
- Hsu Wei: *Ching P'ing Mei*; the first classic Chinese novel, written in the style of social realism.

- François Clouet paints a portrait of Queen Catherine de' Medici of France.
- Jacopo Tintoretto paints "Susannah and the Elders."
- Andrea Palladio designs a Refectory for the church of St. Giorgio Maggiore in Venice.

SOCIETY, EDUCATION

- Domenico Romoli: *La singolare dottrina di M. Domenico Romoli . . . Dell'ufficio dello scaleo* ; Venice. Translated into English as *The Steward*, it contains menus and manners for dining well.
- Peter Whitehorne translates Machiavelli's *The Art of War* into English; published in London.
- Sir William Cecil, chief Secretary of State, reforms the English currency.
- Accademia Secretorum Naturae, the first scientific society, is founded in Naples, Italy.

1561

POLITICS

- Mary Queen of Scots, now a widow, returns to Scotland. Denied overland passage through England, she sails home, landing at Leith in August.
- Sir William Cecil, English Secretary of State, is made Master of the Court of Wards in January.
- The French Estates-General meet at Orleans in January. Michel de L'Hôpital appeals to moderates to rally to the Crown.
- Livonia, fearing Russian attack, transfers its allegiance from the newly secularized Teutonic Knights of the Baltic States to Poland.
- King Erik XIV of Sweden annexes Reval.

RELIGION

- The Edict of Orleans is voted at the Estates-General,

suspending persecution of Huguenot Protestants in France. The Prince of Condé presses for allowing liberty of conscience.

♦ The Baltic states of the Order of the Teutonic Knights are secularized

♦ The Duke of Savoy is forced to grant religious toleration to Protestants in the Vaudois, whom he is unable to subdue.

♦ Scottish Church ministers draw up the *Confessions of Faith*, influenced by the writings of Protestant reformer John Knox.

♦ Thomas Norton translates Protestant John Calvin's *Institutes of the Christian* Religion into English; London.

♦ The first Calvinist Protestant refugees from Flanders settle in England, as cloth workers.

LITERATURE AND THE ARTS

♦ Sir Thomas Hoby translates Baldessare Castiglione's *Il Cortegiano* into English as *The Courtyer of Count Baldesser Castilio*. Published in London.

♦ Thomas Norton and Thomas Sackville: *The tragedie of Gorboduc, or Ferrex and Porrex*; London; an historical tragedy play, of which Norton wrote the first five acts.

SOCIETY, EDUCATION

♦ Tobacco is introduced into France by Jean Nicot, who learned of it as French ambassador to Portugal from 1559 to 1561. The word nicotine derives from his surname.

♦ Portuguese monks at Goa introduce printing into India.

♦ German engineers begin mining for copper and lead in England.

♦ St. Paul's Cathedral, London, is badly damaged by fire.

♦ Francesco Guicciardini: *Historia d'Italia* (The History of Italy from 1494 to 1532) is published posthumously. First written in Italian, by the end of the century it is translated into Latin, French, German, Dutch, Spanish and English.

Guicciardini is considered one of the greatest of all writers of contemporary history.

- Sir Thomas Smith writes *Dialogue on the Queen's Marriage*, containing arguments on the Queen's duty to marry, and the problems involved in her choice.
- The Merchant Taylors' School is founded in London.

1562

GEOGRAPHY

- The French attempt to colonize Florida. A group of French Huguenots is sent to the Carolina coast by their leader Admiral Gaspard de Coligny, but they grow homesick and build a pinnace (a light sailing ship) so they can return to France. Running out of food and water during the voyage, they practice canibalism. Unable to land on the French coast, they are rescued by an English ship and taken to England, where they are entertained by Queen Elizabeth I

POLITICS

- Truce between HRE Ferdinand I and Turkey.
- Irish chief Sean O'Neill, Earl of Tyrone, ends his first rebellion against the English by surrendering to Queen Elizabeth I in January, but in May starts a second rebellion that continues until 1567.
- English troops occupy Le Havre, France.
- The Rajah of Jaipur submits to the Mughal ruler, Akbar the Great, in India.
- Treaty of Hampton Court between Queen Elizabeth I of England and the French Huguenot leader, Louis de Bourbon, Prince of Condé, calls for English troops to occupy Le Havre and Dieppe in France, and to assist in the defence of Rouen.
- Queen Elizabeth I of England falls dangerously ill with

smallpox. Many fear she will die, and she gives instructions in case of her death.

♦ Turin again becomes the capital of Savoy.

♦ Prince John Vasa of Sweden, younger brother of King Erik XIV, marries Katarina Jagellonica, sister of the King of Poland and daugher of Queen Bona Sforza of Poland.

RELIGION

♦ Third session of the Catholic Council of Trent convenes (to 1563).

♦ The Edict of St. Germain, that recognizes the rights of French Huguenots, is promulgated by Michel de L'Hôpital. Opposing it, the Duke of Guise, the Cardinal of Lorraine and the Duke of Montmorency form a military league to prevent the edict from being enforced.

♦ Religious wars begin in France between the Protestant Huguenots and the Catholics. More than 1,200 Huguenots are killed by order of the Duke of Guise at the Massacre of Vassy. This is the first of seven wars of religion that continue until the end of the century.

♦ St. Teresa of Avila establishes the Discalced Carmelite religious order in Avila, Spain. This is an attempt to return to the original, stricter Carmelite rule.

♦ The Articles of Religion of 1552 in England are reduced to the *Thirty-Nine Articles.*

♦ Frederick III, Elector Palatine, the first Calvinist elector in Germany, orders the Heidelberg Catechism to be drawn up.

LITERATURE AND THE ARTS

♦ Pieter Brueghel the Elder paints "Dulle Griet" (Mad Meg); Antwerp.

♦ Paolo Veronese paints "The Marriage Feast at Cana."

♦ Hans Eworth paints a portrait of Thomas, Fourth Duke of Norfolk.

♦ Gasparo da Salo (Bertolotti), maker of violins, violas and other bowed string instruments, moves to Brescia, where he eventually becomes the leading maker of these instruments.

SOCIETY, EDUCATION

- Castrati (castrated male singers) are first used in the Papal Choir in Rome.
- Milled coins are introduced in England.
- A plague epidemic occurs in Paris.
- John Hawkins of England takes his first cargo of slaves from Sierra Leone in West Africa to the Spanish colony Hispaniola (now Haiti) in the Caribbean. Queen Elizabeth I and several Privy Council members are unannounced shareholders in the venture.
- Venice passes a sumptuary law that forbids prostitutes to wear gold, silver, silk, or jewels of any kind, even outside the city.
- William Turner publishes a survey of European spas and watering places in London.
- The Hall of the Middle Temple is erected in London.

1563

GEOGRAPHY

- Portuguese navigator Juan Fernandez discovers the island in the South Pacific Ocean that is named for him.

POLITICS

- The French army regains the port of Le Havre, occupied by the English in 1562.
- The French Duke of Guise is killed at Orleans.
- The English Parliament presses Queen Elizabeth I to marry and settle the succession to the throne.
- King Charles IX of France, now 13, is declared of age. His Mother, Queen Catherine de' Medici, had been acting as Regent.

- Maximilian of Habsburg, ruler of Austria and Bohemia, is crowned King of Hungary.
- Tsar Ivan "the Terrible" " of Russia conquers part of Livonia. The war between Russia and Poland continues through 1582.

RELIGION

- The Thirty-one Articles are promulgated by Parliament in England, completing the establishment of the Anglican Church (Church of England).
- Peace of Amboise ends the first War of Religion in France. The Protestant Huguenots are granted limited toleration.
- The Catholic Council of Trent, first convened in 1545, concludes in December.
- John Foxe: *Actes and Monuments of these latter and perillous dayes touching matters of the Church* (known as "Foxe's Book of Martyrs")—first English edition; London; first published in 1554 in Latin, at Strasbourg, Germany. A copy of this 1700 page history of English Protestant martyrs from the 14th century to Foxe's time was placed in all English cathedrals.

LITERATURE AND THE ARTS

- Giovanni da Bologna begins to build the Neptune fountain in Bologna (to 1567).
- Hans Eworth paints a portrait of Lord Darnley and his brothers. Darnley is the future husband of Mary Queen of Scots.
- William Byrd is named organist at Lincoln Cathedral, England.
- Accademia delle Arti del Disegno is established in Florence; the first formal academy of art.
- John Shute: *First and Chief Grounds of Architecture* ; London.
- King Philip II of Spain begins construction of the Escorial (San Lorenzo del Escorial), that combines royal residence,

monastery, library, church, and mausoleum. It was designed by architect Juan de Herrera and completed in 1584.

SOCIETY, EDUCATION

♦ The English Parliament passes acts for relief of the poor and for regulating apprentices.

♦ The English Parliament passes a law requiring every land-owner with land worth £ 50 a year or more to provide two men to work on the roads every year for six eight-hour days.

♦ Plague breaks out throughout Europe, spreading to England and killing more than 17,000 people in London.

♦ The first printing presses are established in Russia by order of Tsar Ivan IV, "the Terrible."

♦ King Charles IX of France appoints Nostradamus (Michel de Nostradame) as his physician-in-ordinary.

♦ The designation "Puritan" is first used in England.

1564

GEOGRAPHY

♦ The Spanish settle in the Philippine Islands, naming them for King Philip II. They had been discovered by Magellan in 1521 while he sailed around the world.

♦ French cartographer Jacques LeMoyne de Morgues paints a picture of the Huguenot leader Landonniere being welcomed by Native Americans near present-day St. Augustine, Florida.

POLITICS

♦ HRE Ferdinand I dies.

♦ Ferdinand's eldest son, Maximilian of Habsburg, is crowned Holy Roman Emperor as Maximilian II.

♦ The French Queen Mother Catherine de' Medici makes a tour of France to present her son, King Charles IX, to his subjects.

♦ King Philip II of Spain recalls Cardinal Granvelle from the

Netherlands at the request of the Regent, Margaret of Parma, and of the Nationalist Party led by Count Egmont.

♦ The Peace of Troyes ends the war between England and France.

♦ A reign of terror begins in Russia under Tsar Ivan "the Terrible," who is forced by the boyars to withdraw from Moscow.

RELIGION

♦ Pope Pius IV publishes decrees confirming the work of the Council of Trent for settling questions of dogma. These are known as "Tridentine" decrees.

♦ The Catholic Church publishes the Tridentine Index of forbidden books, promulgated at the Council of Trent.

♦ King Philip II of Spain orders that the decrees of the Council of Trent (Tridentine decrees) are to be enforced throughout his dominions.

♦ Pope Pius IV promulgates the *Professio fidei*. This presents a definition of Roman Catholicism.

LITERATURE AND THE ARTS

♦ Jacopo Tintoretto begins work on the Scuola di San Rocco (to 1587).

♦ Pieter Brueghel the Elder paints "The Adoration of the Kings"; Brussels.

♦ Jan Metsys paints "Susanna and the Elders"; Antwerp.

♦ Andrea Amati makes the earliest-dated of his surviving violins in Cremona, Italy. It has the arms of King Charles IX of France painted on the back. Amati is credited with originating and perfecting the present-day forms of the violin, viola and violoncello.

♦ Philibert Delorme begins work on the Tuileries Palace, Paris.

SOCIETY, EDUCATION

♦ Walter Rippon, a Dutchman living in London, builds a coach for Queen Elizabeth I.

♦ Dinghen van den Plasse a Dutchwoman, introduces starch into England. By the 1580's, starched ruffs become enormous and very elaborate.

♦ John Dee: *Monas hierogliphica* (the symbol of oneness expressed in sacred language); Antwerp; in Latin; dedicated to HRE Maximilian II. Using his universal symbol, the Monas, Dr. Dee proceeds through various systems of knowledge toward an understanding of universal truth.

1565

GEOGRAPHY

♦ The Spanish found the city of St. Augustine, Florida, in September. Pedro Menendez de Aviles, while sailing on a mission to stop the French Huguenot colonists in Florida, sights land and names it for the saint on August 28, the feast of St. Augustine of Hippo. There is a battle between Aviles' Spanish troops and the French, near present-day Jacksonville, Florida.

POLITICS

♦ Mary Queen of Scots marries her first half-cousin the Catholic Henry Stuart, Lord Darnley, son of the Earl and Countess of Lennox, in July in Edinburgh. The Protestant nobility strongly oppose the marriage. Unlike Queen Mary I of England, Mary Stuart does not grant the "crown matrimonial" to her husband.

♦ Turks beseige the island of Malta without success. It is defended by the Knights of St. John, formerly of Rhodes, and Spanish troops.

RELIGION

♦ Count Egmont, leader of Protestants in the Netherlands, goes to see King Philip II of Spain, to seek concessions for Protestants in Holland and Zeeland.

♦ Pope Pius IV dies in December.

- The Japanese Emperor issues an anti-Christian edict.

LITERATURE AND THE ARTS

- Pieter Brueghel the Elder paints "The Hunters in the Snow"; Brussels.
- Titian paints "The Penitent St. Mary Magdalene."
- Andrea Palladio constructs the churches of St. Giorgio Maggiore and St. Francesco della Vigna in Venice.

SOCIETY, EDUCATION

- The first graphite pencil is described by the Swiss.
- John Hawkins introduces sweet potatoes and tobacco into England.
- The Spanish bring the game of billiards to St. Augustine, Florida.
- The Royal College of Physicians, London, is empowered to carry out human dissections.
- Basel: The works of Nicholas of Cusa are published posthumously, among them his principal work *De docta ignorantia* (On Learned Ignorance). In this, he suggests the possibility that the earth rotates, that it might not be the center of the universe, that outer space could be infinite rather than bounded by divine decree, and that an understanding of the cosmos was open to rethinking according to mathematical rather than dogmatic rules. His ideas influenced Leonardo da Vinci, Copernicus and Giordano Bruno , who called him "the divine Cusanus."
- Lodovico Guicciardini: *Commentarii . . . delle cose piu memorabili seguite in Europa* (Commentary on the Most Notable Events in Europe); Antwerp.
- Tomas de Santa Maria: *The Art of Playing the Fantasia*; Valladolid, Spain. One of the earliest-known keyboard instruction books, it is chiefly concerned with improvising pieces in contrapuntal style on the clavichord.
- Venice: A catalogue of 210 outstanding courtesans is pub-

lished privately in Venice (*Catalogo di tutte le principali et piu honorate cortigiane di Venezia*) providing names, addresses, specialties and prices. Included on the list is the noted Veronica Franco. A previous catalogue appeared in 1535 entitled *The Price List of the Whores of Venice.*

1566

POLITICS

◆ Compromise of Breda: Louis of Nassau, Philip de Marnix, and Henry, Count of Brederade, organize resistance to Spanish persecution of Protestants in the Netherlands, in the confederation called Les Gueux. They present the Regent with a petition for the withdrawal of the Inquisition, and ask for the right to "liberty of conscience."

◆ War between Turkey and Hungary resumes, in spite of the truce of 1562.

◆ Suleiman I "the Magnificent," Sultan of Turkey since 1520, dies.

◆ Selim II becomes Sultan of Turkey.

◆ The Turks take the island of Chios from Genoa.

◆ June 16: James Stuart, later King James VI of Scotland and King James I of the United Kingdom, is born to Mary Queen of Scots and her husband Lord Darnley.

◆ David Riccio, confidential secretary and musician to Mary Queen of Scots is murdered by a group of conspirators at Holyrood House, Edinburgh, with the complicity of Mary's husband, Lord Darnley.

RELIGION

◆ Pope Pius V (Michiele Ghislieri, later canonized as a saint) is crowned.

◆ Protestant Calvinist riots in the Netherlands.

◆ Regent Margaret of Parma abolishes the Catholic Inquisition in the Netherlands.

- Heinrich Bullinger unites the two Protestant sects of Calvinism and Zwinglianism in the Second Helvetian Confession.
- Martin Luther: *Tischreden* (Table Talks); published posthumously in Eisleben, Germany.

LITERATURE AND THE ARTS

- Performance at Gray's Inn, London, of *The Supposes* , translated and adapted by George Gascoigne from Lodovico Aristo's *Gli Suppositi* . It is considered the earliest English prose comedy. A translation of Euripides' tragedy *Jocasta* is also performed at Gray's Inn.
- Pieter Brueghel the Elder paints "The Wedding Dance in the Open Air"; Brussels.

SOCIETY, EDUCATION

- The Janissaries (the Sultan's personal infantry troop) become a hereditary caste in Turkey.
- Bernard Palissy, "inventeur du rutique figulines du roi" (creator of rustic figures for the King), is commissioned to construct a pottery grotto for the French Queen Mother, Catherine de' Medici.
- Pier Francesco Giambullari: *History of Europe.*
- G. Blundeville: *Faure Chiefest Offices belonging to Horsemanship*; London; a manual of veterinary science.
- *Notizie Scritte* (Written News), one of the first newspapers, appears in Venice.
- The potato is introduced in Rome and Belgium.

1567

GEOGRAPHY

- The Portuguese settle at Rio de Janiero, Brazil, founding a city.
- Alvaro Mendana de Neyra discovers the Solomon Islands in the Pacific Ocean.

♦ John Hawkins makes his third voyage to the West Indies, accompanied by his cousin Francis Drake.

♦ Jesuits missionaries found a mission in Nagasaki, Japan.

POLITICS

♦ Lord Darnley, husband of Mary Queen of Scots, is murdered in February, possibly on the orders of the James Hepburn, Earl of Bothwell.

♦ The Earl of Bothwell carries Mary Queen of Scots off to Dunbar, Scotland.

♦ Mary Queen of Scots marries Lord Bothwell.

♦ The Earl of Moray, illegitimate half-brother of Mary Queen of Scots, discovers the "Casket Letters" that implicate Mary in plotting with the Earl of Bothwell to murder Lord Darnley. Their authenticity has been questioned.

♦ Mary Queen of Scots is forced to abdicate. She appoints the Earl of Moray as Regent.

♦ Mary's son by Lord Darnley, James Stuart, becomes King James VI of Scotland. In 1603, he becomes King of the United Kingdom of England and Scotland.

♦ Irish rebel leader Sean O'Neill, Earl of Tyrone, is assassinated.

♦ The English Parliament is dissolved. Queen Elizabeth I refuses a request to name her successor, but undertakes to pursue marriage negotiations with Charles, Archduke of Austria.

♦ The Duke of Alba, arriving in the Netherlands in August, begins a reign of terror. He arrests alleged rebel leaders Counts Egmont and Hoorn.

♦ Margaret of Parma resigns from her position as Regent of the Netherlands in August. King Philip II of Spain appoints the Duke of Alba to succeed her, which puts him in complete command of the Netherlands.

♦ Mughal Emperor Akbar the Great conquers Chitor in India

♦ Jiajing, 12th Emperor of the Ming Dynasty in China, dies.

LITERATURE AND THE ARTS

◆ Nicholas Udall: His comic play *Ralph Roister Doister* is published posthumously (written c. 1553) in London. Considered the first original comedy in English literature, it was written for Eton College's St. Andrews Day celebrations.

◆ Pieter Brueghel the Elder paints "The Land of Cockaigne"; Brussels.

◆ Giovanni Pierluigi da Palestrina: *Missa Papae Marcelli* (Mass of Pope Marcellus) appears in his second book of masses; Rome.

◆ The Red Lion, a building for use in staging plays, is built in London.

RELIGION

◆ Edward Hake translates Thomas à Kempis's *The Imitation of Christ* into English.

◆ John Casimir leads an army of German Protestants to fight for the French Huguenot Protestants.

SOCIETY, EDUCATION

◆ Two million natives die of typhoid fever in South America. Approximately 20% of the South American natives die during the early years of the Spanish occupation.

◆ Santa Trinita Bridge in Florence, Italy, is constructed.

◆ Ulisse Aldrovandi establishes a botanical garden at the University of Bologna.

◆ Rugby School is founded by Laurence Sheriff in England.

◆ Helmstedt University, Brunswick, is founded in Germany.

1568

GEOGRAPHY

◆ England takes possession of Newfoundland.

POLITICS

◆ Mary Queen of Scots, defeated in battle at Langside by the

Earl of Moray, escapes to England where she is confined by Queen Elizabeth, whom she will never meet face to face during her 19 years of captivity there.

♦ The York Conference is convened to inquire into the conduct of Mary Queen of Scots, reconvening later at Westminster.

♦ The Duke of Alva declares William of Orange an outlaw.

♦ Counts Egmont and Hoorn of the Netherlands are convicted of high treason, and beheaded in Brussels.

♦ Three Spanish treasure ships carrying pay for the Duke of Alva's trrops in the Netherlands are driven by a storm into the English port of Plymouth and are impounded by the English. Commercial relations between England and Philip II's dominions are severed until 1574.

♦ Spanish forces destroy three of John Hawkins' five ships at San Juan de Ulua, the Vera Cruz harbor, and force him to turn back to England.

♦ England permanently recalls its ambassador to Spain.

♦ Peace is concluded between Sultan Selim II of Turkey and HRE Maximilian II. The Turks cede some territory in return for an annual tribute of 30,000 ducats.

♦ Oda Nobunaga seizes Kyoto, Japan, displacing the Emperor and making himself dictator of central Japan. He breaks the power of the Buddhist monasteries.

RELIGION

♦ The Treaty of Lonjumeau ends the second War of Religion in France.

♦ Construction is begun in Rome on a mother church, called "Il Gesu," for the Jesuit order.

♦ The Muslim Moors revolt in Granada, Spain. King Philip II orders the slaughter of the Moorish population.

LITERATURE AND THE ARTS

♦ Pieter Brueghel the Elder paints "The Peasant Wedding Banquet"; Brussels.

♦ A "corral" (an outdoor "yard play") is presented in Madrid. This is possibly the first public theatrical presentation there.

SOCIETY, EDUCATION

♦ Construction is begun on Longleat House, an Italian-style manor house in Wiltshire, England, under the direction of Robert Smythson, for Sir John Thynne, Marquis of Bath.

♦ Queen Elizabeth I purchases Mary Queen of Scots' six-strand pearl necklace and 25 black pearl drops from the Scottish Regent, the Earl of Moray. Elizabeth is later depicted wearing it in the "Armada," "Ditchley," and other portraits.

♦ Marnix de Ste. Aldegande composes the "Wilhelmuslied," that soon comes to be regarded as the national anthem by the Dutch provinces in revolt against Spain.

♦ Alexander Nowell, Dean of St. Paul's Cathedral, London, is the first to put beer in bottles.

1569

GEOGRAPHY

♦ Gerardus Mercator: *Nova et aucta orbis terrae descriptio ad usum navigantium accomodata (Cosmographia)*; Duisbeug, Germany. A map of the world for navigational use, this is the first comprehensive map of the world using the projection that bears his name, with the parallels and meridians at right angles.

♦ Francisco de Toledo is appointed Viceroy of Peru by King Philip II of Spain, serving until 1581. He executes Tupac Amaru, the last recognized Inca prince.

POLITICS

♦ The Swedes declare King Erik XIV unfit to reign, and

proclaim his brother king as John III. Erik is imprisoned until his death in 1577 at Gripsholm Castle in Sweden.
- Poland and Lithuania merge, in the Union of Lublein.
- Mughals attack the Portuguese colony at Goa, India.
- Pope Pius V makes Cosimo de' Medici Grand Duke of Tuscany.

RELIGION
- Don Juan of Austria, illegitimate half brother of King Philip II of Spain, surpresses the Moorish rebellion in Granada.
- During a Catholic uprising in northern England, Durham Cathedral is sacked.

LITERATURE AND THE ARTS
- Hans Eworth paints "Queen Elizabeth Confounding Juno," the first of the propaganda paintings supporting the Tudor dynasty and the legitimacy of Elizabeth's monarchy.
- Daniele Barbara: *La practica della perspettiva* (The Practice of Perspective); Venice. A manual for developing the skill of drawing in perspective for artists and architects, it refers to Durer's manual of 1525.

SOCIETY, EDUCATION
- 50,000 inhabitants of Lisbon, Portugal, die in a carbuncular fever epidemic.
- A public lottery is held in London to finance repairs to the harbors.
- Tycho Brahe begins construction of a 19-foot quadrant and a celestial globe, five feet in diameter; Augsburg, Germany.

1570-1579

1570

GEOGRAPHY

♦ Abraham Ortelius: *Theatrum Orbis Terraram* ; Plantin Press, Antwerp; dedicated to Philip II of Spain. This is **the first atlas of maps**, containing 70 maps by various cartographers. A second edition follows three months later. Eventually, there are 40 editions in various languages.

♦ Nagasaki, Japan's principal port, is opened to foreign trade, the only port in Japan open to foreign ships.

POLITICS

♦ The Earl of Moray, Regent of Scotland, is assasinated in January, leaving the Scottish Protestant party leaderless. Shortly afterward, English troops are sent into Scotland to harass Queen Mary's Catholic supporters.

♦ The Earl of Mar becomes the Regent of Scotland.

♦ In April, the French ambassador to England warns Queen Elizabeth I that the French will support Mary Queen of Scots in her claim to the English throne..

♦ Queen Elizabeth I of England opens negotiations with the French for a marriage with Henri, Duke of Anjou, son of Catherine de' Medici and King Henri II. Henri is brother to King Charles IX.

♦ Princess Marguerite de Valois, sister of King Charles IX of

France, is betrothed to King Henri of Navarre, a leading Protestant Huguenot.

♦ King Charles IX of France marries Princess Elisabeth of Austria, daughter of HRE Maximilian II.

♦ King Philip II of Spain marries his fourth wife, a cousin, Princess Anna of Austria, daughter of HRE Maximilian II. She becomes the mother of the future king of Spain (Philip III).

♦ Peace of Stettin: Denmark recognizes the independence of Sweden.

♦ The Imperial Diet convenes in Speyer, Germany.

♦ Tsar Ivan "the Terrible" of Russia massacres the people of the city of Novgorod.

♦ The Turks attack the island of Cyprus, sacking the city of Nicosia.

♦ The Turks declare war on the Republic of Venice.

RELIGION

♦ In February, Pope Pius V issues the bull *Regnans in excelsis* , depriving Queen Elizabeth I of England of her throne and excommunicating her, as well as absolving her subjects from allegiance to her. The bull does not become known in England until late May.

♦ In July, Pope Pius V proclaims that the *Missale Romanum* (Roman Missal), a group of prayers formalized at the Council of Trent for use during the celebration of the Mass, is to be used in all chruches from that time on.

♦ The third War of Religion in France ends. Huguenot Protestants are given conditional freedom of worship by the Peace of St. Germain-en-Laye.

LITERATURE AND THE ARTS

♦ *The Journey to the West* is written in China, a famous novel recounting the adventures of the monk Hsuan-tsang and the monkey Sun Wu-K'ung.

- Titian paints "The Fall of Man" and "Christ Crowned with Thorns."
- The magnificent gold saltceller Benvenuto Cellini made for King François I of France in 1543 is given to Archduke Ferdinand of Austria when his neice Elisabeth marries King Charles IX of France.
- Andrea Palladio *I Quattro Libri dell'Architettura* or*Architettura*; Venice; four Books on Architecture.
- William Baldwin: *A Marvellous History intituled Beware the Cat* is published in London. Considered the first English novel, it was written in 1553.
- HRE Maximilian II confers a patent of nobility on Franco-Flemish composer Orlande de Lassus .

SOCIETY, EDUCATION

- The stock of money in the treasury of the Kingdom of Naples is 700,000 ducats.
- Nuremberg, Germany: postal services begin.
- First importation of silver from the Americas to China (apx. date). Taxation based on silver ingots becomes general.
- Alfonso de Ulloa: *Le historie di Europa* (The History of Europe), Book I; Venice.
- Roger Ascham: *The Scholemaster*, London; intended as "a plaine and perfite way of teachying children to understand, write and speake in Latin tong." Tutor to the future Queen Elizabeth I for two years in the 1540's, Ascham intended his book "for the private brynging up of youth in gentlemen and noblemens houses."
- Cardinal Carlo Borromeo, Archbishop of Milan, founds the Helvetic College at Milan.

1571

GEOGRAPHY

- The city of Manila, present capitol of the Philippine Islands, is founded by the Spanish.

POLITICS

♦ Pope Pius V signs an alliance with Spain and the Republic of Venice to fight the Turks, in May.

♦ The Turks take Famagusta, Cyprus, after an 11-month siege, and massacre its inhabitants, in August.

♦ The **battle of Lepanto** , the largest naval battle of the century, is fought in the Gulf of Corinth on Saint Justina's Day in September. Don Juan of Austria, illegitimate half-brother of King Philip II of Spain, leads combined papal and Venetian forces with about 200 ships, defeating the Turks under Ali Pasha, with about 300 ships. Thousands are killed. The Turks lose 117 ships. This is the last large naval battle of the century using fleets of galleys (boats propelled by oarsmen).

♦ Sir William Cecil, Principal Secretary of State in England and Queen Elizabeth's chief advisor, is created Baron Burghley.

♦ Negotiations for a marriage between Queen Elizabeth I of England and the French Duke of Anjou are opened. They are abandoned in January '72.

♦ A peace treaty is concluded between Altan Khan, leader of the Mongols, and the Chinese.

♦ The Bornu Empire in the Sudan reaches its greatest height under King Idris III.

RELIGION

♦ King Charles IX of France and the Protestant Huguenot party are reconciled.

♦ An English Act of Parliament enforces subscription to the Thirty-Nine Articles by the clergy.

LITERATURE AND THE ARTS

♦ Andrea Gabrielli: *Canzoni alla francese* (Songs in the French Style); Venice.

♦ Thomas Whythorne: *Songs for Three, Fower and Five Voyces*;

London; This is the first book of madrigals published in England, all composed by Whythorne, who was inspired by the popularity of Italian madrigals. As a result of this book, he was appointed Master of Music in the chapel of Archbishop Parker.

SOCIETY, EDUCATION

♦ The Royal Exchange in Cornhill, London, is opened by Queen Elizabeth I. Built by Sir Thomas Gresham, it becomes the hub of commercial activity.

♦ English Act of Parliament forbids the export of wool from England. To protect the wool industry, all commoners over age six are required to wear a wool cap on Sundays and holidays.

♦ The Blacksmiths and Joiners Companies are incorporated in London.

♦ A royal edict in France imposes uniform prices, sizes and qualities for cloth.

♦ Bibliotheca Laurenziana, Florence, Italy, is opened to the public as a public library

♦ Harrow School, England, is founded by John Lyon.

♦ Jesus College of Oxford University, England, is founded by Hugh Price.

1572

GEOGRAPHY

♦ Francis Drake becomes the first Englishman to see the Pacific Ocean, after crossing the Isthmus of Panama.

POLITICS

♦ Thomas Howard, 4th Duke of Norfolk, is beheaded for treason in February. Norfolk, Queen Elizabeth's cousin, was the last duke in England, and no other dukedoms were created during the remainder of Elizabeth's reign (to 1603). In a trial before a panel of twenty-six high-ranking noblemen, he was accused of plotting with Florentine banker Roberto Ridolfi (the "Ridolfi Plot") to remove Queen Elizabeth I, marry Mary Queen of Scots, and put her on the English throne with the help of a Spanish invasion. Following this, the English Parliament demands the execution of Mary Queen of Scots.

♦ Negotiations for a marriage between Queen Elizabeth and the French Duc d'Anjou break down. Queen Catherine de' Medici suggests her next younger son, the Duc d'Alençon.

♦ Treaty of Blois between England and France is concluded in April, with assurances that if either is attacked, the other will lend assistance.

♦ William Cecil, Lord Burghley, becomes Lord Treasurer of England in July (until 1598).

♦ King Henri of Navarre marries Princess Marguerite de Valois, sister of King Charles IX of France in August.

♦ St. Bartholomew's Day massacre of Protestant Huguenots in Paris and the provinces of France begins during the celebrations for the royal wedding (see Religion).

♦ England sends 1,000 soldiers to help the Protestant rebels in their fight against the Spanish Catholic forces in the Netherlands, while officially denying it.

♦ The Earl of Mar, Regent of Scotland, dies in December and is succeeded by the Earl of Morton, a supporter of England.

RELIGION

♦ Pope Pius V dies on May 1. He is cannonized as a saint in 1712.

♦ Pope Gregory XIII (Ugo Buoncampagni) is elected pope on May 13.

♦ **St. Bartholomew's Day massacre** of Huguenot Protestants in Paris on August 24-25 during the festivities for the marriage of Princess Marguerite de Valois, daughter of Queen Catherine de' Medici, with Protestant King Henri of Navarre. Alleging a conspiracy by the Huguenots against the

Catholic monarchy, Queen Catherine orders all Huguenots out of Paris on August 23 after their leader Marshal Gaspard de Coligny is wounded in an attack. She is supposed to have secretly ordered the assasination of Coligny on August 24, which escalates into a killing spree, with two to three thousand Huguenots killed in Paris. The killing spreads to the provinces, including the towns of Rouen, Lyons, Bourges, Orleans and Bordeaux, and lasts for some months, with a death toll as high as 8,000. One Huguenot leader claims that a total of 70,000 were killed. In Rome, Pope Gregory XIII is informed merely that a Huguenot conspiracy has been foiled, and orders a celebration.

♦ Fourth War of Religion between Catholics and Huguenot Protestants begins in France.

LITERATURE AND THE ARTS

♦ Luiz Vaz de Camoens: *Os Lusiades* (The Lusiads); Lisbon; an epic poem describing the voyages of Vasco da Gama.

♦ Pierre de Ronsard: *La Franciade* ; an unfinished epic poem about the Kings of France.

♦ Nicholas Hilliard paints his first portrait of Queen Elizabeth I of England in "the open alley of a goodly garden where no tree was near, nor any shadow at all," establishing the pattern and lighting that she came to prefer for her portraits.

♦ Paolo Veronese paints "The Battle of Lepanto." (apx. date)

♦ Andrea Amati makes his earlist 'cello still extant, "Il Re" (The King), in Cremona, Italy.

♦ English composer William Byrd and his mentor, composer Thomas Tallis, become organists of the Chapel Royal.

SOCIETY, EDUCATION

♦ Danish astronomer Tycho Brahe observes a new star in Cassiopeia (the nova now known as "Tycho's star"), without the aid of any magnification.

- One third of the population of the city of Algiers dies in an epidemic.
- The English Parliament enacts an "Acte for the punishement of Vagabondes and for the Releif of the Poore & Impotent," an effort to enlarge government's control of its subjects and minister to their welfare. A system of national taxation financed weekly doles to poor householders.
- Carrier pigeons are used by the Dutch during the Spanish seige of the city of Haarlem.
- Ambroise Paré: *Cinq Livres de chirurgie*; Paris. Considered the father of modern surgery, Paré improved the treatment of gunshot wounds, and substituted ligature of the arteries for cauterization with a red-hot iron after amputation. He served as surgeon to the French crown for almost forty years.
- Georg Braun and Frans Hagenberg begin to issue *Civitates Orbis Terrarum*; Cologne, Germany; six volumes of maps of towns and cities all over the world. Publishing continues to 1618.

1573

POLITICS

- The Peace of Constantinople ends the war between Turkey and the Republic of Venice in March. Venice abandons Cyprus. Crete (Candia) is now her only important eastern possession.
- The Spanish Duke of Alba resigns as Regent of the Netherlands, leaving Brussels and returning to Spain. Alba is replaced by Don Juan of Austria, illegitimate half-brother of King Philip of Spain, and leader of the victorious European forces at the battle of Lepanto.
- The Spanish capture the city of Haarlem in the Netherlands, after a seven-month siege.
- Sir William Drury leads an English army into Scotland, capturing Edinburgh Castle. The leader of Queen Mary's

supporters (Maitland) dies. Scotland is no longer a military threat to England.

♦ Henri, Duke of Anjou (later King Henri III of France), is elected King of Poland, and goes there to rule.

♦ Sir Francis Walsingham becomes Principal Secretary of State in England.

♦ Wan-Li begins his reign as 13th emperor of the Ming Dynasty in China, reigning until 1620.

♦ End of the Ashikaga shogunate in Japan, as the last shogun is expelled from Kyoto.

RELIGION

♦ The Pacification of Boulogne ends the Fourth French War of Religion. Protestant Huguenots are granted amnesty and they are free to worship in La Rochelle, Nimes and Montauban.

♦ The Inquisition in Rome calls painter Paolo Veronese to account for his painting of profane subject matter.

LITERATURE AND THE ARTS

♦ Johann Fischart: *Floh Haz, Weiber Traz;* Strasbourg; an account of a battle between fleas and women.

♦ Thomas Bedingfield: English translation of *Cardanus Comfort*; London. It was sponsored by, and dedicated to, Edward de Vere, 17th Earl of Oxford.

♦ Paolo Veronese paints "Feast in the House of Levi."

♦ Orlande de Lassus : *Patrocinium musices . . . cancionum . . . prima pars, 4-6vv* ; Munich. This is the first of five magisterial volumes of sacred music, that were printed together in 1589.

♦ Thomas Tallis composes (probable date) the 40 voice motet *Spem in alium* (Sing and glorify). This unique experimental work was probably used during the enactment of the liturgical drama of Judith for the celebration of Queen Elizabeth I's 40th birthday.

- Giovanni de' Bardi begins to host meetings of Florentine musicians and noblemen in his home. They come to be known as the "Camerata" and are credited with providing the main impetus toward the development of opera.

SOCIETY, EDUCATION

- John Hawkins is appointed treasurer of the English navy, and begins to reorganize the fleet, designing the "race built" ship, commanded by the sailors rather than soldiers.
- King Philip II of Spain promulgates laws explicitly forbidding the enslavement or abuse of the native peoples in the Americas, and restricting Spanish settlements to "untilled" lands.
- First mention of the cultivation of maize by the Chinese.
- First German cane-sugar refinery, at Augsburg.
- Sir Reginald Scott: *Perfect Platform of a Hop-garden*; London. Scott is credited with the systematic development of hop growing in England, and this is the first manual on hop culture in the country.
- François Hofman: *Francogallia*; a treatise arguing for the people's right to elect and depose kings.
- Construction is begun on the Cathedral in Mexico City (completed in 1813).

1574

GEOGRAPHY

- ThePortuguese begin to settle the coast of Angola, Africa, founding the city of Sao Paolo.
- William Bourne: *A Regiment for the Sea*—the first English book on navigation; London.

POLITICS

- King Charles IX of France dies in May.
- Henri of Valois, Duke of Anjou and King of Poland, secretly leaves Poland to return to France to become King as Henri

III (to 1589). Enroute, he meets HRE Maximilian II in Vienna, who counsels a policy of religious toleration. The Polish Assembly deposes Henri as King of Poland. He arrives in France in September and is met by King Henri of Navarre and his brother, the Duke of Alençon.

♦ Zeeland falls to the Dutch rebels.

♦ Louis of Nassau is defeated at the battle of Mookden Heath.

♦ In June, Protestant rebel leader William of Orange ("William the Silent") persuades the Estates of Holland to open the dykes to hinder the Spanish siege of Leyden in the Netherlands. By October, he raises the siege.

♦ Bernardino de Mendoza arrives in England as Spanish Ambassador.

♦ Selim II, Sultan of Turkey, dies and is succeeded by Murad III.

♦ John the Terrible, Prince of Moldavia, is killed during his attack on the Turks. His principality is laid waste.

♦ Spain loses Tunis to the Turks. Tunis becomes a Turkish Regency with an elective Bey.

RELIGION

♦ The Fifth French War of Religion begins in February (to 1576).

♦ Damville, Marshal of France, issues a manifesto from Languedoc in November, calling for religious toleration, administrative reforms and the expulsion of the Guises.

♦ The first "Auto-da-fé" is held in Mexico (burning of heretics at the stake).

LITERATURE AND THE ARTS

♦ The Chinese print an edition in movable type of a large collection of stories, *T'ai-p'ing kuang-chi.*

♦ Tintoretto paints "Paradiso" at the Doge's Palace in Venice, Italy.

- The manor of Longleat House in Wilshire, England, is completed.
- Queen Elizabeth I of England grants a license to the Earl of Leicester 's Men, the Earl's private theatrical company.
- Pope Gregory XIII makes the composer Orlande de Lassus a Knight of the Golden Spur. De Lassus was the best known composer of the century, and was honored many times, beginning with a grant of nobility from HRE Maximilian II in 1570.

SOCIETY, EDUCATION

- Conrad Dasypodius builds the Strasbourg clock, which displays a series of scenes.
- Stefano Guazzo: *La Civil Conversatione* (Civil Conversation); Venice; published in Italian; translated into French, English, German, Latin, and Spanish.
- Justus Lipsius edits *The Histories* and *The Annals* of the ancient Roman historian Tacitus; Antwerp, Plantin Press; notes and commentaries are included; a landmark in classical scholarship.
- Ulisse Aldrovandi: *Antidotarii Bononiensis Epitome* ; Bologna; a treatise on drugs that was a model for many subsequent pharmacoepias. Aldrovandi had successfully urged his home city, Bologna, to establish a botanical garden in 1568.
- Fabricius (Girolamo Fabrici) discovers that valves in our veins assist the circulation of human blood, and explores other aspects of blood circulation as well. Fabricius was a Professor at the University of Padua, Italy.
- Jacob Verzellini, a Venetian residing in London, uses soda ash from seaweed instead of crude potash for the manufacture of glass.
- The University of Berlin is founded.

1575

POLITICS

♦ Henri of Valois is crowned King Henri III of France at Rheims Cathedral in February.

♦ King Henri III of France marries Louise de Vaudemont of Lorraine, thereby allying himself with the House of Guise.

♦ Breda Conference: King Philip II of Spain refuses to grant the concessions sought by the Dutch Protestant rebels.

♦ Queen Elizabeth I of England declines the sovereignty of the Netherlands, offered to her by William of Orange.

♦ Stephen Bathory of Transylvania is elected King of Poland (to 1586). The Polish Estates had deposed Henri of Valois as King after he left the country to claim the French crown.

♦ Mughal Emperor Akbar the Great of India conquers Bengal.

♦ Japanese warlords Oda Nobunaga and Tokugawa Ieyasu are victorious at the battle of Nagashino.

RELIGION

♦ The Mongols of China are converted to Tibetan Buddhism.

♦ Two Dutch Anabaptists are burned at the stake in Smithfield, England.

♦ John Casimir, son of the Elector Palatine, signs a treaty with the French Huguenot Protestant leaders for bringing an army of 16,000 German and Swiss mercenaries into France to fight in the Fifth War of Religion.

♦ Edmund Brindal becomes Archbishop of Canterbury in England (to 1583).

LITERATURE AND THE ARTS

♦ Torquato Tasso completes the writing of *Gerusalemme Liberata* (The Liberation of Jerusalem) at the court of the Duke of Ferarra. This is a group of epic poems about the First Crusade.

♦ George Gascoigne: *Posies*; London; "corrected and completed," it contains *Jocasta*, the second tragedy in English

blank verse, parapharased from the *Phoenissae* of Euripides;
also *Certain Notes of Instruction Concerning the Making of
Verse,* the earliest critical essay of its kind in English literature; and "a tragicall comedie," *The Glasse of Government*

♦ Johann Fischart: *Affentheuerliche und ungeheuerliche
Geschichtschrift vom Leben, Rhate und Thaten der . . . Helden
und Herren Grandguisier Gargantoa und Pantagruel;*
Strasbourg; an adaptation of Rabelais' *Gargantua and
Pantagruel.* Fischart levelled his satires at all the perversities,
public and private, of his time.

♦ First use of a "broken consort" of musical instruments in
England when Queen Elizabeth is entertained by the Earl of
Leicester at Kenilworth Castle. The English think it a
"heavenly sound," and broken consorts come to be especially
associated with English music.

♦ William Byrd and Thomas Tallis: *Canciones Sacrae* (Sacred
Songs); London; motets dedicated to Queen Elizabeth.

SOCIETY, EDUCATION

♦ The Spanish crown declares bankruptcy. In September, King
Philip II suspends all payments to his troops in the Netherlands.

♦ First European imitations of Chinese porcelain are made in
Venice and Florence.

♦ Abraham Ortelius becomes geographer to King Philip II of
Spain.

♦ Freedom from arrest is granted by the English Parliament to
its members and their servants.

♦ Plague breaks out in Sicily, spreading through Italy as far
north as Florence, Milan and Venice (to 1577).

♦ Archbishop Matthew Parker leaves his collection of historical
documents to Corpus Christi College of Cambridge University, England.

♦ Ambroise Paré: *Oeuvres;* Paris; first edition of his collected
works. There were 13 editions through 1685.

♦ The University of Leiden is founded in the Netherlands by William of Orange, to commemorate the siege.

1576

GEOGRAPHY

♦ The English navigator Martin Frobisher sets off on an expedition to find the Northwest Passage. He reaches Labrador and discovers Frobisher Bay.

♦ Bernal Diaz del Castillo writes *La historia de la conquista de la Nueva Espana* (translated into English as *The Discovery and Conquest of Mexico)*. It is first published in Madrid in 1632, based on a copy of the original MS stored in Guatemala. Diaz accompanied Cortez during his conquest of Mexico, and this is considered the most complete account of the conquest, the country, and the people conquered.

POLITICS

♦ Louis, Prince of Condé and John Casimir of the Palatinate invade France near Sedan and move toward Vichy in January. By March, they are united with the Duke of Anjou's army at Moulins.

♦ King Henry of Navarre escapes from Paris and renounces Catholicism at Tours.

♦ King Philip II of Spain makes his illegitimate half brother Don Juan of Austria the Governor of the Netherlands after the death of Don Louis Requesens.

♦ Louis VI becomes Elector Palatine (to 1580) upon the death of Frederick III.

♦ Diet of Ratisbon: HRE Maximilian II obtains support for an expedition to Poland to dispute the election of Stephen Bathory as King.

♦ HRE Maximilian II dies.

♦ Rudolf of Habsburg , HRE Maximilian II's son, becomes Holy Roman Emperor as Rudolf II (to 1612). A great patron of the arts and arcane sciences, Rufolf transfers the royal court from Vienna to Prague in 1583. In 1606 he is declared unfit to rule by the Habsburg family.

◆ An Act of Federation between the Netherlands provinces of Holland and Zeeland is signed in Delft. They unite in the hope of driving the Spaniards out.

◆ William of Orange calls the Congress of Ghent in October, to discuss pacification of the Netherlands.

◆ Spanish soldiers in the Netherlands, unpaid because of the crown's bankruptcy, mutiny and sack Antwerp. Known as the "Spanish Fury" , during the course of the mutiny 8,000 people are killed and 1,000 buildings are destroyed by fire.

◆ Pacification of Ghent : all 17 provinces of the Netherlands are united. They agree to require King Philip II of Spain to recall his troops, grant religious toleration and summon a representative assembly. Archduke Matthias is to be invited to become Governor. Pacification is ratified by the States-General at Antwerp in November.

◆ The French Duc d'Alençon, son of King Henri II and Queen Catherine de' Medici, begins a courtship of Queen Elizabeth I of England.

RELIGION

◆ The Peace of Monsieur (after the Duke of Anjou) ends the Fifth War of Religion in France. The Edict of Beaulieu grants toleration for the Huguenot Protestants, except in Paris, and allows them to garrison eight strongholds. The Duke of Anjou gains estates in Anjou and Tourraine, and John Casimir receives a pension from King Henri III.

◆ Henri, Duke of Guise, forms a Catholic League to overthrow the French Huguenot Protestants.

◆ The League of Torgau is formed between the Elector of Saxony and the Landgrave of Hesse to support the opinions of the Lutherans. It draws up the Article of Faith ("The Torgau Book").

◆ A Puritan party in the English Parliament attempts to promote a radical reform of the Church of England. It fails and leader Peter Wentworth is imprisoned in the Tower for attacking Queen Elizabeth's interference with the Commons claim to freedom of speech.

LITERATURE AND THE ARTS

◆ James Burbage, father of actor Richard Burbage, begins construction of the first theatre in London, in Shoreditch, with a 21-year lease on the land. It is first known as "The Theatre," (the first use of the name, a shortening of ampitheatre) and completed in 1577. Shortly afterwards, "The Curtain" theatre is built in the same neighborhood. Burbage is also credited with building the Blackfriars Theatre.

◆ *The Paradise of Dainty Devices*; an anthology of 99 poems by Richard Edwards, the Earl of Oxford, Lord Vaux, and others; London.

◆ Palladio designs Il Redentore Church in Venice.

◆ Tomas Luis de Victoria : *Liber primus* (Book One) of masses, psalms and a Magnificat; Venice. A Catholic priest, from 1552 to 1586 Victoria studied and worked in Rome, returning to Spain to be Chaplain for the Dowager Empress Maria, sister of King Philip II.

SOCIETY, EDUCATION

◆ Danish astronomer Tycho Brahe establishes Uraniborg ("Castle of the Heavens") Observatory on the island of Hveen, Denmark, for the Danish King Frederick II.

◆ Jean Bodin: *Six Livres de La republique*; Paris; a treatise examining the definition and limits of sovereignty, arguing for a limited form of monarchy.

◆ Charles de Lécluse (Carolus Clusius; French botanist; 1525-1609) publishes a treatise on the flowers of Spain and Portugal.

- Thomas Digges: *A perfit description of the caelestiall orbes*; London. Influenced by the thinking of Copernicus, Digges posits an infinite, sun-centered universe.
- King Henri III of France founds the Academie du Palais in Paris. Pierre Ronsard, elected to membership, gives the introductory address: *Les vertus intellectuelles et morales* (Intellectual and moral virtues).
- The English Parliament passes a statute for the punishment of vagrants, ordering the establishment of houses of correction to set vagrants and thieves to hard labor.
- The University of Warsaw is founded in Poland.

1577

GEOGRAPHY

- **Francis Drake begins a circumnavigation of the globe** in his ship "The Golden Hind" (to 1580), sailing via the Cape of Good Hope. This will be the second circumnavigation. He captures the Spanish treasure ship "Cacafuega" off the west coast of South America, that carried 26 tons of silver, 80 pounds of gold, and many jewels and precious stones.

POLITICS

- A "Perpetual Edict" to settle the civil war in the Netherlands issued by Don Juan of Austria is rejected by William of Orange, leader of the Protestant rebels.
- Don Juan of Austria seizes Namur. His plan to invade England, depose Queen Elizabeth and marry Mary Queen of Scots, fails.
- Don Juan of Austria is formally deposed by the States General in the Netherlands. William of Orange enters Brussels. Don Juan is still Regent as far as the Spanish are concerned.
- The city of Danzig surrenders to Stephen Bathory, King of Poland, ending opposition to his reign.

♦ Mughal ruler Akbar the Great completes the annexation and unification of northern India.

RELIGION

♦ King Henri III of France announces to the States-General at Blois that the Edict of Beaulieu (May 1576) granting toleration to the Protestant Huguenots was obtained by force, and therefore is not binding upon him.

♦ King Henri of Navarre, husband of Princess Marguerite de Valois, is recognized as the leader of the Huguenot Party in France.

♦ Sixth French War of Religion breaks out in March. Fighting is principally in the west. The war is ended by the Peace of Bergerac, signed in August.

♦ Edward Grindal is sequestered (taken away) from the Archbishopric of Canterbury for refusing to suppress the Puritan "prophesying" movement in the Church of England.

♦ Jacob Andrae of Tubingen, Martin Chemnitz, and others, draft the Lutheran Book of Concord; Germany.

♦ The Cathedral of Milan, Italy, is consecrated by Cardinal Carlo Borromeo.

LITERATURE AND THE ARTS

♦ Greek artist Domenico Theotocopoulos ("El Greco ") moves to Toledo, Spain, after a period of study in Italy.

♦ Nicholas Hilliard paints a miniature self-portrait; London.

SOCIETY, EDUCATION

♦ Raphael Holinshed: *The Chronicles of England, Scotland and Ireland*, 2 vols, folio; London. Holinshed was assisted by William Harrison, Richard Stanyhurst (who wrote the section on Ireland) and John Hooker. Shakespeare is thought to have used Holinshed as a source for his history and legend plays.

♦ William Harrison: *The description of England*—an introduction to Holinshed's *Chronicles*; natural, social, economic, legal, ecclesiastical, folk, and architectural history; reissued in 1587.

1578

GEOGRAPHY

- George Best: *A True Discourse of the late voyages of discoverie, for the finding of a passage to Cathaya, by the Northwest*; London; within 5 years translated into French, Latin and Italian. Best had been Martin Frobisher's navigator.
- Thomas Nicholas publishes an English translation of Francisco Lopez de Gomara' s account of the conquest of the West Indies: *The Pleasant Historie of the Conquest of the Weast India, now called a new Spayne*; Henry Bynneman, London. Lopez de Gomara was secretary to Hernan Cortez, and first published his account in 1522 in Spain.

POLITICS

- Don Juan of Austria, Regent of the Netherlands, is aided by Alexander Farnese, Duke of Parma, and succeeds in defeating the Dutch federal army at the battle of Gembloux.
- The Duke of Anjou invades the southern Netherlands with a French army and takes the city of Mons.
- Queen Elizabeth I of England pays a subsidy of £ 20,000 to John Casimir of the Palatinate to aid the Dutch rebels.
- Queen Elizabeth I of England offers to mediate between the Spanish Governor of the Netherlands, Don Juan of Austria, and the Dutch rebels.
- Don Juan of Austria dies of a fever, and is succeeded by the Duke of Parma as Regent of the Netherlands.
- The Duke of Parma subdues the southern provinces of the Netherlands.
- John Casimir holds the city of Ghent with a largely Calvinist army.
- James VI (b.1566), son of Mary Queen of Scots, takes over

the government of Scotland after the Earl of Morton resigns the regency.

♦ Robert Dudley, Earl of Leicester, chief favorite of Queen Elizabeth I, secretly marries Lettice Knollys, Dowager Countess of Essex. Lettice Knollys was Elizabeth's first cousin once-removed, and mother of Robert Devereux, Earl of Essex, and Penelope Devereux, later Lady Rich.

♦ The Swedish army defeats the Russians at Wenden in the battle for control of the Baltic Sea.

♦ Sebastian I, King of Portugal, is killed at Alcazar (Al Kasr Al-Kabil) during his invasion of Morocco. Seven candidates claim the throne of Portugal, including King Philip II of Spain.

♦ King Sebastian I's Uncle Henry, a Cardinal who had been Regent during Sebastian's minority, becomes King of Portugal.

♦ Mohammed Khudabanda becomes Shah of Persia (to 1586). He is the father of the great Shah Abbas I.

♦ The first Portuguese ambassador is accredited to the court of Akbar the Great in Delhi, India.

RELIGION

♦ Otomo Yoshishige, one of the chief daimyos (warlords) of Japan, is converted to Christianity.

♦ Cardinal Carlo Borromeo, Archbishop of Milan, founds the religious order that becomes known as the Oblates of St. Ambrose. Borromeo is canonized as a saint by the Catholic Church in 1610.

♦ King John III of Sweden secretly becomes a Catholic.

LITERATURE AND THE ARTS

♦ Guillaume de Salluste, Seigneur du Bartas : *La Sepmaine* , *ou Creation du monde* ; Paris; a religious epic on the creation, part of his collected works (*Les Oeuvres*) in 10 volumes.

- Pierre de Ronsard: *Sonnets pour Helène* ; Paris; poems for Helène de Surgères.
- John Lyly: *Euphues, The Anatomie of Wit*; London.
- Antonio de Cabezon: posthumous publication of *Obras de musica para tecla, arpa y vihuela* (Musical works for keyboard, harp and vihuela); Madrid. King Philip II of Spain's favorite composer, Cabezon was an innovator who may have influenced the English composer William Byrd during his stay in London as part of Philip's entourage from 1554 to 1555.
- The Curtain Theatre in Finsburg, London, is opened. This is the second theatre in London.

SOCIETY, EDUCATION

- The Levant Trading Company is founded in London for trade with Turkey.
- Work is begun on Pont Neuf, the oldest bridge over the Seine River in Paris.
- The Royal Order of the Holy Spirit is founded by King Henri III of France. This was France's principal order of chivalry until the Revolution of 1789.
- The catacombs underneath Rome are discovered.
- Manufacture of faience pottery is begun in Nevers, France, by the Conrade brothers.
- The *Pen-ts'ao kang-mu*, the famous treatise on pharmacopoeia by Li Shih-chen, is completed in Ming Dynasty China.
- The English College of Douai is removed to Rheims.

1579

GEOGRAPHY

- Francis Drake proclaims English sovereignty on June 17 at New Albion, California, usually presumed to be located somewhere above San Francisco in present-day Marin County. However, some recently uncovered evidence suggests the landing really may have been as far north as Whale Bay, Oregon.

♦ English Jesuit Father Thomas Stephens is the first Englishman to settle in India, at Goa.

♦ Portuguese merchants set up a trading station in Bengal.

POLITICS

♦ The Union of Utrecht is formed by the northern provinces of the Netherlands in January (Holland, Zeeland, Utrecht, Gelderland, Friesland, Groningen, Overyssel). They pledge to defend their rights and liberties against Spain and to establish complete freedom of worship. William of Orange, hoping that the southern provinces also will sign, withholds his signature until May. This is considered the foundation of the Dutch Republic.

♦ Treaty of Arras : the deputies of Hainault, Douai and Artois (the southern provinces of the Netherlands) undertake to protect the Catholic faith and to effect a reconciliation with Spain; in May.

♦ An English-Dutch military alliance is signed.

♦ A small force of Spanish, Portuguese and Italian recruits under the command of exiled chieftan Desmond Fitzmaurice sails from Ferrol and lands in Ireland, officially fighting in the Pope's name, to aid the rebellion led by James Fitzmaurice Fitzgerald.

♦ Duke Albert of Bavaria dies, and is succeeded by Duke William V(to 1597).

♦ Jean de Simier, the French Duc d'Alençon's representative, arrives in England in January to initiate Alençon's courtship of Queen Elizabeth I. She is delighted with him, and gives him the pet name "monkey."

♦ The Duc d'Anjou (known to history as Duc d'Alençon, his previous title, when he was second in line to the throne) pays a supposedly secret visit to England in August to pursue his courtship of Queen Elizabeth. She is captivated and calls him her "frog."

♦ The English Privy Council fails to give Queen Elizabeth the support she expected in proceeding with a marriage treaty with the Duc d' Alençon. A preliminary treaty is signed in November, but negotiations are delayed as a result of the Catholic duke's unpopularity in England, especially with Puritains.

RELIGION

♦ Spanish mystic John of the Cross (Juan de Yepes; canonized 1726) writes *The Dark Night of the Soul*. The title comes from the first line of a poem (*En una noche oscura*) that appears together with his extensive commentary on it in *The Ascent of Mt. Carmel.*

♦ The first Christian religious service is held in California, as Rev. Francis Fletcher, Drake's chaplain on Francis Drake's ship the "Golden Hind" reads from the Book of Common Prayer of the Church of England on June 24.

♦ Faustus Socinus goes to Cracow to teach, in opposition to Luther and Calvin, and helps to found the Polish sect of Socinians.

LITERATURE AND THE ARTS

♦ Thomas North: English translation of Plutarch's *Lives of the Noble Grecians and Romanes Compared,* from the 1559 French translation of James Amyot; London.

♦ Edmund Spenser: *The Shepheards Calender*; London; twelve eclogues.

♦ John Lyly: *Euphues, The Anatomie of Wit*; London.

♦ Stephen Gosson: *The Schoole of Abuse*; London; a pamphlet attacking the theatre on moral and religious grounds.

♦ Thomas Lodge: *A Defence of Poetry, Music and Stage Plays*; London; an answer to Gosson, and against the Puritan view in general.

183

- Andrea Palladio designs the Teatro Olimpico in Vicenza, Italy.

SOCIETY, EDUCATION

- The English Eastland Company is founded for trading with Scandinavia.
- The English Levant Company signs a treaty with the Turkish Ottoman Sultan protecting their passage to Europe from Syrian ports.
- The Genoese-dominated business fair moves to Piacenza, Italy, convening four times a year as a "clearing house" where European exchange rates are fixed. Genoa now replaces Antwerp as the center of finance in Europe.
- Martin Hubblethorne, an English dyer, is sent overland to Persia by a group of English merchants to learn of "great colouring of silks" in "all the countreys that you shall passe thorow."
- Christopher Saxton: *Country Atlas of England and Wales* ; London.
- The English College is removed from Rheims to Rome.

1580-1589

1580

GEOGRAPHY

◆ Francis Drake reaches England after circumnavigating the globe. His is the second circumnvigation. The first, by Magellan, was completed in 1522. Queen Elizabeth I knights him aboard his ship, "The Golden Hind," at Deptford. Drake receives £ 10,000, plus £ 8,000 for his crew, and he gives the Queen a magnificent emerald and gold crown and a diamond cross.

POLITICS

◆ Cardinal/King Henry of Portugal dies, and the Portuguese throne is claimed by the Infante Dom Luis, and three others. Dom Luis's claim is not recognized by King Philip II of Spain, who is also a claimant.

◆ Portugal is absorbed into Spain, after a Spanish invasion led by the Duke of Alba, who was recalled from the Netherlands to command the army.

◆ Spanish forces in Ireland, sent there to support the Irish rebels, surrender to the English. The surviving officer says they were sent there on direct orders of King Philip II.

◆ John Casimir provokes civil strife in the southern Netherlands.

◆ Tsar Ivan IV (Ivan "the Terrible") of Russia kills his son and

185

heir with his own hands, an indication of his escalating descent into madness.

♦ England signs a commercial treaty with Turkey.

RELIGION

♦ The Seventh French War of Religion between Catholics and Protestant Huguenots begins in April, ending in November with the Peace of Flax, that renewed the terms of the Peace of Bergerac.

♦ Jesuits Father Edmund Campion and Father Robert Parsons land in England to begin a mission to Catholics there, who were not permitted to hear Mass. They maintain that their work of conversion cannot be considered as treason against Queen Elizabeth.

♦ Johann Fischart: *Das Jesuiterhutlein*; Strasbourg; a harsh, satirical attack on the Jesuits.

♦ The first Jesuit mission arrives in the capitol of Mughal Emperor Akbar the Great at Delhi, India.

♦ Robert Browne founds the first English Protestant Separatist congregation in Norwich, England, in defiance of the established Church.

LITERATURE AND THE ARTS

♦ Michel de Montaigne: *Essais* (Essays); Bordeaux; the first two books of the collected essays. The 3rd book, written 1586-88, is published together with the first two in 1588.

♦ John Lyly: *Euphues and his England* ; London.

♦ The English folksong "Greensleeves" is mentioned in print for the first time. Entered in the Stationers' Register in London as "a new Northern Dittye of the Lady Greene Sleeves," the ballad appears to have been popular for some time before this. It is mentioned twice in Shakespeare's play, "The Merry Wives of Windsor" ."

♦ Edward de Vere 17th Earl of Oxford and Lord Great Chamberlain of England takes over the Earl of Warwick's Players, a

theatrical company that performs both at court and at public venues.
- French essayist Michel de Montaigne travels through Germany and writes a record of his experiences and observations.

SOCIETY, EDUCATION
- A strong earthquake occurs in London, just before Easter.
- The potato is introduced in the cities of Dublin, Vienna, and Frankfurt, imported from Chile.
- Venice imports coffee from Turkey.
- Whalebone is first used for constructing the hoops of a farthingale (a voluminously wide skirt) in England, thus enabling skirts to become even wider and stiffer. Women's skirts, and ruffs as well, become progressively larger and more exaggerated throughout the 80's and 90's.
- A proclamation to restrict the growth of London forbids new building.

1581

GEOGRAPHY
- Richard Hakluyt: *Divers Voyages touching the Discoverie of America* ; London. The publication attracts the notice of Lord Howard of Effingham, and secures Hakluyt the position of chaplain to Sir Edward Stafford, English ambassador at Paris.

POLITICS
- The Portuguese Cortes (courts in which high ranking nobles and churchmen were represented) submit to King Philip II as King of Portugal.
- Poland, led by King Stephen Bathory, invades Russia.
- Act of Abjuration: the Union of Utrecht (the Protestant northern provinces of the Netherlands) declares itself a

Dutch Republic, independent of Spain, and elects William of Orange as its ruler.

♦ Don Antonio of Portugal, claimant of the Portuguese crown, escapes to England.

♦ A marriage treaty is signed in November between Queen Elizabeth I of England and the French Duc d'Anjou (generally known in history as Alençon). There is strong opposition from the English people, especially the Puritans, to her proposed marriage with a Catholic Frenchman.

♦ Russia begins its conquest of Siberia.

♦ Sigismund Bathory, nephew of Stephen Bathory, becomes Prince of Transylvania (to 1602).

♦ Peace between Spain and Turkey, based on the status quo.

♦ Mughal Emperor Akbar the Great of India conquers Afghanistan.

RELIGION

♦ Pope Gregory VIII attempts to reconcile the Roman Catholic and Russian Orthodox churches.

♦ The English Parliament enacts severe legislation against Roman Catholics, in January, aimed at retaining their obedience to the Queen. It is described as "an Act to retain the Queen's Majesty's subjects in their due obedience." Anyone who deliberately induces a person to withdraw allegiance from the Queen by converting that person to Catholicism is guilty of treason. Punishments include fines of 200 marks (approximately £ 133) for saying Mass, and £ 20 per month for refusing to attend Church of England services (recusancy).

♦ Jesuit Father Edmund Campion, in England to perform religious services for Catholics there, is seized in July. He is imprisoned and brutally tortured, then publicly hanged, drawn and quartered in London on December 1, on a charge of conspiracy.

- King James VI of Scotland signs the Second Confession of Faith, affirming his position as a Protestant.
- Acrobats, bankers and brothel keepers are excluded from communion to churches in the Union of Utrecht, in the northern provinces of the Netherlands.

LITERATURE AND THE ARTS

- Tarquato Tasso: *Gerusalemme Liberata* (The Liberation of Jerusalem); Parma: the first complete edition. An idealized story of the First Crusade, it was completed in 1575 and published as *Il Goffredo* without Tasso's consent, and with many errors, while he was imprisoned for insanity at the Court of Ferrara.
- Fabritio Caroso: *Il Ballarino*; Venice; an illustrated compendium of dance steps and dancing etiquette, with melodies notated in Italian lute tablature.
- Balthasar de Beaujoyeulx produces what is thought to be **the first ballet**, for the French royal court. A multidisciplinary 5 1/2 hour spectacle titled "Ballet Comique de la Reine," it is staged in October in the presence of King Henri III of France and his court to celebrate a royal marriage. Beaujoyeulx says of it: "As for the Ballet, it is a modern invention or is, at least, a revival from such distant antiquity that it may be called modern; being, in truth, no more than the geometrical groupings of people dancing together, accompanied by the varied harmony of several instruments."
- Hans Ruckers of Antwerp builds a muselar "mother and child" virginal (a box-shaped harpsichord with one keyboard). This is the oldest of his instruments still extant.
- The *Geuzenliedbock* is compiled in the Netherlands, an anthology of Dutch marching, military and historical songs, including the national anthem, *Wilhelmus*.

SOCIETY, EDUCATION

- First black African slaves are imported to the Spanish colony at St. Augustine, Florida.
- Queen Elizabeth I of England orders one of the first match-

ing sets of furniture: 10 chairs, 6 high stools, 24 square stools and 11 footstools, all upholstered in the same material.

♦ Richard Mulcaster, Headmaster of the Merchant Taylors' School in London: *Positions . . . necessarie for the Training up of children*; London; a treatise on education. Mulcaster advocates broader access to education, less emphasis on Latin, study of English literature, and vigorous physical exercise. One of the 45 chapters says that girls also should be trained, another suggests that even tradesmen should learn some Latin.

1582

POLITICS

♦ The Peace of Jam-Zapolski is concluded, among Russia, Poland and Sweden, through the mediation of Pope Gregory XIII. Russia loses access to the Baltic Sea and abandons Livonia and Estonia to Poland.

♦ The Duc d'Anjou ("Alençon") leaves England for Flushing (in the Netherlands) in February. Later in the month, he is inaugurated in Antwerp as the Duke of Brabant. In July, he is inaugurated as Lord of Friesland, Duke of Gelderland and Count of Flanders, through the efforts of William of Nassau, son of William of Orange.

♦ An unsuccessful attempt is made in March to assassinate William of Orange, leader of the Protestant Union of Utrecht in the Netherlands.

♦ The Imperial Diet is summoned by HRE Rudolf II to provide money for repairing forts on the Turkish frontier.

♦ King James VI of Scotland is kidnapped in August by Protestant nobles, in the "Raid of Ruthven." He escapes from them in June 1583.

♦ The Venetian constitution is amended: the authority of the Council of Ten is restricted.

- Oda Nobunnaga, the ruler of Japan, is overwhelmed in a surprise raid on his home and commits suicide. His chief general, Toyotomi Hideyoshi, becomes dictator as his successor.

RELIGION

- Italian Jesuit Father Matteo Ricci arrives in China for missionary work. Ricci introduces European clocks to the Chinese, and becomes the tutelary deity of Chinese clockmakers. By 1601, he is established in Beijing, where he is placed in charge of the government's bureau of astronomy.

LITERATURE AND THE ARTS

- El Greco paints "The Martyrdom of Saint Maurice and the Theban Legion" (apx 1580-82).
- Pierre Phalèse the Younger: *Harmonia celeste*; Antwerp; a collection of Italian madrigals; reprinted five times between 1589 and 1628.

SOCIETY, EDUCATION

- **Pope Gregory XIII reforms the Julian calendar** (first established by Julius Caesar) by omiting 10 days. Previous to the new calendar, the year had begun on March 25. Now it begins on January 1. The new calendar is adopted by the Catholic countries (the Papal states, Spain and Portugal) in October; and by France, the Netherlands and Scandinavia in December), but not by Protestant nations (e.g., England does not adopt it until 1752). HRE Maxamilian I had suggested this calendar reform at the very beginning of the century. In addition to the different reactions based on religion, some people were concerned because they were "losing" 10 days.
- Akbar the Great, Mughal Emperor of India, abolishes slavery.
- Urbain Hemand investigates the anatomy of the teeth.

♦ London's first waterworks is founded. Waterwheels are installed on London Bridge.

♦ Richard Mulcaster: *The first part of the Elementarie which treateth of right writing of our English tung* ; London. Mulcaster advocates phonetic spelling, and the book contains a list of 7000 words in his reformed spelling; e.g.: guide = "gide."

♦ Graduated pay, based on rank, is introduced into the English Royal Navy.

♦ The Utrecht Library is founded in the Netherlands.

♦ The University of Edinburgh is founded in Scotland.

1583

GEOGRAPHY

♦ England takes possession of Newfoundland. Sir Humphrey Gilbert, Sir Walter Ralegh's half brother, arrives at St. John's, the site of a fishermen's camp, and claims it for the Queen. This is the first English possession in the New World. Gilbert drowns on the voyage home.

♦ Ralph Fitch, together with Ralph Eldred and two other London. merchants, is sent on commercial reconaissance overland to the East, bearing letters from Queen Elizabeth to the Emperor of China. Captured by the Portuguese in India, Fitch is imprisoned in Goa. Escaping, he visits the court of Mughal Emperor Akbar the Great in India, and goes on to Burma and Malacca, returning via Bengal and Cochin (to 1591).

♦ The settlement at Buenos Aires, Argentina, is first called by that name.

♦ Lucas Janszoon Waghenaer of Enchuysen: *Speculum nauticum super navigatione maris Occidentalis* (The Mariners' Mirror); Leiden;Volume I of the first atlas of seacharts of western and northern Europe, covering Cadiz to Zuider Zee; published in the Netherlands in Dutch. Vol. II appears in 1586.

POLITICS

- The Duke of Anjou, Spanish Regent of the Netherlands, sacks the city of Antwerp (the "French fury"), and then retires from the Netherlands.
- King James VI of Scotland, son of Mary Queen of Scots, escapes from the Ruthven Raiders after ten months in captivity. He takes refuge in St. Andrews, and recalls the Earl of Arran.
- The "Sommerville" plot to assassinate Queen Elizabeth I of England is uncovered in October. John Sommerville is executed in December.
- The "Throckmorton" Plot (alt. Throgmorton) for a Spanish invasion of England, is discovered in December, and Francis Throckmorton is arrested.
- Duke William V of Bavaria signs a concordat with Pope Gregory XIII.

RELIGION

- Archbishop Gebhard of Cologne, Germany, having married and changed his religion from Lutheranism to Calvinism attempts to return to his See, but is opposed by the Lutherans in the "Cologne War."
- John Whitgift is elected Archbishop of Canterbury in England (to 1604), following the death of Edmund Grindal.

LITERATURE AND THE ARTS

- Queen Elizabeth I of England starts her own theatre company, "The Queen's Men" with Sir Edmund Tilney as Master of the Revels.

SOCIETY, EDUCATION

- HRE Rudolf II relocates his royal court from Vienna to Prague. It develops into a major cultural center in a short time..
- The first known life insurance policy is issued in England,

on the life of William Gibbons, for one year at an eight per
cent premium.

♦ General Toyotomi Hideyoshi lays the foundations of Osaka
Castle in Japan.

♦ Justus Lipsius: *On Constancy in a Time of Public Evils.*

♦ Sir Thomas Smith: *De Republica Anglorum (Discourse on the
Commonwealth of England)*; London. This is the only
contemporary survey of Elizabethan government and
institutions. Written in 1565, while Smith was ambassador
to France, it discusses the class divisions of English society,
from nobles, knights, squires and gentlemen, to citizens and
burgesses, yeomen, and day laborers, to merchants and
retailers, copyholders and artificers.

♦ Italian heretic philosopher Giordano Bruno visits England.
Among the works he writes while there is *Specio della Bestia
Trionfante*, an allegory dealing with moral philosophy and
expressing his opposition to religion. Bruno espoused a
pantheistic philosophy in which God animates the whole of
creation as "world soul."

♦ Galileo Galilei's experiments at the University of Pisa, Italy,
lead him to deduce the value of a pendulum for the exact
measurement of time.

1584

GEOGRAPHY

♦ The Dutch establish a trading post at Archangel on the
White Sea.

POLITICS

♦ Mendoza, the Spanish ambassador in London, is expelled for
his complicity in the Throckmorton Plot to depose Queen
Elizabeth.

♦ Fyodor I is crowned Tsar of Russia (to 1598), after the death
of his father Tsar Ivan IV "the Terrible." Fyodor is the last of

the Rurik dynasty, and he is dominated by his brother-in-law, Boris Godunov.

◆ William of Orange, the "Silent," is assassinated at the instigation of King Philip II of Spain, and is succeeded by his son Maurice of Nassau as leader of the Union of Utrecht (the Protestant provinces in the northern portion of the Netherlands).

◆ England sends aid to the Protestant rebels in the Netherlands.

◆ The French Duc d'Anjou ("Alençon") dies at Chateau-Thiery, leaving the Protestant Henry of Navarre as heir to the French throne. He had been Queen Elizabeth's favorite suitor, whom she nicknamed "frog."

◆ An alliance is formed by the Protestant Swiss cantons of Bern, Geneva and Zurich against Savoy, because it is threatening Geneva.

◆ The Turkish fleet fails to capture the coast of Zanzibar from the Portuguese.

RELIGION

◆ The first Christian catechism, *T'ien-chu shih-lu*, is printed in China.

◆ The Duke of Guise consolidates the Catholic factions in France into a Catholic League to oppose Protestant leader Henry of Navarre's claim to the throne.

◆ The English Parliament frames legislation for expelling Jesuits and seminary priests within 40 days.

LITERATURE AND THE ARTS

◆ John Lyly: 2 plays: *Alexander and Campaspe* , and *Sapho and Phao* ; London.

◆ Prince Imperial Chu Tsai-yu of China defines the tempered scale in music.

◆ The Accademia di Scienze, Lettere ed Arte is founded in Lucca, Italy.

SOCIETY, EDUCATION

♦ The Tiepolo Pisani land bank fails in Venice.

♦ The Banco di Rialto is established in Venice.

♦ André Thevet: *Les vrais pourtraits et vies des hommes illustres, grecz, latins, et payens* (True Portraits and Lives of Illustrious Men); Paris. A Who's Who of the European 16th century, it contained biographies, with engraved likenesses of most biographees. No artists, musicians, or sculptors and few writers are included; for example, Sir Thomas More 's biography makes no mention of *Utopia.*

♦ Justus Lipsius: *De constantia* (On Constancy in a Time of Public Evils); Antwerp.

♦ Giordano Bruno: *Della Causa, Principio ed Uno*; London; an exposition of his pantheistic, anti-Aristotelian philosophy of an infinite universe and the oneness of matter and spirit. Also published: *La cena de le ceneri*; London; in support of the Copernican heliocentric theory of the universe. While Bruno espoused the Copernican system, he added many of his own concepts to it.

♦ Reginald Scott: *The Discoverie of Witchcraft*; London; an exposure of the absurdities that formed the basis of the witchcraft craze. Scott incurred the antipathy of King James VI of Scotland, who later had his book burned. James believed in witches, and later wrote a book about witchcraft.

♦ Jose de Acosta publishes a catechism in Quichua, the language of the Incas, the first book to be printed in Peru.

♦ Sir Walter Mildmay founds Emmanuel College of Cambridge University. Nicholas Hilliard paints the charter, with a beautiful miniature portrait of Queen Elizabeth enthroned.

♦ Construction begins on the tomb of the Chinese Ming Dynasty Emperor Wan-li (to 1590).

♦ The oldest still-surviving wave-swept lighthouse is erected at Cordanau, France, at the mouth of the Gironde River.

1585

GEOGRAPHY

♦ Roanoke Island, off the coast of what is now North Carolina, is colonized by the English under Grenville and Lane, on behalf of Sir Walter Ralegh.

♦ Francis Drake of England sails to the West Indies where he raids Hispaniola (present day Haiti). He continues on to South America, capturing the city of Cartagena where the Spanish store their South American gold (in present-day Venezuela), and after that to the coast of Florida, where he sacks the Spanish city of St. Augustine. He brings 190 English colonists home from the Roanoke Island settlement, together with potatoes and tobacco (to 1586).

♦ John Davis of England explores the sea passages between Greenland and the Canadian mainland, searching for a northwest passage to eastern Asia.

♦ Gerardus Mercator: first part of *Atlas, sive cosmographicae meditationes de fabrica mundi* ; the first part of a projected atlas of the entire globe, containing maps of Germany, France and Belgium. This is **possibly the first time the word "Europe" is used**, and is also **the origin of the use of the word "atlas" to describe a book of maps**, since the cover shows Atlas holding a globe on his shoulders. It was completed by Mercator's son Rumold in 1595.

♦ Lucas Janszoon Waghenaer of Enchuysen publishes Volume II of *The Mariners' Mirror*, the first atlas of seacharts of western and northern Europe, covering the North Sea to the Baltic; in Dutch. Vol. I appears n 1584.

POLITICS

♦ King Henri III of France refuses the sovereignty of the Netherlands in February

♦ The Catholic League declares that the Protestant leader King

Henri of Navarre is not elegible to succeed to the French throne

♦ Treaty of Joinville between the Catholic League in France, led by the Guises, and King Philip II of Spain. Philip agrees to support Henri, Cardinal of Bourbon's claim to succeed to the French throne instead of the Protestant leader King Henri of Navarre, and will acquire Navarre and Bearn in return for doing so..

♦ English shipping in Spanish ports is confiscated in May, as a reprisal for English piracy in Spanish waters. This equates to a declaration of war against England.

♦ Queen Elizabeth I of England declines the sovereignty of the Netherlands in June.

♦ The Treaty of Nemours in July: King Henri III of France is forced to capitulate to the demand of the Guise Catholic party to revoke all toleration of the Protestant Huguenots.

♦ The "War of the Three Henrys" in France, precipitated by the Treaty of Nemours: King Henri III of France, Duke Henri of Guise, and King Henri of Navarre dispute the succession to the throne.

♦ Spanish troops under the Duke of Parma sack the city of Antwerp in August, ending its days as an interntional port and the hub of the international money market.

♦ Henry Percy, 8th Earl of Northumberland, is accused of being involved in the "Throckmorton Plot" against the life of Queen Elizabeth I of England. He commits suicide while imprisoned in the Tower of London.

♦ Queen Elizabeth I of England issues a Declaration, taking the Protestant Netherlands under her protection.

♦ The Treaty of Nonsuch : Queen Elizabeth agrees to supply 1000 cavalry and 5,100 foot soldiers under a proved general to aid the Dutch Republic. They are placed under the command of the Earl of Leicester.

♦ Akbar the Great, Mughal Emperor of India, annexes Afghanistan.

RELIGION

◆ Pope Gregory XIII dies in April.

◆ Pope Sixtus V (Felice Peretti) is crowned (d. 1590).

◆ Pope Sixtus V issues a "Bull of Deprivation," declaring that the Protestant King Henri of Navarre forfeits his rights to the throne of France.

◆ Jesuit missionaries are sent to South America.

LITERATURE AND THE ARTS

◆ Miguel de Cervantes Saavedra: *La Galatea*; Alcala; a pastoral romance, his first important work.

◆ Battista Guarini: *Il Pastor Fido*; Ferrara; a pastoral play, much influenced by Tasso's *Aminta*.

◆ Teatro Olympico, Vicenza, Italy, is opened.

◆ The Lord Admiral's Company, an acting troupe, is formed in London, led by actor Edward Alleyn.

◆ William Shakespeare of Stratford-upon-Avon goes to London to live and work.

SOCIETY AND EDUCATION

◆ Simon Stevin (Stevinus): *De Thiende*; Plantin Press, Leiden; a pamphlet arguing that a decimal system should be used for calculations, instead of common fractions, as well as for coinage and weights and measures.

◆ The Jesuits found a University at Graz, Austria.

1586

GEOGRAPHY

◆ Thomas Cavendish leaves Plymouth, England, in July on a voyage of circumnavigation, returning in 1588. This is the **third circumnavigation of the globe.**

◆ Both volumes of Lucas Janszoon Waghenaer's atlas of seacharts of western and northern Europe are translated into Latin and published in Leiden, the Netherlands .

◆ The German merchant banking house of Welser leases from

the Portuguese the exclusive rights to purchase pepper in the
East Indies.

POLITICS

♦ The Earl of Leicester accepts the title of Governor and
Captain-General of the Netherlands, but Queen Elizabeth I
of England insists that he resign it.

♦ Mary Queen of Scots recognizes King Philip II of Spain as
her heir to the thrones of Scotland and England, both of
which she claims as hers by right.

♦ Treaty of Berwick , July 1: Queen Elizabeth I of England
and King James VI of Scotland form a league of friendship.
James is to receive an annual pension from England.

♦ The "Babbington" plot " plot to murder Queen Eliazbeth I
and put Mary Queen of Scots on the English throne is
uncovered by Sir Francis Walsingham, implicating Mary
Queen of Scots.

♦ Anthony Babbington and other conspirators are tried,
convicted, and executed.

♦ The English attempt to establish plantations in Munster,
Ireland.

♦ Sir Philip Sidney dies from wounds received in the Netherlands. The English consider him a great hero, and he is
given an enormous ceremonial funeral..

♦ Mary Queen of Scots is tried for treason and convicted by a
special commission convened at Fotheringhay Castle,
following which sentence is pronounced against her in the
Star Chamber in London.

♦ The Earl of Leicester returns to England, leaving Sir John
Norris in command in the Netherlands.

♦ "The "Sixteen" establish a revolutionary government in Paris,
pledged to support the Duke of Guise and the Catholic
League.

♦ The death sentence for Mary Queen of Scots is reluctantly

confirmed by Queen Elizabeth in December, but she delays signing the death warrant until February 4, 1587.

♦ Stephen Bathory, King of Poland, dies in December. Elected as King in 1575, he is considered one of Poland's greatest rulers.

♦ Olivarez, Spanish ambassador to Pope Sixtus V, obtains the Pope's pledge to help finance sending an armada against England.

♦ The French Queen Mother Catherine de' Medici and Protestant leader King Henri of Navarre hold a meeting near Cognac.

♦ Christian I becomes Elector of Saxony after the death of Elector Augustus.

♦ Colonel Pfyffer forms the Borromean League of the Seven Swiss Catholic Cantons.

♦ Abbas I becomes Shah of Persia (until 1629). He is considered one of the greatest rulers in the history of Persia.

RELIGION

♦ Pope Sixtus V fixes the number of Cardinals at 70.

♦ Pope Sixtus V issues a bull, *Detastabilis,* forbidding usury.

♦ Claudius Aquaviva, General of the Society of Jesus from 1581: *Ratio atque institution studiorum*; expounds the Jesuit system of education.

♦ An English Star Chamber decree, instigated by Archbishop Whitgift, forbids publication of pamphlets and books unless previously approved by church authorities (this produced the *Martin Marprelate* pamphlets of 1588, arguing against this practice). This could be considered a Protestant version of the Roman Catholic *imprimatur* requirement.

LITERATURE AND THE ARTS

♦ Pierre de Ronsard: *Les Oeuvres*, ed. by Jean Galland and Claude Binet; published posthumously in Paris.

♦ William Warner: *Albion's England,* Books I-IV; London; a

metrical history of England in sixteen books, publication completed in 1606.

♦ Composer John Bull is sworn in as a Gentleman of the Chapel Royal in England.

♦ The beginning of Kabuki theatre in Japan.

SOCIETY, EDUCATION

♦ The first man smokes tobacco on the streets of London: Ralph Lane, recently returned from being governor of the Roanoke Island colony.

♦ There is a severe corn shortage in England.

♦ Galileo Galilei publishes a paper describing his invention of the hydrostatic balance; Florence, Italy.

♦ Jost Amman: *Gynaeceum, siveTheatrumMulierum* ; translated into English as "The Theatre of Women: wherein may be seen the Female Costumes of all the Principal Nations, Tribes and Peoples of Europe." Published in Frankfurt, Germany.

1587

GEOGRAPHY

♦ The first child is born in what is now the United States of America. Virginia Dare is born on August 18 in the Roanoke Island Colony, in present day North Carolina. She is the Grandaughter of Gov. John White, who leaves for England nine days after her birth.

POLITICS

♦ Queen Elizabeth I of England signs the death warrant of Mary Queen of Scots on February 4

♦ Mary Queen of Scots is executed at Fotheringay Castle on February 8. Mary, granddaughter of the English King Henry VIII's sister Margaret Tudor, wife of King James IV of Scotland, was Queen Elizabeth's first cousin, once removed,

and had claimed the English crown. Catholics throughout Europe considered her the rightful ruler of England.
- ♦ Queen Elizabeth I heavily fines William Davidson, a Secretary of State, for his share in sending the death warrant of Mary Queen of Scots to Fotheringay Castle, and Lord Treasurer Burghley remains in disgrace for his part in this, until July
- ♦ Francis Drake of England destroys the Spanish fleet at Cadiz
- ♦ Sir Christopher Hatton is named Lord Chancellor of England (to 1591)
- ♦ Sigismund III, son of King John III of Sweden, is elected King of Poland in August, as successor to Stephen Bathory
- ♦ Savoy and the Catholic Swiss cantons form an alliance with Spain.
- ♦ King Henri III of France forbids the Duke of Guise to enter Paris, and the Duke retires to Nancy.

RELIGION
- ♦ The Basilica of St. John Lateran in Rome, which functions as the papal cathedral, is rebuilt.
- ♦ The first Native American baptized as a Protestant Christian is Manteo, Chief of the Hatteras tribe. He becomes a member of the Church of England at the Roanoke Island Colony.
- ♦ Shogun Hideyoshi of Japan issues an edict ordering all foreign priests to leave the country within 20 days on pain of death. He does not enforce the law, however. Portuguese merchants are allowed to stay.
- ♦ French political philosopher Jean Bodin writes his *Colloquium Heptaplomeres* at about this time; not published until 1857. It is a strong plea for religious tolerance, that contains discussions among a Jew, a Mohammedan, a Roman Catholic, a Lutheran, a Zwinglian and a Theist, among others, resulting in the conclusion that it may be best for them all to stop disputing about religious beliefs.

LITERATURE AND THE ARTS

♦ Christopher Marlowe's play *Tamburlaine the Great* is produced in London.

♦ English dramatist Thomas Kyd writes *The Spanish Tragedy* play. (apx date)

♦ El Greco paints "The Burial of Count Orgaz" (c1586-88); Toledo, Spain.

♦ Giovanni Gabrielli: *Concerti . . . continenti musica di chiesa, madrigali, & altro . . . libro primo et secondo* ; Venice, Italy.

♦ Claudio Monteverdi: *Il primo libro di madrigali 5 vv.* (The First Book of Madrigals, in 5 voices); Venice. Books of madrigals followed in 1590 and 1592.

♦ The Rose Theatre is built in London.

♦ A company of English actors visits Germany for the first time.

♦ Construction begins on the Rialto Bridge, Venice, designed by Antonio da Ponte (completed 1591).

SOCIETY, EDUCATION

♦ Colonists at Sir Walter Ralegh's Roanoke Island Colony in present-day North Carolina brew beer from maize and hops (described in the writings of settler Thomas Hariot).

♦ William Bourne: *The Arte of shooting in Great Ordnance* ; London; a treatise on the theory of gunnery and the handling of large cast guns; London.

♦ Raphael Holinshed: *The Third volume of Chronicles (of England, Scotlande, and Irelande) . . . now newlie recognised, augmented, and continued*; revised by John Stow; London.

♦ Everard Digby: *De Arte Natandi* (The Art of Swimming); London; T Dawson; translated into English by Christopher Middleton in 1595 and published in London by James Roberts for Edward White. This is the first swimming treatise in English.

1588

GEOGRAPHY

♦ The English translation of Lucas Janszoon Waghenaer's atlas of seacharts of western and northern Europe, entitled *The Mariners Mirror*, is published in October in London, commissioned by the Lord High Admiral Lord Howard of Effingham. The book itself is not dated, but the dedication at the front is dated October 1588. The atlas is also an almanac and a manual of navigation, and each chart has a "rutter" (a book of sailing directions). It was in use for more than 100 years afterward, during which time English seamen called all sea charts "Waggoners."

♦ Robert Parke: English translation of Juan Gonzalez de Mendoza's *The Historie of the great and mightie kingdome of China*; London. It was written at the request of English geographer, Richard Hakluyt, and first published in Spanish in 1585 in Rome. This is a serious account of Chinese history, customs and religion: "for the increase of the knowledge of the subjects of Englande, and specially for . . . those, that are to take the voyage next in hand to Japan, China, and the Philippines . . ."

POLITICS

♦ Christian IV becomes King of Denmark and Norway after the death of his father, King Frederick II, in April. He rules under Regents until 1596. In 1624, he founds the city of Kristiania (now Oslo) in Norway.

♦ King Henri III of France summons Swiss mercenary soldiers to the outskirts of Paris in April, to defend himself against the Catholic League, led by the Duke of Guise.

♦ In May, the Duke ofGuise becomes the master of Paris, and King Henri III escapes to the city of Chartres.

♦ The Spanish Duke of Medina-Sidonia sets sail from Lisbon

on June 9, commanding the first Armada sent against England

♦ In July, King Henri III of France agrees to all of the Duke of Guise's demands, including the summoning of the States-General to Blois in October

♦ In August, the **first Spanish Armada is defeated by the English fleet** in a battle in the English Channel. The war between England and Spain continues until 1603, and three other armadas are mounted by Spain. Queen Elizabeth makes one of her most famous speeches to the troops assembled at Tilbury. English naval forces are commanded by the Queen's cousin, Lord High Admiral, Lord Howard of Effingham, with the Earl of Leicester as Lieutenant-General for the defense of the realm. English Vice Admiral is Sir Francis Drake; Rear Admiral is Martin Frobisher; naval treasurer is John Hawkins. Spanish forces of 130 ships and 30,000 men are commanded by the Duke of Medina-Sidonia as Admiral and the Duke of Parma as commander of the land troops, that never appear to do battle. The English force numbers about 140 vessels and 10,000 men. Of the Spanish forces, one third to one half of the ships are lost, and about 20,000 men die, most through privation, disease and shipwreck in Ireland, rather than in battle. John Hawkins and Martin Frobisher are both knighted by Lord High Admiral Howard for their services.

♦ Robert Dudley, Earl of Leicester, dies in September. Queen Elizabeth's chief favorite since her coronation, she nick-named him "spirit." Elizabeth keeps his last letter to her in a special little box by her bedside until her death in 1603.

♦ The French States-General meet at Blois in October and suggest the surrender of the French crown to the Duke of Guise.

♦ King Henri III of France arranges for the assassination of Henri, Duke of Guise, at Blois, in December, and Louis

Cardinal of Guise is also assassinated. The leadership of the Catholic League then passes to the Duke of Mayenne.

RELIGION

◆ In January the Catholic League asks King Henri III of France to remove Huguenot Protestants from his court and council, confiscate Huguenot property, and implement the decrees of the Council of Trent (Tridentine decrees).

◆ William Morgan translates the Bible into Welsh.

◆ The *Martin Marprelate* tracts are issued by a secret press in London. They defend Presbyterianism, and are published in defiance of the Star Chamber decree instigated by Archbishop Whitgift in 1586. Suspected authors John Penry and John Udall are arrested. Penry is executed in 1593, and Udall dies in prison.

◆ Luis de Molina, Spanish Jesuit theologian: *Liberi Arbitrii cum Gratiae Donis . . . Concordi* (The Reconciliations of Free Will with Received Grace). Molina asserts that predestination to eternal happiness or punishment is consequent on God's foreknowledge of the free determination of man's will. God knows beforehand the choices humans will make. This leads to a dispute on the nature of free will between Molina's adherants and the followers of 13th century philosopher St. Thomas Aquinas, whose thought still dominates Catholic theology.

◆ Thomas Stapleton: *Tres Thomae (Three Thomases)*; collective biographies of St. Thomas the Apostle, St. Thomas of Canterbury, and Sir Thomas More .

LITERATURE AND THE ARTS

◆ Tintoretto paints "Paradise," an enormous work for the Sala del gran Consiglio in the Doge's palace, Venice.

◆ Nicholas Hilliard paints a miniature portrait of Sir Christopher Hatton holding a miniature of Queen Elizabeth I of

England, and his most famous miniature: "Young Man Leaning Against a Tree among Roses."

♦ Thoinot Arbeau: *Orchesographie* ; Langres, France; a compendium of dance steps and melodies. A second edition was published there in 1589. "Arbeau" (an anagram of Jehan Tabourot) was Canon of Langres. He believed that dance was a healthy pastime.

♦ Claudio Monteverdi: *First Book of Madrigals* ; Venice .

♦ William Byrd: *Psalmes, Sonets and Songs of sadnesse and pietie*; London; dedicated to Sir Christopher Hatton.

♦ Nicholas Yonge: *Musica Transalpina*; London; an anthology of 57 Italian madrigals with English translations apparently written by "a Gentleman for his private delight." This was the most influential of five Italian madrigal collections to appear in England between 1588 and 1598.

♦ Nicholas Hilliard designs and makes the "Armada Jewel"—a jeweled and enameled gold locket containing his miniature portrait of Queen Elizabeth, and several Latin mottos, celebrating the Queen and the English victory. It was presented to Sir Thomas Heneage , who was Treasurer of War at the time of the English Armada victory, and is also known as the Heneage Jewel. It is now in the British Museum.

SOCIETY, EDUCATION

♦ Galileo Galilei writes a treatise on the center of gravity in solids.

♦ Warlord Hideyoshi of Japan orders the weapons of the peasantry confiscated in an effort to put an end to warfare and popular uprisings (Hideyoshi's "sword hunt").

♦ Giovanni Botero: *Delle cause della grandezza delle citta* (On the Causes of the Greatness of Cities); Rome. Botero discusses the advantageous sites for the location of cities.

♦ Timothy Bright: *Characterie.An Arte of Shorte, Swifte, and Secrete Writing by Character*; London; a manual of shorthand.

♦ Thomas Hariot: *Brief and True Report of the New Found Land of Virginia*; London. Hariot recommends tobacco as a medicine.

♦ The Vatican Library is opened in Rome.

1589

GEOGRAPHY

♦ Richard Hakluyt: first edition of *The Principall Navigations, Voiages and Discoveries of the English Nation* in 1 volume; London.

♦ Walter Bigges: *A Summarie and True Discourse of Sir Frances Drakes West Indian Voyage*, ed. Thomas Cates; London; one reprint in '89, and two more within 10 years. Bigges sailed with Drake in in 1585, but died during the voyage.

POLITICS

♦ The French Queen Mother Catherine de Medici dies.

♦ The Duke of Mayenne enters Paris and is declared Lieutenant-General of the Kingdom by the Catholic League.

♦ The Peace of Benten : Archduke Maximilian of Habsburg renounces his claim to the Polish throne.

♦ King Henri III of France and King Henri of Navarre, leader of the Huguenot Protestants, meet in Tours to sign a truce to oppose the objectives of the Catholic League.

♦ Sir Francis Drake of England, at the head of 150 ships and 18,000 men, leads an expedition to Portugal. He attacks, but fails to take, Lisbon. The attempt to place Don Antonio on the Portuguese throne ends in failure.

♦ King Henri III of France leads an army that takes the bridge at St. Cloud and begins to threaten Paris in July.

♦ King Henri III of France is assassinated at St. Cloud in August by Jacques Clement, a Jacobin monk. On his deathbed, he recognizes King Henri of Navarre as his successor to the throne of France. His death marks the end of the Valois dynasty in France.

- King Henri of Navarre becomes King of France as Henri IV. He makes his headquarters at Tours. This is the beginning of the Bourbon dynasty in France.
- King Philip II of Spain lays claim to the throne of France for his daughter Princess Isabel, daughter of Elisabeth of Valois, sister of King Henri III of France.
- King Henri IV of France repulses the Catholic League at the Battle of Arques.
- Sir Francis Vere becomes chief commander of the English forces in the Netherlands.
- Peregrine Bertie, Lord Willoughby, of England lands in France with 4,000 English troops to aid King Henri IV.
- Maurice of Nassau is elected Stadtholder of Utrecht, Gelderland and Overyssel.
- King James VI of Scotland, son of Mary Queen of Scots, marries Princess Anne of Denmark.

RELIGION

- Tsar Boris Godonov of Russia asserts Moscow's religious independence of the Eastern Church based in Constantinople (Istanbul).
- Thomas Kett is burned at the stake in Norwich, England, for denying the divinity of Christ (the Arian heresy).
- Gebhard, Archbishop of Cologne, deposed by Pope Gregory XIII in 1583, retires to Strasbourg to end his struggle with the Papacy.

LITERATURE AND THE ARTS

- Christopher Marlowe's play *The Jew of Malta* is performed in London.
- George Puttenham: *The Art of English Poesie* ; London.
- Robert Greene: *Menaphon*; London, a romance; reprinted in 1599 as *Greene's Arcadia*.
- The English composer John Bull receives a Doctor of Music

degree from Cambridge University and, therefore, a D.Mus. by incorporation from Oxford University in 1592.

SOCIETY, EDUCATION

- ◆ Galileo Galilei establishes through experiments the first principles of dynamics. Legend has it that he demonstrates by throwing things off the Leaning Tower of Pisa that bodies of different weights fall at the same velocity (through 1591).
- ◆ Forks for individual diners are first used at the French court, imported from Italy. Their use does not become general in Europe until the middle of the 18th century.
- ◆ William Lee invents the stocking frame.
- ◆ The English House of Commons first appoints a Standing Committee for Privileges.
- ◆ In January, King Henri III of France purchases diamonds and other jewels from Nicholas Harlay de Sancy. Among them is the large diamond that becomes known as the "Sancy," and is described as a "great flawless diamond, facet cut, weight 37 to 38 carats." The stone was purchased in 1604 by King James I of Great Britain.
- ◆ Sir Thomas Smith: *Discourse on the Commonweal of England*; London. Formerly attributed to John Hales, this is the most celebrated tract in Tudor social history. "Women were "those whom nature hath made to keepe home and to nourish their familie and children, and not to meddle with affairs abroad."
- ◆ Giovanni Botero: *Reason of State*; Rome.
- ◆ Giovanni Battista (Giambattista) della Porta : *Magia naturalis*, in 20 books; Naples; first published in four volumes in 1558. The most notable sections are those about the experiments on magnetism and the optical experiments, including a description of the *camera obscura*.
- ◆ Sidney Sussex College of Cambridge University is founded in England.
- ◆ Kiev Academy is founded in Russia.

1590-1600

1590

GEOGRAPHY

♦ The English Roanoke Island Colony in Virginia (present day North Carolina) is found mysteriously deserted, having disappeared almost without a trace. Gov. John White returns to find everyone gone, including his grandaughter, Virginia Dare.

♦ Jose de Acosta: *Historia natural y moral de las Indias.*

POLITICS

♦ King Philip II of Spain agrees to support the Catholic League in France, providing that ports and some other towns are placed under Spanish control.

♦ Prince Maurice of Nassau takes the city of Breda in the Netherlands.

♦ King Henri IV of France defeats the Catholic League at the Battle of Ivry.

♦ Charles, Archduke of Inner Austria, dies and is succeeded by the future Emperor Ferdinand II, then aged 12.

♦ Sir Francis Walsingham, English Secretary of State and head of English espionage activities, dies in poverty and in debt.

♦ Shah Abbas I of Persia, abandoning Tabriz, Shirva, and Georgia, makes peace with Turkey.

- The Emperor of Morocco annexes Timbuctu and the Upper Niger in Africa.
- Akbar the Great, Mughul Emperor of India, conquers Orissa.
- Japan is unified under the powerful warlord Hideyoshi.
- Tokugawa Ieyasu is established in Edo, Japan, as lord of the Kanto. Edo is present day Tokyo.

RELIGION

- King Christian of Saxony and Elector John Casimir of the Palatinate present a list of German Protestant grievances to HRE Rudolf II.
- A critical edition of the Latin Vulgate translation of the Bible is issued by order of Pope Sixtus V (to 1592). It is considered to be very inaccurate.
- Pope Sixtus V dies in August. His most notable achievements are building up a large surplus in the papal treasury, extending liberty to the Jews, and fixing the number of the College of Cardinals at 70. He instigated the building of the Vatican Library at the Lateran Palace.
- Cardinal Giovanni Battista Castagno is elected Pope Urban VII on September 15, dying on September 27.
- Niccolò Sfondrato is elected Pope Gregory XIV (to 1591) in December. He is a forceful supporter of the Catholic League in France.

LITERATURE AND THE ARTS

- Edmund Spenser: *The Faerie Queene;* London. Spenser died before completing planned additions to the lengthy poem, which was written to glorify Queen Elizabeth.
- Sir Philip Sidney: *The Countesse of Pembrokes Arcadia*, now known as *The New Arcadia*, is published posthumously in London.
- Anthony Munday translates from the French the Spanish (or

perhaps Portuguese?) chivalric romance *Amadis of Gaul*, written c. 1508.

♦ El Greco paints "St. Jerome."

SOCIETY, EDUCATION

♦ Coal mining begins in the Ruhr Valley area of Germany.
♦ The first English paper mill is opened at Dartford.
♦ Justus Lipsius: *Politicorum sive civilis doctrinae libri VI* (translated into English as *Politicke Discourses*); London.
♦ Alfonso Orozo establishes the College of Doña Maria de Aragon in Madrid, later known as Madrid University.

1591

GEOGRAPHY

♦ Sir James Lancaster leaves from Plymouth, England, in April on his first voyage to the East Indies.

POLITICS

♦ Queen Elizabeth of England sends Sir John Norris with 3,000 men to aid King Henri IV of France. Later in the year, the Earl of Essex is sent to help Henri with the siege of Rouen.
♦ Antonio Perez, former private secretary to King Philip II of Spain, defects to France.
♦ Dmitri, son of Ivan "the Terrible," is assassinated at the instigation of Boris Godunov, Regent under Tsar Fyodor. In 1601, a "false Dmitri" appears in Poland.
♦ The English ship *Revenge* is captured by the Spaniards in an action off the Azores and Sir Richard Grenville is mortally wounded
♦ Prince Christian, age 8, becomes King Christian II of Saxony upon the death of his father, Christian I. His guardians, John George, Elector of Brandenburg, and the Duke of Saxe-Weimar, uproot Calvinistic Protestantism in Saxony.

- The Kingdom of Navarre and the counties of Foix and Albret are annexed to the Crown of France.
- The Songhai Empire, Africa, is defeated in battle by Spanish and Portuguese mercenary soldiers in the pay of Morocco. The black African culture of Timbuktu is destroyed.
- Hideyoshi, warlord ruler of all Japan, is given the title Taiko by the Emperor. Taiko is translated as "retired chancellor."

RELIGION

- King Henri IV of France, still a Huguenot Protestant, is excommunicated by Pope Gregory XIV in March.
- Pope Gregory XIV dies in October.

LITERATURE AND THE ARTS

- John Lyly: *Endimion, the Man in the Moon*; London; published anonymously; an allegorical prose comedy.
- John Harington: metrical English translation of Ariosto's *Orlando Furioso*; London. Harington, Queen Elizabeth's godson, was later knighted in the field in Ireland by the Earl of Essex.
- Sir Philip Sidney: *Astrophel and Stella* poem (posthumous publication); London. Stella is thought to be based on Penelope Devereux, Lady Rich, sister of the Earl of Essex. The first edition, containing sonnets by another writer, an epistle by Newman, and a preface by Nash, was suppressed, and the edition containing only Sidney's poem was published later in the year.
- Giuseppe Archimbaldo paints a portrait of HRE Rudolf II as Vertumnus, the guardian spirit of gardens. Rudolf's head, neck and chest are entirely composed of fruits, flowers and vegetables.
- William Byrd: *My Ladye Nevells Booke*—a manuscript containing 42 virginal pieces by Byrd; copied by John Baldwin, a Gentleman of the Chapel Royal. This is the most beautiful surviving keyboard MS of the period. Always

-MOSH

privately owned, it now belongs to the Marquis of Abergavenny, whose ancestor supposedly presented it to Queen Elizabeth in 1591.

♦ The first printed collection of Danish ballads appears.

SOCIETY, EDUCATION

♦ Hideyoshi of Japan orders all warriors, peasants and merchants to remain in their current occupations and positions.

♦ François Viète: *In Artem Analyticam Isagoge*—the earliest known work on symbolic algebra. Viète is credited with introducing decimal fractions, obtaining the value of P (Pi) as an infinite product, and devising methods for solving algebraic equations up to the fourth degree.

♦ Robert Greene: *A notable discovery of coosenage* and *The Second part of Conny-Catching* ; London; two pamphlets describing the devices used by thieves and confidence men.

♦ Giordano Bruno: *De immenso et innumerabilis seu de universo et muncis.*

♦ Simon Forman: *The Grounds of the Longitude, with an admonition to all those that are incredulous and believe not the truth of the same*; Thomas Dawson, London. Astrologer, unlicensed doctor and magician, Forman left a manuscript containing accounts of the earliest performances of Shakespeare's plays.

♦ Trinity College in Dublin, Ireland, is founded by Queen Elizabeth I of England.

1592

GEOGRAPHY

♦ Juan de Fuca of Spain discovers the area now known as British Columbia, on the western coast of Canada.

♦ Sir James Lancaster of England sails around the Malay Peninsula in June.

♦ The Portuguese settle at Mombassa, Africa.

POLITICS

♦ Frederick IV succeeds as the Elector Palatine on the death of John Casimir.

♦ HRE Rudolf II makes peace with Poland.

♦ The English, led by Sir John Burrows, capture a Spanish treasure ship, the 1600 ton Portuguese carrack "Madre de Deus" sailing from the East Indies with a cargo estimated at £ 850,000 in value, one of the largest captured treasures in history.

♦ Archduke Matthias is sent by HRE Rudolf to govern Hungary.

♦ King John III of Sweden dies, and is succeeded by his son, King Sigismund III of Poland, thus uniting the crowns of Sweden and Poland. Sigismund resides in Warsaw, appointing his brother Charles as Regent of Sweden.

♦ The provinces of Perigord and Bearn are annexed to the French crown.

♦ Hideyoshi of Japan invades Korea with an army of 150,000, planning to go on to conquer China, but he is forced to withdraw in 1593.

♦ Akbar the Great, Mughal Emperor of India, conquers Sind.

RELIGION

♦ Pope Clement VIII (Ippolito Aldobrandani) is crowned (to 1605). After the death in 1590 of Sixtus V, there had been three very brief papacies: Urban VII in 1590; Gregory XIV in 1591, and Innocent IX in 1592.

♦ Giordano Bruno is arrested in Venice by the Inquisition, the principal charge being his support of the Copernican heliocentric theory of the universe.

♦ Spanish Franciscan missionaries arrive in the Philippines on their way to begin a mission in Japan.

LITERATURE AND THE ARTS

♦ Shakespeare's *Henry VI, Part III* is performed in London, the first Shakespeare play to be publicly performed. A complete edition of Shakespeare's plays does not appear until the First Folio of 1623.

♦ Christopher Marlowe writes a play entitled *The Tragical History of the Life and Death of Doctor Faustus;* London.

♦ Thomas Nash: two satires: *Strange Newes of the intercepting certaine letters*; dedicated to "Gentle Master William," the "most copius" poet in England and*Pierce Penilesse His Supplication to the Divell*; London.

♦ John Lyly: *Midas*, a play; London; first performed in 1590. "Traffic and travel hath woven the nature of all nations into ours, and made this land like arras, full of device, which was broadcloth, full of workmanship."

♦ Robert Greene: *The thirde and last part of conny-catching* and*A Quip for an Upstart Courtier*; London; two pamphlets. Only later did the first pamphlet about "conny catching" (1591) become known as *The art of conny-catching*.

♦ Robert Greene: *A Groatsworth of Wit Bought with a Million of Repentance*; an autobiographical narrative containing the attack on "an upstart crow" . . . who . . . "is in his owne conceit the only Shake-scene in a Countrey." Henry Chettle edited the pamphlet, and some scholars believe that he wrote it as well.

♦ Philip Henslowe, manager of the Rose Theatre in London, begins to write his *Diary* and account book, now held in Dulwich College Library; to 1603.

♦ Lodovico Zacconi: *Prattica di musica utile ei necessaria si al compositore per comporre i canti suoi regolatamente, si anco al cantore* ; Venice; comprehensive treatise on music theory, notation, and rules for singers. It contains much information about the performance practices of 16th c. music, and was reissued in 1596. A second part was published in Venice in 1622.

SOCIETY, EDUCATION

♦ Galileo Galilei resigns his chair at the University of Pisa, because of the hostility of Aristotelians (followers of the philosophy of Aristotle), moving to Padua to become professor of mathematics at the university there.

♦ Queen Elizabeth I of England visits Sir Henry Lee at his manor Ditchley in Oxfordshire. Marcus Gheeraerts the Younger paints a portrait of her standing on the globe of the world, with her feet resting on Oxfordshire, to commemorate the visit. Elizabeth is wearing the enormous pearl necklace which once belonged to Catherine de' Medici, and later to Mary Queen of Scots. Sir Henry Lee was Elizabeth's "Champion," and organized the November 17 Ascension Day ceremonial tournaments beginning in 1577 until his retirement in 1590.

♦ A plague epidemic kills at least 15,000 people in London.

♦ Windmills are used in the Netherlands to drive mechanical saws.

♦ The ruined Roman city of Pompeii, destroyed by the eruption of Mt. Vesuvius in A.D. 79, is uncovered for the first time since the catastrophe. Even its name had been forgotten, as it lay buried under lava deposits and ash. Serious work of excavation does not begin until the 18th century.

♦ Queen Elizabeth I of England reacquires the palace of Nonsuch from the Arundel family. Built by her father King Henry VIII, it becomes her favorite palace.

1593

GEOGRAPHY

♦ Barent Erikszen leads a voyage to the coast of Guinea.

♦ Gerard de Jode: *Speculum orbis terrarum,* in 2 volumes; posthumously published in Antwerp. An enlargement of a world atlas first produced in 1578, it shows both the north and south polar regions.

POLITICS

- The French States-General, meeting at the Louvre Palace in Paris, refuse to accept King Philip II of Spain's claim to the throne on behalf of his daughter, Isabel, and agree to support the Duke of Guise.
- King Henri IV of France becomes a Catholic in July, hearing Mass at the monastery of St. Denis, and remarking that "Paris is worth a mass." He considered that security in his kingship required the change in religion. He reasoned that since he had been the leader of the Huguenot Protestants, they would continue to support him, while now that he was a Catholic, the Catholic opposition to his Kingship was neutralized.
- Archduke Albert of Austria is appointed Viceroy of Portugal by King Philip II of Spain.
- The war between Austria and Turkey is renewed by HRE Rudolf II.
- The Japanese leader Hideyoshi makes a truce with the Chinese armies in Korea.

RELIGION

- The English Parliament passes an act directed against Puritans, for "restraining the Queen's subjects in obedience."
- Henry Barrow, a Puritan, is convicted of slandering Queen Elizabeth I of England, and is executed.
- Spanish Franciscans arrive in Japan to begin a mission there, coming from Manila in the Philippines.
- The Japanese begin to kill and persecute Christians. Hideyoshi orders all Jesuits to leave the country.
- King Sigismund III's attempt to restore Roman Catholicism in Sweden is opposed by the Convention of Uppsala, which upholds Martin Luther's doctrines.

LITERATURE AND THE ARTS

♦ *Venus and Adonis*—the **first work published with Wm. Shakespeare listed as author**; London. It is dedicated to Henry Wriothsley, 3rd Earl of Southampton.

♦ El Greco paints "The Crucifixion" and "The Resurrection."

♦ Rowland Lockey paints "Sir Thomas More , his Household and Descendants," a posthumous tribute.

♦ Thomas Morley: *Canzonets, or Little Short Songs to Three Voices*; London; the first publication by this very prolific composer.

♦ London theatres are closed throughout the year because of a plague epidemic that began in 1592. They remain closed until 1594.

♦ Henry Chettle publishes a pamphlet called *Kind Harts Dreame* in London. Without naming them, Chettle apologizes to two playwrights who were satirized in the 1592 pamphlet, *A Groatsworth of Wit*.

♦ Dramatist Christopher Marlowe is murdered in Deptford in a private room at an Inn owned by Eleanor Bull. All three witnesses allege that he was the aggressor in a dispute over the bill (the "reckoning"). Marlowe had worked as a spy, and so had his three companions.

SOCIETY, EDUCATION

♦ Banco Sant' Ambrogio is founded in Milan.

♦ The Purana Pul Bridge of 23 arches is built across Musi River in Hyderabad, India.

♦ The first French botanical gardens are established by the University of Montpellier.

♦ The English Parliament passes legislation promoting parish collections as a fund for wounded soldiers and seamen.

♦ Galileo Galilei: *Della scienza mechanica* (Of Mechanical Science); translated as "concerning the problems of raising weights"; a syllabus of lectures on mechanics written for his private pupils in Padua. This was not a university subject at the time.

♦ Giovanni Battista (Giambattista) della Porta: *De refreactione, optices parte* ; Naples; a treatise on refraction including an account of binocular vision.

1594

GEOGRAPHY

♦ English navigator Sir James Lancaster breaks the Portuguese monopoly of trade in India.

♦ English traveler Ralph Fitch returns from an overland journey to India and Ceylon.

POLITICS

♦ Archduke Ernest of Austria arrives in Brussels as Governor of the Netherlands, in January.

♦ The city of Lyons declares support for Henri IV as King of France.

♦ Henri IV, after being crowned King of France at Chartres Cathedral in February, enters Paris. The power of the Catholic League disintegrates, and the country gradually submits to him. Throughout the year, the cities of Rouen, Havre, Harfleur and Laon, and the province of Champagne, come under the King, leaving only Brittany as a Catholic stronghold, where the Spanish come to aid the resistance.

♦ King Henri IV of France disburses 32 million livres to Catholic League generals and nobles, in an effort to create an atmosphere of accord.

♦ Roger Lopez, physician to Queen Elizabeth I of England, is arrested in February for participating in a conspiracy to poison the Queen. He is executed in June.

♦ German Protestant princes, led by Frederick IV of the Palitinate, meet at Heilbronn in March, to oppose HRE Rudolf II.

- Jean Chastel, a pupil of the Jesuits, attempts to assassinate King Henri IV of France.
- HRE Rudolf II meets the Diet at Ratisbon in May. A vote approves supplies for the Turkish war, despite opposition by the Protestant party.
- Hugh O'Neill, Earl of Tyrone, in alliance with O'Donnell, Earl of Tyrconnell, leads a rising in Ulster, Ireland, against Queen Elizabeth I of England. He appeals to King Philip II of Spain for aid.
- An Anglo-French force recaptures the city of Brest, Brittany, from the Spaniards. Sir Martin Frobisher of England is killed.
- The Turks conquer Raab at the Austro Hungarian border.
- The Mughal Emperor Akbar the Great takes Kandahar in India.

RELIGION

- King Henri IV of France issues the Edict of St. Germain-en-Laye, granting Huguenot Protestants freedom of worship in France. At an assembly in Sainte-Foy, the Huguenots demand securities for its observance and full equality with Catholics in public life.
- King Henri IV of France expels the Jesuits from certain areas of France in December. They return in 1603.
- Pierre Charron: *Les Trois Vérités* (The Three Truths); Bordeaux, France; a theological treatise vindicating Catholicism. The three truths are the existence of God, the rightness of Christianity, and the supremacy of the Catholic faith.
- Richard Hooker: *Of the Laws of Ecclesiastical Polity*, Books 1-4: London. The fifth book appears in 1597, and another three appear posthumously. Hooker presents a defense of the Church of England that gives tone and direction to the Anglican Church.

LITERATURE AND THE ARTS

- *The Rape of Lucrece*—2nd work published under the name

William Shakespeare; London; a long narrative poem dedicated to the 3rd Earl of Southampton. Shakespeare's 154 sonnets are published in 1609, and a full edition of the plays is not published until 1623 ("The First Folio").

♦ Richard Carew translates Cantos 1-5 of Torquato Tasso's *Jerusalem Delivered*, as *Godfrey of Bulloigne*; London.

♦ Thomas Nash: *The Unfortunate Traveller*, or *The life of Jack Wilton*; London; an early picaresque novel.

♦ Michelangelo Merisi da Caravaggio paints "The Musical Party."

♦ Giovannia da Bologna makes equestrian statues of Cosimo I de' Medici and Fernando de' Medici.

♦ Carlo Gesualdo: First and Second Books of Madrigals; Ferrara (*Madrigali libro primo, 5vv* and *Madrigali libro secondo*, 5 vv); the third and fourth books follow in 1595 and 1596, also published in Ferrara.

♦ Jan Pieterszoon Sweelinck: *Chansons . . . de M Jean Pierre Sweelingh organiste, et Cornille Verdonq nouvellement composées . . . accommodées tant aux instruments comme a la voix, 5vv*; Antwerp. Principally an organist, Sweelinck was the leading composer of the Netherlands School, and many of his keyboard pieces are in the *Fitzwilliam Virginal Book*. Most of his compositions were published in the early 1600's.

♦ Actor Richard Burbage and others organize the Lord Chamberlain's Men theatrical company in London. William Shakespeare provides part of the investment capital. From 1599 on, they perform at the Globe Theatre.

♦ London theatres reopen in May after being closed during the plague epidemic of 1592-3.

SOCIETY, EDUCATION

♦ The Dutch East India Company is founded in Amsterdam.

♦ The Lisbon spice market is closed to Dutch and English

merchants, which results in future voyages to the Far East by Dutch and English traders.

◆ The forgotten city of Herculaneum, buried together with the city of Pompii by the eruption of Mt. Vesuvius in A.D. 79, is uncovered for the first time since the catastrophe.

◆ Harvest failures and high grain prices (continuing until 1597) cause crises in parts of England and the continent.

◆ Pierre Matthieu: *Histoire des derniers troubles de France sous Henri III et Henri IV*; Paris. Matthieu was the official royal historiographer of King Henri IV.

1595

GEOGRAPHY

◆ The Dutch begin settlements on the Guinea Coast of Africa and the East Indies.

◆ Sir Walter Ralegh explores 300 miles up the Orinoco River in South America.

◆ Sir Walter Ralegh: *The discoverie of the large, rich, and beautifull Empire of Guiana, with Manoa (which the Spaniards call El Dorado)*; London.

◆ Sir Francis Drake and his kinsman Sir John Hawkins leave Plymouth on their last voyage to the Spanish Main (the east coast of Spanish America, from Panama to Venezuela); to 1596. Sir John Hawkins dies at sea in November.

POLITICS

◆ King Henri IV of France declares war on Spain.

◆ Following the death of Archduke Ernest, King Philip II of Spain appoints Archduke Albert as Governor of the Netherlands.

◆ King Philip II of Spain sends aid to the Irish Earl of Tyrone's rebellion against England.

◆ The English send Sir John Norris to Ireland to put down

the rebellion, and the Earl of Tyrone is officially proclaimed a traitor.

♦ Beaune, Dijon and Autun revolt against King Henri IV of France, who marches east through Burgundy. The Duke of Mayenne, Protestant Huguenot leader, signs a truce with King Henri.

♦ Spanish forces land in Cornwall, England, burning the towns of Penzance and Mousehole.

♦ Treaty of Teusina between Sweden and Russia. Sweden gains Estonia.

♦ Sigmund Bathory, King of Poland, defeats the Turks at Giurgevo.

♦ Gustavus Vasa, the future King Charles IX, is appointed Lieutenant-General of Sweden. Sweden ends its war with Lithuania, and acquires Estonia and Narva.

♦ Warsaw becomes the capital of Poland.

♦ Sultan Murad III of Turkey dies, and is succeeded by Mohammed III (to 1603).

RELIGION

♦ English Jesuit priest and poet Robert Southwell is hanged at Tyburn in February, after prolonged torture and imprisonment.

♦ Pope Clement VIII absolves King Henri IV from excommunication, and recognizes him as King of France.

LITERATURE AND THE ARTS

♦ Robert Southwell: *St. Peter's Complaint* (and other poems); London; also *The Triumphs over Death*; ("a consolatorie epistle"); London.

♦ El Greco paints "The Penitent St. Peter." (apx. date; possibly as late as 1600)

♦ Johannes Ruckers of Antwerp, eldest son of Hans Ruckers, builds a "child" virginal (a box-shaped harpsichord), the oldest of his instruments still extant.

♦ The Swan Theatre is built in London in Paris Gardens, Bankside, outside the reach of the City of London authorities.

SOCIETY, EDUCATION

♦ The English army officially abandons the bow and arrow as a weapon of war.
♦ First appearance of heels on shoes.
♦ Smoking tobacco becomes very popular in London.
♦ Peasants revolt in Upper Austria.
♦ Queen Elizabeth I of England appoints Dr. John Dee as Warden of Manchester College of Cambridge University.
♦ Thomas Beddingfield makes the first English translation of Machiavelli's *Florentine History* of 1525.

1596

GEOGRAPHY

♦ Willem Barents, Dutch navigator, discovers Spitzbergen and the Barents Sea.
♦ Jan Huyghen van Linschoten: *Itinerario* ; Amsterdam; a geographical description of the world, including information gained from his stay in India (1583-89), with sailing directions for reaching America and India.
♦ Richard Eden: English translation of Martin Cortes's 1551 *Breve compendio de la spehra y de la arte de navigar*, published in English as *The Arte of Navigation* ; London. Commissioned by the English Muscovy Company merchants, it contained instructions for making charts and navigational instruments, and how to plot the course of a ship.
♦ Davila y Padilla Augustin ("Chronicler of the Indies"): *History of Mexico* .
♦ Sir Francis Drake dies while on an expedition to the West Indies and the Spanish Main.

-MOSH

POLITICS

- The war between King Henri IV of France and the Catholic League concludes. The Duke of Guise prevents the Spanish capture of Marseilles. The only remaining opposition to King Henri is in Brittany.

- The Spanish take Calais from the French in April, under Archduke Albert of Habsburg.

- Treaty of the Hague: France, England and the Netherlands form an alliance against Spain, planning to combine their seaborn operations to dismember the Spanish empire.

- English ships, with assistance from the Dutch, capture and sack Cadiz in June, under the joint command of Lord High Admiral Lord Howard of Effingham and the Earl of Essex. The English poet John Donne, then only 24, sails with the expedition, as do Sir Walter Ralegh and Sir Francis Vere. Because of his courteous treatment of 1,500 nuns, King Philip says of Essex: "Such a gentleman has not been seen before among the heretics."

- England "pacifies" Ireland. Irish leader Hugh O'Neill, the Earl of Tyrone, refuses to abide by it and appeals to Philip II of Spain for help.

- The Second Spanish Armada, under the command of Don Martin de Padilla Manrique, leaves Lisbon for Ireland in October, carrying troops and supplies to assist the Earl of Tyrone, but is scattered and substantially destroyed by storms off Cape Finistere, Portugal.

- Christian IV, now of age, is crowned King of Denmark and Norway.

- The Turks under Sultan Mohammed III defeat the Imperial army under Archduke Maximilian at Keresztes, near Erlau in North Hungary.

- Peace between Japan and China, after the Japanese fail to invade Korea.

RELIGION

◆ Decrees of Folembray end the wars of the Catholic League in France; January.

◆ Luis de Carvajal ("El Mozo"), a Mexican Jew, is burned at the stake with his mother and sisters in an auto-da-fe in Mexico City; December.

◆ Caesar Baronius: *Martyrologium Romanum.* Baronius also wrote the first critical church history, the *Annales Ecclesiastici* (1588-1607), proving that the Catholic Church of Rome was identical with the Christian Church of the first century.

LITERATURE AND THE ARTS

◆ John Harington: *A new discourse of a stale subject, called the Metamorphosis of Ajax* (containing the earliest design for a water closet, a type of flush toilet); also *An Anatomie of the Metamorphosed Ajax* ; and *Ulysses upon Ajax* ; London; three pamphlets in the style of François Rabelais. The titles are puns on "a jakes," an Elizabethan name for a toilet.

◆ Edmund Spenser: Books 4 and 5 of *The Faerie Queene*; London. Books 1 to 3 were published in 1590.

◆ Peter Philips: *Il primo libro di madrigali,* 6vv (The First Book of Madrigals, for 6 Voices); Antwerp. Next to Byrd, Philips was the most published English composer of his time. A Catholic, he spent most of his life in Europe.

◆ The Blackfriars Theatre is opened in London, built by actor Richard Burbage. William Shakespeare of Stratford-upon-Avon is one of the shareholders.

SOCIETY, EDUCATION

◆ First water closets, designed by John Harington, are installed at Richmond Palace, England. Queen Elizabeth called Richmond her "warm box" for the winter.

◆ Acquavite (brandy) is first mentioned in Venice customs reports.

◆ Tomatoes are introduced in England.

-MOSH

♦ Galileo Galilei invents the thermometer.

♦ King Henri IV of France summons an Assembly of Notables to discuss public revenue. The assembly adopts a 5 per cent sales tax on all goods except corn.

♦ The Spanish coinage is further devalued to stave off bankruptcy.

♦ A rising of peasant farmers in Oxfordshire, England, against landlords who fence property, is suppressed.

♦ Johan Kepler: *Prodromus Dissertationum Cosmographicarum seu Mysterium Cosmographicum*; Tubingen. Convinced that for the actual disposition of the solar system some abstract intelligible reason must exist, Kepler posits that five kinds of regular polyhedral bodies govern the five planetary orbits.

♦ Rhaeticus (Georg Joachim von Lauchen): *Opus palatinum de triangulis*; Neustadt an de Haardt; trigonometric tables; published posthumously.

♦ Ludolph van Ceulen: *Van den Circkel* ; Delft. He works out the value of "pi" (the ratio of the diameter to the circumference of a circle) to 35 decimal places. This is known as "Ludolph's number."

♦ *A profitable booke declaring dyvers aprooved remedies, to take out spotts and staines in Silkes, Velvets, Linnen, and Wollen Clothes* ; translated from the Dutch by Leonard Mascall; London.

1597

GEOGRAPHY

♦ The Dutch found Batavia, Java.

POLITICS

♦ Archduke Albert of Austria takes Amiens for Spain.

♦ King Philip II of Spain opens peace talks with King Henri IV of France.

♦ In July and August, an English fleet sets sail for Spain but is deterred by bad weather, proceeding to the Azores instead, leaving England undefended and returning empty-handed during the height of the Armada scare.

♦ The third Spanish Armada sets out for Falmouth, England, in September, but is scattered by storms off Lizard.

♦ William V, Duke of Bavaria, abdicates in favor of his son Maximilian I, then retires to a monastery.

♦ The Irish rebel against England under the leadership of Hugh O'Neill, Earl of Tyrone. The insurrection spreads through the provinces of Ulster, Connaught and Leinster.

♦ Sigismund Bathory, Prince of Transylvania, cedes Transylvania to HRE Rufolf II.

♦ Duke Alfonso II d'Este dies. Alfonso was the last of the main branch of the Este family, which had been one of the most powerful in Italy for over two centuries, with possibly the most splendid court in all of Europe. Although Alfonso bequeathed his duchy to a cousin, it was taken over by the Pope in 1598.

♦ Hideyoshi, ruler of Japan, resumes his Korean campaign with a second invasion.

RELIGION

♦ Upper Austria is forced to become Catholic.

♦ First executions of European missionaries and Japanese converts to Christianity in Japan.

LITERATURE AND THE ARTS

♦ Francis Bacon: *Essays; Religious Meditations*, First Edition, now known as *Essays, Civil and Moral* ; London.

♦ John Lyly: *The Woman in the Moone;* a play; London.

♦ Thomas Nash's satiric play *The Isle of Dogs* is closed by the authorities in London after only a few performances, and Nash is thown into Fleet Prison. Ben Jonson, who acted in and co-authored the play, is confined in Marshalsea Prison and interrogated, but he reveals nothing. The play, now lost, focused attention on abuses in government, and thus was considered potentially seditious or treasonous.

♦ Thomas Morley: *A Plaine and Easie Introduction to Practicall Musicke;* London; dedicated to William Byrd; second edition in 1608. Morley says that it is expected that all educated people could read music, and sing at sight from a page of printed vocal music.

♦ English composer and virginalist John Bull is elected the first Public Reader in Music at newly organized Gresham College in London, receiving the Queen's permission to give his lectures in English rather than Latin.

♦ John Dowland: *The Firste Booke of Songes or Ayres of Foure Partes with Tableture for the Lute*; London.

♦ Aldine Press, Venice, founded in 1494, closes after publication of 908 works.

SOCIETY, EDUCATION

♦ English Acts of Parliament pass laws abolishing the death penalty for vagabonds, giving relief to the deserving poor, and prescribing sentences of transportation to the colonies for convicted criminals.

♦ The Spanish crown declares bankruptcy.

♦ Hardwick Hall is completed in Derbyshire, England, by Bess of Hardwick (Elizabeth Talbot, Countess of Shrewsbury). The windows contain the most extensive use of glass to date in a private residence.

♦ The Lord High Admiral of England, Lord Howard of Effingham, is given the title Earl of Nottingham. Cousin to Queen Elizabeth, he commanded the victorious English naval forces in the Armada battle of 1588.

♦ The Spanish send almost 12 million pesos in gold bullion from Acapulco, Mexico, to Manila in the Philippines.

♦ Field hospitals and field dispensaries are first used in Europe.

♦ John Gerard: *The Herball, or general historie of plants*; London. Beautifully and profusely illustrated, it includes information on the medicinal properties of plants, and is dedicated to William Cecil Lord Burghley, whose gardens Gerard superintended for twenty years, from 1577 to 1598.

♦ Andreas Libavius: *Alchemia*; Rothenberg an der Taube; a richly illustrated book credited with being the first published textbook on chemistry.

♦ James VI of Scotland: *Daemonologie*; Edinburgh; a prose treatise denouncing witchcraft and calling on the civil authorities to suppress it vigorously.

♦ The London house of Sir Thomas Gresham, by the terms of his will, becomes Gresham College, with professors for astronomy, geometry, physics, law, divinity, rhetoric, and music.

1598

GEOGRAPHY

♦ Olivier van Noort of the Netherlands becomes the **fourth explorer to circumnavigate the globe.**

♦ A permanent Spanish colony is established at San Juan Pueblo (now in the state of New Mexico, USA).

♦ The Dutch take the island of Mauritius, in the Indian Ocean east of Madagascar.

♦ English translation of Jan van Linschoten's *Voyages into the East and West Indies*; London; a detailed survey of trade routes and translations of Portuguese and Spanish documents on geography, statistics and navigation.

POLITICS

♦ The Treaty of Vervins is signed in April: the French leave their alliance with England and the Netherlands (Treaty of The Hague of 1596) and make peace with Spain. King Philip II of Spain resigns his claim to the French crown. France is united under King Henri IV as their single sovereign. The Spanish agree to evacuate Picardy, Calais, Brittany and Blavet.

- The Treaty of Ponts de Cé ends civil wars in France.
- Tsar Fyodor I of Russia dies. Boris Godunov seizes the throne.
- Boris Godunov is formally elected Tsar of Russia by the National Assembly, ruling until 1605. The story of his rise to power and reign is the basis for the libretto of Modest Moussorgsky's 19th century opera "Boris Godunov."
- Taiko Hideyoshi, leader of Japan, dies.
- Japanese forces withdraw from Korea.
- Tokugawa Iyeyasu becomes the chief of a group of five regents who are empowered to rule Japan during the childhood of Hideyoshi's infant son, Hideyori. Tokugawa takes his first steps to restore the shogunate, which will endure until the revolution of 1867-68.
- Pope Clement VIII seizes the Duchy of Ferrara, vacant since the last of the main branch of the Este family died in 1597.
- Charles Vasa, Regent for his brother King Sigismund III, is hailed as King of Sweden. He is chosen King by the Swedish Diet of 1599, receiving formal title from the Riksdag in 1604, to be crowned in 1607.
- William Cecil Lord Burghley dies on August 4. He was the most prominent statesman of Elizabethan England, serving as Chief Secretary of State from 1558 and Lord High Treasurer from 1572. He was created Baron Burghley in 1571. Elizabeth called him her "Spirit." His son Robert became the most powerful man in England under King James I.
- English forces in Ireland are annihilated in mid August at the Battle of the Yellow Ford, by the Irish under the Earl of Tyrone. King Philip II of Spain sends congratulations to the Earl, and the Pope sends him a crown of peacock feathers.
- King Philip II of Spain dies on September 13.
- Philip II's son Philip is crowned King of Spain as Philip III (to 1621).

♦ Steelyard, the London headquarters of the Hanseatic League, is closed.
♦ English merchants are expelled from the Holy Roman Empire in retaliation for their treatment of the Hanseatic League in London.

RELIGION

♦ The **Edict of Nantes** grants equal right of worship to French Huguenot Protestants. It is revoked under King Louis XIV in 1685, and cruel persecutions ensue.
♦ François de Sales, cannonized as a Catholic saint 1665, is appointed coadjutor Bishop of Geneva.
♦ Jesuit Father Matteo Ricci visits Peking, China, bringing clocks, globes and maps as presents for the Emperor.

LITERATURE AND THE ARTS

♦ Lope de Vega: *La Dragonetta*—a fanciful poem celebrating the death of Sir Francis Drake; the first work published under his own name. De Vega sailed with the first Spanish Armada in 1588, and wrote more than 1500 plays.
♦ Ben Jonson: first public performance of the play *Every Man in His Humour* at the Curtain Theatre, London.
♦ Francis Meres: *Palladis Tamia*; London; anthology of quotations from 125 English authors.
♦ Jacopo Peri: *Dafne*, usually called **the first opera**, is performed in Florence.

SOCIETY, EDUCATION

♦ Korean Admiral Visunsin invents the iron-clad warship.
♦ Sir Thomas Bodley begins rebuilding the library at Oxford University, England.
♦ King Henri IV of France reorganizes the University of Paris.
♦ John Stow: *Survey of London*; London; a detailed description of the city and its suburbs; enlarged in 1603. It has been almost always in print since its first publication.

- Abbé Philibert Maréschal (Sieur de la Roche): *Le Guide des arts et des sciences* ; Paris.
- John Florio: *A World of Words* ; London; an English-Italian Dictionary.
- Justus Lipsius: *Politicorum sive civilis doctrinae libri VI* (translated into English as *Politicke Discourses*); London.
- Tycho Brahe: *Astronomicae Instauratae Mechanica* ; Wandbeck; an account of his astronomical discoveries and a description of his instruments.

1599

POLITICS

- Confederation of Vilna: an alliance is formed between Orthodox and Dissident factions in Poland.
- The Agreement of Gera is signed between branches of the Hohenzollern family concerning mutual succession.
- King Henri IV of France obtains a divorce from his wife Marguerite de Valois.
- The Swedish Diet deposes King Sigismund III of Poland as King of Sweden and proclaims his brother Charles of Sodermanland ruler as King Charles IX.
- The Earl of Essex is chosen to lead the English forces in Ireland. He leaves in March with the largest expeditionary force sent out during Elizabeth's entire reign—17,000 infantry and 1,300 cavalry.
- Irish rebels defeat the Earl of Essex. He signs a truce with the Earl of Tyrone. In September he returns to England against orders, and is arrested and imprisoned after paying a surprise visit to Queen Elizabeth. Lord Mountjoy succeeds Essex as commander in Ireland, and is successful.
- The Spanish begin to mount a Fourth Armada, but it does not sail for England.

RELIGION

♦ The church of St. Cecilia in Rome is rebuilt. Upon examination, the body of the saint, martyred in A.D. 176, is found to be still intact. Stefano Moderno's statue of the saint as patron of music is placed at the high altar.

LITERATURE AND THE ARTS

♦ Ben Jonson writes the play *Every Man out of his Humour*, published in 1601 in London.

♦ The Globe Theatre is built in London by actor Richard Burbage, supposedly with some timber that had been used in his father's 1576 construction of The Theatre (later known as Shoreditch Theatre). The Globe is intended as a summer venue, while Blackfrairs was to be a winter playhouse. William Shakespeare of The Lord Chamberlain's Men, a professional theatrical company, provides 10% of the financing. Other partners include actors John Heminge and Henry Condell.

♦ James VI of Scotland: *Basilikondoron*; Edinburgh; an essay on the divine right of kings, in Greek (a first edition of seven copies).

♦ Michelangelo Merisi da Caravaggio paints "Judith and Holofernes" in Rome.

♦ Thomas Morley: *The First Booke of Consort Lessons, made by Divers Exquisite Authors, for 6 Instruments to Play Together, the Treble Lute, the Pandora, the Cittern, the Base-Violl, the Flute and Treble Violl* ; London; corrected and enlarged in 1611. This is the typical grouping of the English "Broken Consort."

♦ John Farmer: *The First Set of English Madrigals: to Foure Voices*; London; dedicated to the Earl of Oxford.

♦ Queen Elizabeth I of England sends a mechanical organ and clock made by Thomas Dallam to the Sultan of Turkey. It is described in the state papers as "a Great and Curious present . . . which will scandalise other nations, especially

237

the Germans." Dallam's diary of his journey to Constantinople with the organ was published by the Hakluyt Society in 1893.

SOCIETY, EDUCATION

♦ The Duke of Sully, French Superintendent of Finances, reforms taxation, economic policy, overseas trade, and agriculture.

♦ The first chamber of commerce is founded in Marseilles, France.

♦ Plague breaks out in Spain.

♦ First known depiction of the use of a table fork appears in a painting of the "Last Supper" by Jacopo Bassano.

♦ Tycho Brahe becomes a guest at the royal court of HRE Rudolf II at Prague.

♦ The potato is introduced in London.

♦ The first postal rate is fixed in Germany.

♦ Count Francesco Cenci of Rome is murdered. His entire family, including his daughter Beatrice, is arrested. A man of great cruelty and brutal habits, Francesco was tried for sodomy in 1594, and merely fined because of his high rank. All the Cencis are found guilty, and all but the youngest son are executed by order of Pope Clement VIII.

♦ Ulisse Aldrovandi: *Natural History* ; the first three volumes, dealing with ornithology; plentifully and beautifully illustrated. A fourth volume, dealing with insects, is published in 1602. Other volumes, compiled from his notes, are published posthumously.

♦ Edward Wright: *Certaine errors in navigation*—the first explanation of the theoretical construction of Mercator's projection.

1600

GEOGRAPHY

♦ English navigator William Adams, the first Englishman to

visit Japan, arrives on a Dutch vessel, the first Dutch ship to visit Japan, and becomes a trusted agent and advisor on shipbuilding to the Shogun, Tokugawa Ieyasu.

♦ Queen Elizabeth I of England incorporates the East India Company by royal charter on December 31, conferring on "The Governor and Company of Merchants of London, trading into the East Indies" the sole right of trading with the East Indies for 15 years. There are 125 shareholders and an initial capital of £ 72,000. The first governor is Sir Thomas Smythe.

♦ Richard Hakluyt: the final, revised, much enlarged edition of *Principal Navigations, Voyages and Discoveries of the English Nation* (publication begun in 1598); London. This contains a map using mercator projections drawn by Edward Wright and Emery Molyneux, that includes the results of Francis Drake's circumnavigation of the globe.

POLITICS

♦ The Irish Earl of Tyrone resumes his rebellion against Queen Elizabeth I of England (until March 1603).

♦ Peace negotiations at Bergen op Zoom and Boulogne between Spain and the United Provinces of the Netherlands, and between Spain and England, prove unsuccessful.

♦ Robert Devereux, Earl of Essex, is tried for misdemeanors committed in Ireland while commander of the English forces there, and is forced to relinquish his offices at court. After the Queen refuses to renew his right to receive the duties on imported sweet wines, he plans a coup d'etat against her, attempting to gain the support of King James VI of Scotland.

♦ Prince Maurice of Nassau, commanding the forces of the Protestant Netherlands and with an army including English volunteers led by Sir Francis Vere, defeats the Archduke Albert's Spanish and Italian troops at the battle of Nieuport. Maurice subsequently retires into Holland.

♦ King Henri IV of France marries Maria de' Medici. Their son will reign as King Louis XIII.

♦ The Tokugawa Shogunate period begins in Japan, lasting until 1870. Tokugawa Ieyasu defeats his rivals at the battle of Sekigahara, Japan's most famous battle in which 160,000 Samurai fight. Tokugawa becomes ruler of all Japan and establishes his military and administrative headquarters at Edo (present day Tokyo).

RELIGION

♦ Giordano Bruno is burned at the stake for heresy by Catholic authorities in Rome on February 17, after a seven-year imprisonment. The chief reason given is his support of Copernicus's theory that put the sun as the center of earth's system, also his belief in an infinite universe and a plurality of worlds. In 1889, a statue of him is erected at Campo dei Fiori, the site of his execution.

♦ Persecution of Catholics begins in Sweden under King Charles IX.

♦ Vincent de Paul, cannonized as a Catholic saint in 1737, is ordained a priest in France.

LITERATURE AND THE ARTS

♦ Edward Fairfax translates Torquato Tasso's *Gerusalemme Liberata* into English as *Godfrey of Bulloigne; or, The Recoverie of Jerusalem*; London: the first complete translation. Richard Carew had translated the first five cantos in 1595, in heroic verse, dedicated to Queen Elizabeth.

♦ Nicholas Hilliard: *Treatise concerning the Art of Limning*; London.

♦ Michelangelo Merisi da Caravaggio paints "The Supper at Emmaus." Caravaggio is noted for his use of the technique called *chiaroscuro*, that conjoins areas of light and dark in pronounced contrast, as seen in this painting.

♦ Robert Peake (attributed) paints the "Blackfriars Portrait" of

Queen Elizabeth I of England and her court in procession (sometimes called "Eliza triumphans").

♦ Jan Brueghel the Elder paints "The Sense of Hearing," that illustrates most of the musical instruments in use at the time. (some sources date the painting a bit later)

♦ Peter Paul Rubens of the Netherlands goes to Italy to study painting, after about twelve years of study in Antwerp.

♦ Fabritio Caroso: *Nobilità di Dame*; Venice; a compendium of Italian dance steps and etiquette, with melodies notated in Italian lute tablature.

♦ The first opera for which the entire score survives, *Euridice*, with music by Jacopo Peri and libretto by Ottavio Rinuccini, is published in Florence in February 1601, five months after its first performance at the wedding festivities of King Henri IV of France and Maria de' Medici. Giulio Caccini (called Giulio Romano) also wrote an opera to the same text that was published in December 1600, but not performed until 1602.

♦ Thomas Morley: *The First Booke of Ayres, or Little Short Songs to Sing and Play to the Lute with the Base Viole*; London.

♦ John Dowland: *Second Booke of Songs or Ayres of 2, 4, or 5 parts with Tableture for the Lute or Orpherian, with the Violl de Gamba*; London. This collection includes his song "Flow My Tears," usually known as *Lachrimae*, since it uses a melody of that name that Dowland first composed for lute in 1596. This became the most famous melody of the period. In1604, Dowland composed a group of seven pavans for viols and lute, each pavan using the *Lachrimae* melody.

♦ The Fortune Theatre opens in London, on Golden Lane.

♦ Women appear on stage in London.

SOCIETY, EDUCATION

♦ The Amsterdam Bank is founded.

♦ Dutch opticians begin experiments leading to the development of the telescope. In 1608, German-born Dutch optician Hans Lippershey applies for a patent. In 1609, Italian mathematician and natural scientist Galileo Galilei makes several small telescopes ("spyglasses") for astronomical observation, in Padua, Italy.

♦ Athenasius Kircher of Germany invents the magic lantern.

♦ Caspar Lehmann, jewel cutter to HRE Rudolf II, begins the craft of cutting glass at the royal court in Prague.

♦ Johan Kepler goes to the court of HRE Rudolf II at Prague to work as assistant to the court astronomer, Tycho Brahe (whom he succeeds in 1601).

♦ Construction begins on the Royal Palace in Naples, Italy.

♦ The amount of gold extracted from the New World to this date is estimated to be about 750,000 lbs. Annual average imports to Spain had been 6,000-7,000 lbs.

♦ World gold production from all sources during the 16th century is between 1,500,000 and 2,000,000 lbs. By the 18th century it will be 2 1/2 times greater.

♦ Approximate populations in the year 1600 (in millions): France, 16; German states, 14.5; Poland, 11; Spain, 8; Austrian Habsburg dominions, 5.5; England and Ireland, 5.5; Netherlands, 3; Portugal,2; Sweden, 1.5; Scotland, 1.

♦ England: an inventory of the Royal Great Wardrobe of Queen Elizabeth I itemizes more than 1900 items of clothing and jewelry.

♦ William Gilbert: *De Magnete*; London; a treatise on magnetism and electricity.

♦ The Scottish College is founded in Rome.

FIRSTS AND UNUSUAL EVENTS

1500

The first map of the New World is drawn

The Mastersingers of Nuremberg are permitted to write songs on worldly subjects

The first Caesarian operation is performed on a living woman

Silver guilders are introduced as coinage in Germany

The first black lead pencils are used in England

The first American cat is bred; beginning of the American Short Hair breed

The first commercial colleges are founded in Venice, Italy

1501

Amerigo Vespucci explores the coast of Brazil

Shah Ismail I founds the Safavid dynasty in Persia

The first printing of polyphonic vocal music from movable type

Aldine Press, Venice, first uses italic type

1502

Jao de Nova discovers St. Helena Island

Muslims in Castile and Leon, Spain, are ordered to choose between conversion to Christianty or exile

Leonardo da Vinci is appointed chief engineer for Caesare Borgia

The first watch is constructed: called the "Nuremberg egg"

1503
Mines are used in warfare
The Portuguese send African slaves to South America
Leonardo da Vinci begins to paint the Mona Lisa

1504
Michelangelo completes his statue of David
Postal service between Vienna and Brussels is extended to Madrid
Venice proposes the construction of a Suez Canal to Turkey

1505
Albrecht Dürer travels from Germany to Venice in 14 days
Scipione del Ferro solves a form of cubic equation

1506
The first printed map of the Americas
The Laocoön statue group is unearthed in Rome
Pope Julius II lays the cornerstone for a new St. Peter's Basilica in
    Rome
Niccolò Machiavelli creates the first national army in Italy, the
    Florentine militia

1507
The first use of the name "America" in a map of the world
The Diet of Constance recognizes the unity of the Holy Roman
    Empire
The second epidemic of the "sweating sickness" in England

1508
Michelangelo begins to paint the ceiling of the Sistine Chapel

1509
The first European manual of navigation is printed
An earthquake destroys Constantinople

The first wallpaper is produced

1510
Ludovico de Varthema is the first Christian known to enter the
    Muslim holy city of Mecca and leave alive
Leonardo da Vinci designs a horizontal water wheel
A French upholsterer makes the first air bed

1511
Mathias Grunewald begins to paint the Isenheim altar triptych
The first German book on organ building and playing is pub-
    lished

1512
The English Parliament bans tennis, bowls and skittles, and re-
    quires all men between 17 and 60 to keep a longbow and four
    arrows in his house
The first use of the word "masque" to describe the multidisciplinary
    court entertainment in England
English troops mutiny in Spain because of lack of beer

1513
Balboa discovers the Pacific Ocean
Ponce de Leon lands in Florida
Niccolò Machiavelli writes *The Prince*
Alfonso d'Alboquerque, Portuguese Governor General on the
    Malabar coast of India, sends a performing elephant to the
    Pope
King Manoel I of Portugal offers the Pope a lifesize sugar effigy of
    himself surrounded by 12 cardinals, one and a half meters
    high

1514
Cardinal Thomas Wolsey begins to build Hampton Court Palace
Silver mines are opened in western China

Pineapples are imported to Europe

1515

The Lateran Council forbids the printing of books without church permission

Erasmus publishes *The Praise of Folly*

Lodovico Ariosto writes *Orlando Furioso*

The first recorded use of the "Iron Maiden" torture device

The first nationalized factories are established in France, for manufacture of weapons and tapestries,

1516

Dominican monk Johann Tetzel sells indulgences in Germany

Sir Thomas More publishes *Utopia*

King François I of France brings Leonardo da Vinci to live in France

Indigo blue dye comes to Europe

1517

Martin Luther posts 95 theses protesting the sale of indulgences

The wheel-lock musket is invented

The third epidemic of the "sweating sickness" in England

1518

Juan de Grijalva explores the Yucatan coast of Mexico

East Asian porcelain is imported to Europe

The Royal College of Physicians is founded in London

1519

Magellan sets sail on the first circumnavigation of the globe

Hernan Cortez brings horses to Mexico, the first horses in North America

King François I of France begins the construction of the Chateau of Chambord

1520

King Henry VIII of England and King François I of France meet at

the "Field of the Cloth of Gold" in France
Pope Leo X excommunicates Martin Luther
The Chinese first use cannon
Michelangelo designs the Medici Chapel in Florence
Chocolate is brought from Mexico to Spain
Rifling on firearms is invented
Aztec jewels and gold items are put on display in Brussels

1521

Hernan Cortez conquers the Aztecs in Mexico
The Papal States declare bankruptcy
Machiavelli writes *The Art of War* for Lorenzo de' Medici
The manufacture of silk is introduced in France

1522

A German physician is executed for dressing as a woman so he can
    observe childbirth
The Knights of St. John are forced off the island of Rhodes by the
    Turks
Albrecht Dürer designs a flying machine for use in war

1523

Gustavus Vasa is elected King of Sweden, beginning the Vasa dy-
    nasty
The first maritime insurance policies are issued, in Florence, Italy
The first manual of agricultural practice is published, in London

1524

Giulio Romano's explicitly erotic drawings, later known as *I Modi*,
    begin to circulate in Rome
Turkeys from South America are eaten at the English court
Peasants revolt in southern Germany
Zwingli abolishes the Catholic Mass in Zurich, Switzerland

1525

Spanish troops use muskets

Hops are introduced in England

The Chinese government orders the destruction of all oceangoing
ships and the arrest of their owners

1526

Babar ("the tiger") founds the Mughal empire in India and acquires the Koh-i-noor ("mountain of light") diamond

The first printed New Testament in English, translated by William Tyndale

Peasants revolt in Austria

1527

Rome is sacked by German and Spanish troops; the Pope is imprisoned

The Medici family is expelled from Florence

Pietro Aretino writes the sonnets to accompany the erotic pictures
of *I Modi*

1528

The first "rutter" is printed in English

Baldassare Castiglione publishes *Il Cortegiano* (The Courtier)

The fourth epidemic of the "sweating sickness" in England

1529

Women appear on stage in Italy for the first time

Henry VIII begins to cut England's ties to the Church of Rome

Michelangelo designs fortifications for the city of Florence

A new English law requires an inventory of possessions be drawn
up at the death of every man or woman

1530

The first "crown jewels": King François I of France declares that
some of his jewels are the property of the crown

The Venice arsenal builds the first galleon capable of sailing on the
high seas

Cardinal Wolsey is arrested as a traitor

A criminal code and police regulations are established for the Holy Roman Empire

The Knights of St. John relocate to the island of Malta and change their name to the Knights of Malta

Reinerus Gemma Frisius suggests that longitude can be found by means of a difference of times

1531

Our Lady of Guadalupe appears to Juan Diego, a Mexican peasant

Andrea Alciato publishes the first emblem book

Pope Clement VII forbids Henry VIII to remarry, and founds the Inquisition in Portugal

The Antwerp Stock Exchange is founded

1532

Francisco Pizarro captures the King of the Incas in Peru

Machiavelli's *The Prince* is published

Pope Clement VII warns Henry VIII to break off with Anne Boleyn or be excommunicated

King Henry VIII of England founds the "Gentlemen of the Chapel Royal," a men's choir

Thelast sailing of the "Flanders Galleys," an annual convoy of merchant ships that began in 1314

1533

The first Inca treasure arrives in Spain

Spanish in Peru encounter the potato for the first time

King Henry VIII of England and Anne Boleyn marry

Hans Holbein the Younger paints "TheAmbassadors"

1534

Ignatius Loyola of Spain founds the Society of Jesus (the Jesuits)

Henry VIII is declared the supreme head of the church in England

St. Basil's Cathedral is built in Moscow

1535

A Price List of the Whores of Venice is published, listing 110 courtesans

The Spanish explore Chile

Niccolò Tartaglia works out a general solution for mathematical equations of the third degree

Sir Thomas More is beheaded

1536

Hernan Cortez reaches Southern California

An English act of Parliament makes the first laws providing subsidies for the poor

Queen Anne Boleyn is beheaded

John Calvin arrives to lead the Protestants in Geneva

English monasteries are suppressed and their wealth is confiscated

1537

The Portuguese obtain Macao

The complete works of Cicero are published in Venice

The first copyright library is established by law, in Paris

Niccolò Tartaglia develops the science of ballistics

1538

Mercator uses the names "America" and "North America" for the first time in his maps

Pope Paul III excommunicates and deposes King Henry VIII of England

France begins to persecute Protestants

King Henry VIII of England begins to build the Palace of Nonesuch

1539

Persian weavers begin to make the "Ardabil" carpets

The first Christmas tree is erected, in Strasbourg, Germany

A public lottery is held in France

1540

Coronado explores the Rio Grande area of North America

Authorities in Chester, England, ban an annual football game as too violent

Five members of the Bassano family leave Venice to work for King Henry VIII of England

1541

Hernan de Soto discovers the Mississippi River

John Knox goes to Scotland to preach Protestantism

Ignatius Loyola is elected General of the Jesuit Order

1542

Cabrillo explores Upper and Lower California

Pope Paul III calls a church council to meet in Trento, Italy, and establishes the Inquisition in Rome

The first Christian missionary is killed in what is now Kansas, USA

1543

Portuguese traders introduce firearms in Japan

Pope Paul III issues the *Index Librorum Prohibitorum* (List of Forbidden Books)

The Spanish Catholic Inquisition burns its first Protestant martyrs

Pisa lays out the first botanical garden in Europe

1544

Silver is discovered at Potosi, Peru

Mercator is imprisoned for heresy, but released for lack of evidence

Ivan IV ("the Terrible") of Russia takes the government into his own hands at the age of 14

-MOSH

1545

The Council of Trent is convened

Claude Garamond designs his antique typography

Conrad Gessner begins to compile the first bibliography—a list of
all known authors, with the titles of their works

A botanical garden is opened in Padua, Italy

The "Mary Rose," the finest new ship in the English navy, sinks
immediately after being launched

1546

Mayas revolt against the Spanish in Mexico

Michelangelo designs a dome for St. Peter's Basilica in Rome

Construction begins on the Louvre Palace in Paris

Mercator says he believes the earth has a magnetic pole

1547

Kings Henry VIII of England and François I of France both die

Ivan IV ("the Terrible") is crowned as the first Tsar of Russia

English statute authorizes punishing convicted vagrants by slavery

1548

Silver is mined in Mexico

Mary Queen of Scots, age 5, is betrothed to the French Dauphin

The first roofed theatre is opened in Paris

The South American pepper plant is grown in England

1549

Jesuit Father Francis Xavier lands in Japan, and Jesuits go to South
America

The Villa d'Este is built at Tivoli

The theories of the "Pléiade" poets are published in Paris

1550

King Gustavus Vasa of Sweden founds the city of Helsinki, Finland

Pierre de Ronsard publishes his *Odes*

The first written reference to the English game of cricket appears in the wardrobe accounts of King Edward VI of England

Cattle are introduced in South America

1551

Palestrina is appointed Director of Music at St. Peter's Basilica, Rome

The first licensing of alehouses and taverns in England and Wales

Girolamo Cardano casts a horoscope for King Edward VI of England

Printing is introduced in Ireland

The Chinese government makes it a crime to go to sea on a multimasted ship, even for trade

1552

Jesuit missionary Father Francis Xavier reaches China, but dies before getting to the mainland

St. Andrew's Golf Club, Scotland, is founded

English physician John Caius writes a book about the "sweating sickness"

1553

Italian authorities order all copies of the Jewish Talmud destroyed

The potato is first described in writing

1554

The city of Sao Paolo, Brazil, is founded

Andrea Palladio writes a guidebook to Roman antiquities

The first known autograph album is begun

1555

Nostradamus publishes the first books of his prophecies

Tobacco is brought to Spain from the Americas

1556
A powerful earthquake in China kills more than 800,000 people
Sultan Suleiman's mosque in Constantinople (Istanbul) is finished

1557
The Sack-Full of Newes is the first English play to be censored
A serious influenza epidemic throughout Europe
National bankruptcy in Spain

1558
England loses Calais to the French, after holding it for 211 years
Elizabeth Tudor comes to the throne of England as Elizabeth I,
    and asks John Dee to name an astrologically propitious day for
    her coronation
Protestant reformer John Knox argues that women are incompe-
    tent to rule
Nostradamus publishes the second book of his prophecies
France declares bankruptcy
The Portuguese introduce Europeans to the habit of taking snuff
Thomas Gresham formulates "Gresham's Law"

1559
The Spanish government forbids Spanish students to attend most
    foreign universities
Printing without permission is made punishable by death in France
The tulip is first mentioned in Western Europe
The first known mention of tea in Europe

1560
Madrid becomes the capital of Spain
Akbar the Great establishes his capital at Agra in India
The Inquisition is established in the Portuguese East Indies
The "Geneva Bible" is published, using William Tyndale's En-
    glish translation
The first Chinese novel is written, in the style of social realism

1561

Tobacco is introduced into France by Jean Nicot
Portuguese monks introduce printing in India

1562

Castrati are first used in the Papal Choir in Rome
Milled coins are introduced in England
Venice passes a sumptuary law that forbids prostitutes to wear
    jewels or silk

1563

The Catholic Council of Trent, convened in 1545, concludes
Foxe's Book of Martyrs is published in English
King Philip II of Spain begins construction of the Escorial
The first printing presses in Russia
The designation "puritan" is first used in England
A severe plague epidemic rages throughout Europe, spreading to
    England

1564

The Spanish settle the Philippine Islands, naming them for King
    Philip II
A reign of terror begins in Russia under Ivan "the Terrible"
The Catholic Church publishes the Index of Forbidden Books
Starch is introduced in England

1565

Sweet potatoes and tobacco are introduced in England
A catalogue of outstanding courtesans is published in Venice
The first graphite pencil is described by the Swiss

1566

Ceramist Bernard Palissy is commissioned to construct a pottery
    grotto for Queen Catherine de' Medici
The potato is introduced in Rome and Belgium

The Inquisition is abolished in the Netherlands

1567

The Portuguese found the city of Rio de Janiero in Brazil
Two million natives die of typhoid fever in South America
A botanical garden is established at the University of Bologna, Italy

1568

Mary Queen of Scots, defeated in battle, flees to England to begin her 19 year captivity there
England permanently recalls its ambassador to Spain
Oda Nobunaga makes himself dictator of Japan
Beer is bottled for the first time

1569

Mercator makes the first world map using his projection
Swedes declare their King unfit to rule
A public lottery is held in London to finance repairs to the harbors

1570

The first atlas of maps is published in Antwerp
Ivan "the Terrible" , Tsar of Russia, massacres the people of the city of Novgorod
The Pope issues a Bull absolving the English from allegiance to Queen Elizabeth I
Beware the Cat, the first English novel, is published

1571

The largest naval battle of the century is fought at Lepanto; the Turks are defeated by an allied European force under Don Juan of Austria
The Spanish found Manila in the Philippine Islands
The Royal Exchange is opened in London

1572

St. Bartholomew's Day Massacre of Huguenot Protestants in Paris, spreading to the provinces and lasting some months
Andrea Amati makes his earliest 'cello still extant
Tycho Brahe spots a new star in Cassiopeia without the aid of magnification
The Dutch use carrier pigeons during the Spanish siege of Haarlem
French surgeon Ambrose Paré recommends ligature of the arteries instead of cauterization with a re-hot-iron after amputations

1573
Spain passes laws forbidding the enslavement or abuse of native people in the Americas
The first mention of the cultivation of maize by the Chinese

1574
Thefirst English book on navigation is published
The first "Auto-da-fé" is held in Mexico

1575
The Mongols of China are converted to Tibetan Buddhism
Torquato Tasso completes writing *Gerusalemme Liberata*
The first use of a "broken consort" of musical instruments in England

1576
James Burbage, father of Richard, begins construction of the first theatre in London—"The Theatre"
Tycho Brahe establishes Uraniborg Observatory on the island of Hveen, Denmark

1577
Francis Drake begins his voyage circumnavigating the globe
Akbar the Great completes his unification of northern India
The Cretan artist "El Greco" moves to Spain

1578

One of Japan's chief warlords is converted to Christianity
Work is begun on the Pont Neuf (New Bridge) in Paris
The catacombs under Rome are discovered

1579

St. John of the Cross writes *The Dark Night of the Soul*
The first Christian religious service is held in California
The first English translation of *Plutarch's Lives*, by Thomas North

1580

Portugal is absorbed into Spain
Tsar Ivan "the Terrible" of Russia kills his son and heir with his own hands
The English folksong *Greensleeves* is mentioned for the first time
The potato is introduced in Dublin
The first use of whalebone for constructing the hoops of women's skirts
New construction is forbidden in London

1581

Russia begins its conquest of Siberia
Acrobats, bankers and brothel keepers are forbidden to receive communion in the Protestant churches of the northern Netherlands
The first ballet is performed at the French royal court
Hans Ruckers of Antwerp builds the oldest of his harpsichords still extant
The first black African slaves are imported to St. Augustine, Florida

1582

Pope Gregory XIII reforms the Julian calendar by omitting 10 days; the Catholic countries adopt the new calendar, but the Protestant nations continue to use the Julian calendar
Akbar the Great abolishes slavery in India

1583

The city of Buenos Aires is named in South America

The first known life insurance policy is issued in England

Galileo Gallilei deduces the value of a pendulum for the exact measurement of time

Holy Roman Emperor Rudolf of Habsburg transfers the royal court from Vienna to Prague

1584

William of Orange is assassinated in the Netherlands

The first Christian catechism is printed in China

Prince Chu Tsai-yu of China defines the tempered scale

1585

Roanoke Island, Virginia (now North Carolina), is colonized by the English

Miguel de Cervantes writes his first important work

1586

Thomas Cavendish leaves on the 3rd circumnavigation of the globe

Pope Sixtus V fixes the number of Cardinals at 70

An English Star Chamber decree forbids publication of books or pamphlets without Church of England permission

The beginning of Kabuki theatre in Japan

Tobacco is first smoked on the streets of London

1587

The first child is born in what is now the continental United States

Mary Queen of Scots is executed

Construction begins on the Rialto Bridge, Venice

1588

The first Spanish Armada sent against England is defeated

The Vatican Library is opened in Rome

Warlord Hideyoshi of Japan orders the weapons of the peasantry confiscated

1589

King Henri III of France is assassinated, and King Henri of Navarre becomes King Henri IV of France

Galileo establishes the first principle of dynamics: bodies of different weights fall at the same velocity

Forks for individual diners are first used at the French court

1590

The English Roanoke Island colony in Virginia is found completely deserted

Japan is unified under warlord Hideyoshi

Coal mining begins in the Ruhr valley of Germany

1591

Giuseppe Archimbaldo paints a portrait of HRE Rudolf II as Vertumnus; Rudolf's head, neck and chest are entirely composed of fruits, flowers and vegetables

Trinity College, Dublin, is founded by Queen Elizabeth I of England

François Viète writes the earliest known work of symbolic algebra

1592

Juan de Fuca discovers British Columbia, Canada

Giordano Bruno is arrested by the Inquisition, in Venice

Shakespeare's *Henry VI, Part III* is performed in London, the first Shakespeare play to be publicly performed

The city of Pompeii, destroyed by the eruption of Mt. Vesuvius in A.D. 79, is uncovered for the first time since its destruction

1593

The Japanese begin to kill and persecute Christians

London theatres are closed because of a plague epidemic

English dramatist Christopher Marlowe is murdered
Purana Pul Bridge is built in Hyderabad, India

1594

Queen Elizabeth I of England sends an organ to the Sultan of Turkey
The Dutch East India Company is founded
The city of Herculaneum buried with Pompeii in A. D. 79, is
uncovered

1595

Warsaw becomes the capital of Poland
The Swan Theatre is built in London
The first appearance of heels on shoes
The English army officially abandons the bow and arrow as a
weapon of war

1596

The second Spanish armada leaves for England, but is scattered by
storms
John Harington of England designs a flush toilet
Blackfriars Theatre opens in London
Tomatoes are introduced in England
Galileo invents the thermometer
Ludolph van Ceulen works out the value of "pi"

1597

Duke Alfonso II d'Este dies; the last member of the principal
branch of the house of Este
Aldine Press, Venice, founded in 1494, closes, after publishing
908 works
Spain declares bankruptcy
The first use of field hospitals and dispensaries in Europe

1598

Olivier van Noort of the Netherlands becomes the fourth explorer
to circumnavigate the globe

The Edict of Nantes grants equal right of worship to French Protestants

Boris Godunov is elected Tsar of Russia

Jacopo Peri's *Dafne*, usually called the first opera, is performed in Florence

1599

The body of St. Cecilia is found on the site of the Roman church bearing her name

The first chamber of commerce is founded in Marseilles, France

The potato is introduced in London

The first postal rate is fixed in Germany

Count Francesco Cenci of Rome is murdered by his family

1600

Queen Elizabeth I of England incorporates the East India Company in London

The Tokugawa Shogunate Period begins in Japan

Giordano Bruno is burned at the stake for heresy at Campo dei Fiori, Rome

Athenasius Kircher invents the magic lantern

Caspar Lehmann begins the craft of cutting glass at the royal court of HRE Rudolf II in Prague

GLOSSARY

alchemy—a chemical science and speculative philosophy originating in the Middle Ages, the practice of which continued throughout the 16th century. The main objectives were finding a method to transform base metals into gold, discovering a universal cure for diseases, and achieving a means to prolong life indefinitely.

Auto-da-fé (Spanish; literally "act of faith")—the ceremony accompanying the pronouncement of judgment by the Roman Catholic **Inquisition** (q.v.) followed by the execution, by secular authorities, of those sentenced as guilty; often used to describe the execution only, which was usually by burning.

basilica—a designation for certain Roman Catholic churches having special privileges. In Roman times, it was a building with a specific floor plan.

beatification—a formal declaration by the Roman Catholic Church that a deceased person is one of the "blessed," and is thus entitled to public religious honor. This is very often a preliminary to canonization as a saint.

broken consort—in instrumental music, a grouping of different types of instruments. In a consort, by contrast, all of the instruments are of the same type, merely different as to size and range.

263

The broken consort originated in England about 1575. A typical broken consort grouping included recorders (flutes), viols, and lutes.

canonize—to declare a deceased person a saint. This is done by the Roman Catholic Chursh, and is preceded by a formal inquiry.

castrati (Ital.)—castrated male singers. Boys with good voices were castrated before puberty so as to preserve their ability to sing in the female vocal range. They were first employed in the Vatican choir in 1562, and were used there until the 19th century.

Chambre Ardente (burning chamber)—a French criminal court for the trial of heretics.

charterhouse—a monastery building, originally only for the Carthusian order of monks.

chiaroscuro (Ital.)—a painting technique in which areas of light and dark are conjoined in marked contrast. The Italian artist Caravaggio is particularly associated with the technique.

Church Council (ecumenical or general council)—a formal meeting of the ruling dignitaries (bishops and cardinals) of the Roman Catholic Church, called by the Pope and presided over by the Pope or his legate, assembled together to make pronouncements on matters of faith or morals. These decrees must receive Papal confirmation to be valid.

coasting—the act or practice of sailing from port to port along a sea coast.

cordiform—heartshaped ,as in a cordiform projection for maps.

corral—a Spanish type of outdoor "yard play."

devising by testament—leaving land to heirs in a will.

Diet—a formal public assembly of the governing bodies of a state or kingdom, or the members so meeting.

emblem—a kind of personal logo or identification device used by royalty and nobility, consisting of a symbolic picture accompanied by a descriptive verse. The first book of emblems appeared in 1534, compiled by Andrea Alciato.

farthingale—a voluminous skirt, supported by a framework of hoops. When whalebone became available for making the hoops in about 1580, skirts began to grow wider and wider. By the 1590's their shape had become very exaggerated, as can be seen in portraits from the period.

galley—a sailing vessel powered by rowers; in classical times, often propelled only by rowers; in the 16th century, generally powered by both sails and oarsmen. A typical war galley would have 20 oars on each side, with a number of rowers for each oar. Types of this vessel are called galleons, galleasses, half-galleys, and galiots.

Golden Horde—the Mongols who inhabited the Qipcaq steppe of Asia.

Gresham's Law—a principle of economics which states that when two coins are equal in face or debt paying power, but unequal in intrinsic value, the one with lesser intrinsic value will remain in circulation, while the other will be hoarded.

heliocentric theory—the theory that the sun is the center of our system of planets, which revolve around the sun. The older theory, supported by the Catholic Church in the 16th century, was that the earth was the center of things. Copernicus is principally associated with the theory, but other thinkers, among them Giordano Bruno, supported it as well.

HRE—Holy Roman Emperor

iconoclasm—the destruction of images (icons). Usually only directed at religious paintings and statues, it has also encompassed the destruction of relics and shrines.

Index Librorum Prohibitorum (**Latin; index of forbidden books**)— a list of books Catholics were forbidden to read, first proclaimed by the Pope in 1557. Catholics were allowed to read only books marked with the **imprimatur** (let it be printed).

indulgence—remission of punishment for the soul of a dead person in Purgatory. Roman Catholics believed that indulgences could be obtained by performing specified good works or prayers.

Inquisition—the systematic pursuit of heresy and the punishment of heretics by the Roman Catholic Church, acting together with the state. Inquisition also refers to a court or tribunal established for that purpose, called the Holy Office. The first Inquisitions date to the 12th century. The most famous Inquisition is the Spanish, which was extremely severe. Established in 1480, it was not formally abolished until 1834.

janissary (**var. janizary**)—a soldier in a body of Turkish infantry that existed from the 14th to the 19th century, which formed the main fighting force of the Turks. The first janissaries were personal slaves of the Sultan, and their ranks included many captured Christians. The janissaries developed a characteristic music employing brass instruments and percussion.

kirk—the Scottish word for church.

Malabar coast—the coastline of a region of southwestern India, generally from Mangalore south to the tip of the subcontinent.

masque—a form of court entertainment involving costumes, scenery, dances, music, and poetry which flourished in England in Tudor and Stuart times. Its roots were in Medieval entertainments, in France and Italy as well as in England. Masques were most often performed for special occasions.

Mass—the principal religious service for Roman Catholics; a ritual commemoration of the Last Supper in which bread and wine are consecrated to become the body and blood of Jesus Christ, which may be then received by the faithful in the sacrament of Holy Communion. Many composers have set the principal parts of the Mass to music, always in Latin during the 16th century.

Meistersinger (German; Mastersinger)—a South German burgher belonging to a guild of singers devoted to perpetuating traditions of medieval Middle High German lyric verse on the topic of love. They were at their zenith from 1500 to 1550.

mosque—a building used for Islamic public worship.

motet—a type of religious choral music, which was a major musical genre from the 13th through the 18th centuries.

mystère—a type of French play about religious subjects.

notes inégales—a French performance practice of playing some evenly notated rhythms unevenly, which continued until the late 18th century.

Papal Bull—a letter from the Pope, distinguished from other letters by its form, materials and type of seal (the "bulla"), opening with specified formal words.

Peter's pence—an annual tax or tribute, established in England before King Alfred's time and abolished in 1534, of a penny payable by each householder to the Pope's see, the bishopric of St. Peter. Several other countries had similar tributes.

pinnnace—a type of light sailing ship.

pogrom—an organized massacre of helpless people, usually with the connivance of officials. Specifically, such a massacre of Jews, a practice originating in Russia.

portolano (from the Italian *porto,* **port)**—a book for navigators, containing descriptions of ports. sailing directions, etc., and illustrated with charts—called **portolan maps or charts.**

prelate—a churchman of superior rank or authority; a dignitary of the church.

principality—a territory governed by a Prince.

recusant—in England, a word used to describe a person who continued to worship as a Catholic. **Recusancy** was punishable by fines and sometimes by imprisonment. People were required to attend Church of England services, and when they did not, they might be investigated for recusancy. In general, a recusant is someone who refuses to submit to authority, someone who is a nonconformist.

rutter (from French *routier,* **a guide to the ways)**—a book of sailing directions for navigators, especially of routes between specific places. The first rutter in English was printed in 1528, but rutters had existed for use in the Mediterranean for centuries before that.

shogun—a title for military governors of Japan. By the 16th century, they were virtual rulers of the country, with the Emperor a mere figurehead.

sive (or seu)—Latin for "or." This appears frequently throughout the century to indicate a sub or alternate title for a work.

Spanish Main—the eastern coast of Spanish America, from Panama to Venezuela.

Star Chamber—an English high court which exercised wide civil and criminal jurisdiction, and did not use a jury. It could proceed against a defendant with a charge based on mere rumor, and use torture to examine witnesses. Extensively used by the Tudors, it was abolished by the Long Parliament of 1641. Its name comes from the stars on the ceiling of the room where it convened.

sumptuary laws—laws aimed at preventing extravagance in private life by restricting specific fabrics and colors of clothing as well as types of furs and jewels to specified classes of society. In practice, they were an attempt, usually unsuccessful, to prevent middle class people from looking like members of the upper classes. Such laws were enacted in classical Greece and Rome as well as Medieval and Renaissance Europe, and sometimes extended to food and furniture as well as clothing and jewels.

tithe—a tenth part of income paid either as a tax or voluntary contribution to church or state authorities.

Union of Utrecht—a confederation of the Protestant provinces of the northern Netherlands, formed in 1579, and including Holland, Zeeland, Utrecht, Gelderland, Friesland, Groningen and Overyssel. It was led by Prince William of Orange until his assassination in 1584 , and is considered the foundation of the Dutch Republic.

usury—an excessive rate of interest charged for the use of money.

vade mecum (Latin, go with me) a handbook or manual.; a book or other thing than a person carries with him as a constant companion.

virginal—a small harpsichord, rectangular or polygonal, usually having a range of about four octaves with a single set of strings and jacks. Although virginals are especially associated with 16th century England, the first English-designed virginal dates from the 1660's in the reign of King Charles II. Thus, in the 16th century the English were playing virginals designed, and usually built by, Italians or Flemish makers.

Waggoner (named for Lucas Janzoon Wahenhaer of the Netherlands)—an atlas of seacharts. The first volume, published in 1584, covered Cadiz to the Zuider Zee. The second volume, in 1585, covered the North Sea and the Baltic. They were also almanacs and manuals of navigation. A Latin edition of both volumes was published in 1586, and an English edition, *The Mariner's Mirrour*, in October 1588. For at least a century afterwards, all sea charts were called "Waggoners" by English seamen.

SOURCES CONSULTED

Some of the books listed have provided only a few specialized bits of information, while others have provided general background for the period, and a few have been useful throughout the entire project for both specific facts and general knowledge. For the reader who is seeking more information on various aspects of the sixteenth century, I have included most of the works I consulted even when their contribution was small, for I consider all of them to be of good quality. Of course, in many instances I also cross checked dates and facts in such larger reference works as the Enclyclopaedia Britannica and the Dictionary of National Biography.

ALLEN, PHILLIP. *The Atlas of Atlases*. Harry Abrams, New York, 1992

ARNOLD, JANET. *Queen Elizabeth's Wardrobe Unlock'd*. Maney, 1988

ASHELFORD, JANE. *The Art of Dress: Clothes and Society 1500-1914*. The National Trust, Great Britain, 1996

ASIMOV, ISAAC. *Asimov's Chronology of the World*. Harper Collins, New York, 1991

AUGHTERSON, KATE, Ed. *Renaissance Woman: Constructions of Femininity in England.* Routledge, New York, 1995

BALFOUR, IAN. *Famous Diamonds.* Second Edition. Gemological Institute of America, Santa Monica, 1992

BLACK, C.F. et al, Eds. *Cultural Atlas of the Renaissance.* Prentice Hall, New York, 1993

BOORSTIN, DANIEL J. *The Discoverers.* Random House, New York, 1983

BRAUDEL, FERNAND. *The Structures of Everyday Life. Civilization & Capitalism 15th-18th Century,* Vol. I. Harper & Row, New York, 1982

BRAUDEL, FERNAND. *The Wheels of Commerce. Civilization & Capitalism 15th*-18th *Century,* Vol. 2. Harper & Row, New York, 1982

BURKE, JAMES. *The Day the Universe Changed.* Little, Brown, New York, 1985

CAMBRIDGE BIOGRAPHICAL DICTIONARY. Chambers, Edinburgh. 1990

CHARTIER, ROGER, ED. *A History of Private Life: Passions of the Renaissance.* Harvard University Press, Cambridge, 1989

CLULEE, NICHOLAS H. *John Dee's Natural Philosophy: Between Science and Religion.* Routledge, London, 1988

COCKS, ANNA SOMERS. *An Introduction to Courtly Jewellery.* Victoria & Albert Museum, London, 1980

DURANT, WILL. *The Renaissance. The Story of Civilization*, Vol. V. Simon & Schuster, New York, 1953.

DURANT, WILL. *The Reformation. The Story of Civilization*, Vol. VI. Simon & Schuster, New York, 1957

ERLANGER, PHILIPPE. *The Age of Courts and Kings: Manners and Morals, 1558-1715*. Doubleday Anchor, New York, 1970

GARRARD, TIMOTHY F. *Gold of Africa*. Prestel, Geneva, 1989

GERNET, JACQUES. *A History of Chinese Civilization*. Trans. J.R. Foster. Cambridge University Press, 1982

GOLDSCHNEIDER, LUDWIG. *Michelangelo: Paintings Sculptures Architecture*. Phaidon, London, 1964

GRAHAM, WINSTON. *The Spanish Armadas*. Collins, London, 1987

GRUN, BERNARD. *The Timetables of History*. Simon and Schuster, New York, 1975

HAGEN, ROSE-MARIE and RAINER. *Pieter Bruegel the Elder: Peasants, Fools and Demons*. Taschen, Koln, 1994

HALE, JOHN. *The Civilization of Europe in the Renaissance*. Athenaeum, New York, 1994

HARLEY, JOHN. *William Byrd: Gentleman of the Chapel Royal*. Scolar Press, Aldershot, England, 1997

HEMMING, JOHN. *The Search for El Dorado*. Dutton, New York, 1978

HIBBERT, CHRISTOPHER. *The Rise and Fall of the House of Medici*. The Folio Society, London, 1998.

HOWARTH, DAVID. *The Voyage of the Armada: The Spanish Story*. Viking Press, New York, 1981

KANE, JOSEPH NATHAN. *Famous First Facts*, 5th Edition. H.W. Wilson, New York, 1997

KWANTEN, LUC. *Imperial Nomads: A History of Central Asia 500-1500*. University of Pennsylvania Press, 1979.

LANDES, DAVID S. *The Wealth and Poverty of Nations*. W.W. Norton, New York, 1998

LANGDON, HELEN. *Holbein*. Phaidon, London, 1993

LASOCKI, DAVID, with Roger Prior. *The Bassanos: Venetian Musicians and Instrument Makers in England, 1531-1665*. Ashgate, Aldershot, England, 1995

LOUDA, JIRI & MACLAGAN, MICHAEL. *Lines of Succession: Heraldry of the Royal Families of Europe*. Orbis, London, 1981

MATTINGLY, GARRETT. *The Armada*. Houghton Mifflin, New York, 1959

McCORQUODALE, CHARLES. *The Renaissance: European Painting 1400-1600*. Studio Editions, London, 1994

McEVEDY, COLIN; *The Penguin Atlas of Modern History (to 1815)*. Penguin Books, London, 19

MONTROSE, LOUIS. *The Purpose of Playing: Shakespeare and*

the Cultural Politics of the Elizabethan Theatre. University of Chicago Press, 1996

MOREL, BERNARD. *The French Crown Jewels.* Fonds Mercator, Antwerp, 1988

MORRIS, T. A. *Europe and England in the Sixteenth Century.* Routledge, London, 1998

MULLER, PRISCILLA E. *Jewels in Spain 1500-1800.* Hispanic Society of America, New York, 1972

PARRY, J.H. *The Age of Reconnaissance: Discovery, Exploration and Settlement 1450 to 1650.* University of California Press, Berkeley, 1981

PRICE, DIANA. *Shakespeare's Unorthodox Biography.* Greenwood Press, Westport Connecticut; 2001

REISCHAUER, EDWIN O. *Japan: The Story of a Nation,* 4th Edition. Knopf, New York, 1989

RIDLEY, JASPER. *The Tudor Age.* Overlook Press, New York , 1990

SADIE, STANLEY, ED. *The New Grove Dictionary of Music and Musicians.* Macmillan, London, 1980

SALGADO, GAMINI. *The Elizabethan Underworld.* St. Martin's Press, New York, 1992

SCARISBRICK, DIANA. *Tudor and Jacobean Jewellery.* Tate Publishing, London, 1995

SMITH, LACEY BALDWIN. *Treason in Tudor England: Poli-*

tics and Paranoia. Princeton University Press, Princeton, 1986

STRONG, ROY. *The Cult of Elizabeth.* Thames and Hudson, London, 1977

STRONG, ROY. *The English Renaissance Miniature.* Thames & Hudson, London, 1983

SOMERSET, ANNE. *Elizabeth I.* Knopf, New York, 1991

SUTHERLAND, C.H.V. *Gold..* McGraw-Hill, New York, 1969

TOLNAY, CHARLES DE. *Hieronymus Bosch.* Wm Morrow, New York, 1966

TWINING, LORD. *A History of the Crown Jewels of Europe.* London, 1960

UKERS, WILLIAM H. *The Romance of Tea: An Outline History of Tea and Tea-Drinking Through Sixteen Hundred Years.* Knopf, New York, 1936

WEATHERFORD, JACK. *Indian Givers: How the Indians of the Americas Transformed the World.* Fawcett Columbine, New York, 1988

WHITFIELD, PETER. *Mapping the World* The Folio Society, London, 2000.

WILFORD, JOHN NOBLE. *The Mapmakers.* Knopf, New York, 1981

WILLIAMS, NEVILLE. *Chronology of the Expanding World 1492 to 1762.* New York, Simon & Schuster, 1994

WILLIAMS, NEVILLE. *Henry VIII and His Court.* Macmillan, New York, 1971

TOPICAL REFERENCES BY YEAR

NB: This is primarily a listing of names—of people, places, political events, objects and substances. Nations, cities or principalities are *not* listed for every war or political situation in which they were involved or which occurred there.

As to alphebetical listings:

Popes and Universities are listed under "P" and "U" respectively (e.g., Rodrigo Borgia, Pope Alexander VI, is listed under "P"); Cathedrals are under "C," while Diets are under "D." (except for the Imperial Diet). Peaces and treaties are listed by the place where they were signed.

Kings, Queens and Emperors are listed under their given names, rather than their family names (e.g., King Henry VIII of England is listed under "H" as Henry Tudor)

When two people have the same name (e.g. Archduke Albert of Habsburg, the elder is listed first, or, if contemporaries, the one with the higher rank.

Members of the English, Scottish, French, Spanish, and most other national nobility are listed under their titles (e.g.,Edward Seymour, Duke of Somerset is listed under "S' for Somerset), while Italian nobles are listed under their under their family names, since they are better known by them (e.g., Francesco Sforza, Duke of Milan is listed under "S")

Church dignitaries are listed under their surnames (e. g. Thomas, Cardinal Wolsey is listed under "W")

Spanish and Portuguese surnames are listed as they generally appear in reference works or indices, even though this may be inconsistent (e.g. Vasco Nunez de Balboa is invariably listed as Balboa, while Juan Ponce de Leon is listed under "P" as Ponce de Leon, since this is the usual version of his name).

Names of visual artists are listed, but generally not their individual works. When literary works are as well known as their authors, the works are listed; otherwise, the authors are listed in the years of publication.

Holy Roman Emperor is abbreviated as HRE throughout the entire Chronology.

* * * *

Aachen expels Protestant immigrants 1560

Abbas I, Shah of Persia to 1629 1586, 1590

Academy of Geneva established by John Calvin 1559

Accademia delle Arti de Disegno established in Florence 1563

Accademia di San Luca founded in Rome 1557

Accademia di Scienze, Lettere ed Arte founded in Lucca, Italy 1584

Accademia Secretorum Naturae founded in Naples 1560

Academie du Palais founded 1576

Acosta, Jose de (Spanish translator and lexicographer) 1584, 1590

Acquavite (brandy) 1596

Act of Federation between Holland and Zeeland 1576

Act of Submission to King Henry VIII as head of English Church 1532

Act of Supremacy declaring King Henry VIII head of English Church 1534

Act of Uniformity, England 1549, 1559

Adams, William (English sailor, counselor to Tokugawa of Japan) 1600

Adrianople, Peace of 1545

Aenid in English 1557

Agnadello, Battle of 1509

Agra diamond 1526

Agricola, Georg (Georgius Agricola; George Bauer; German physician and mining engineer; "father of mineralogy"; 1494-1555)
1546, 1556

Agricola, Martin (real name Sohr or Sore; writer on music theory;
1486-1536) 1529

air bed inflatable mattress 1510

Akan people of Ghana 1502

Akbar the Great, Mughal Emperor of India (Jelal-ed-din-
Mohammed; 1542-1605) 1558, 1560, 1567, 1575, 1577,
1581, 1582, 1590, 1592, 1594

Alarcon, Hernando de (Spanish explorer) 1540

Alba, Fernando Alvarez de Toledo, Duke of (alt. Alva; Spanish general and statesman; 1508-82) 1567, 1568, 1573

Albany, Duke of, named Lord Protector of Scotland 1515

Albert of Habsburg, Archduke of Austria, Viceroy of Portugal ,
Governor of the Spanish Netherlands 1593, 1595, 1596, 1597

Albert, IV, Duke of Bavaria ("the wise"; d.1508) 1504

Albert V, Duke of Bavaria (1528-79) 1558, 1579

Albert of Brandenburg, Grand Master of the Teutonic Knights
1525

Albert I, Duke of Prussia 1544

Alboquerque, Alfonso d' (Governor General of the Spanish hold-
ings on the Malabar coast of India; 1453-1515) 1509, 1511,
1513

Alciato, Andréa (var. Alciatus; Alciati; Italian jurist and leader in
legal humanism; author of the first emblem book; 1492-1550)
1531

Aldrovandi, Ulisse (Italian naturalist; 1522-1605) 1567, 1574,
1599

Aldine Press, Venice 1501, 1502, 1513, 1535, 1537, 1570, 1597

Aldus Manutius (Aldo Manucci, or Manuzio; Italian scholar and
printer; founder of Aldine Press, Venice; c.1450-1515) 1501

Alençon, Duke of 1576

Alfonso of Aragon, Duke ofBisceglie, husband of Lucretia Borgia 1500

Alfonso II, Duke of Este 1597

Algiers founded 1518

Alleyn, Edward (English actor; 1566-1626) 1585

Almagro, Diego de Almagro (Spanish conquistador; sometime partner of Francisco Pizarro; 1475-1538) 1530, 1531, 1538

Almeida, Francisco de, Viceroy of Portuguese territory in India (1450-1512) 1505

Altdorfer, Albrecht (German painter, engraver and architect; c.1480-1538) 1520, 1529

Algiers epidemic 1572

Altan Khan 1542. 1571

Alva, Ferdinand Alvarez de Toledo, Duke of (var. Alba; Spanish general and statesman; 1508-82) 1567, 1568, 1573

Alvarez de Pineda, Domenico (Spanish explorer) 1519

Alvarez, Jorge (Portuguese explorer) 1513

Amati, Andréa (Italian maker of stringed instruments; b.before 1511-d.before 1580) 1564, 1572

Amazon River discovered in South America 1542

Amboise, Peace of 1563

Amboyna 1511

"America" used for the first time on a map 1538

Amicable Loan 1525

Amyot, Jacques (French humanist writer; 1513-93) 1559

Amsterdam Bank founded 1600

Anabaptists in Austria 1528

Anabaptist movement in Germany 1520, 1534, 1535

Anabaptist movement in Switzerland 1526

Andagoya, Pascual de (Spanish explorer; discoverer of Peru) 1522

Andrae, Jacob, of Tubingen 1577

Anglo-Portuguese syndicate 1501, 1502

Angola coast, Africa, settled by Portuguese 1574

Anjou, François of Valois, Duke of (son of King Henri II and Catherine de' Medici; brother of King Henri III; formerly Duke of Alençon; d.1584) 1578, 1579, 1581, 1582, 1583, 1584

Anjou, Henri of Valois, Duke of (King Henri III of France from 1574; 1551-89) 1570, 1571, 1572, 1573

Anna of Habsburg, Queen of Spain from 1570 (daughter of HRE Maximilian II, fourth wife of King Philip II) 1570

Anne of Brittany, Queen of France (wife, successively, of Charles VIII and Louis XII; 1476-1514) 1514

Anne of Cleves, Queen of England 1540 (German Princess; fourth wife of King Henry VIII; 1515-57) 1539, 1540

Anne of Denmark, Princess, wife of King James VI of Scotland, who becomes King James I of the United Kingdom in 1603 (1574-1619) 1589

Antico, Andréa (var. Anticho, Antigo, Antiquo, Antiquus; Italian composer, music engraver and publisher; c.1480-after 1539) 1513, 1517

Antwerp has 19 sugar refineries 1550

Antwerp sacked by French (cf "French Fury) 1583

Antwerp sacked by Spanish (cf "Spanish Fury") 1576; 1585

Antwerp stock exchange founded 1531

Aquaviva, Claudius, General of the Jesuits from 1581; 1543-1615) 1586

Aragon Canal begun in Spain 1529

Arbeau, Thoinot (Jehan Tabourot, Canon of Langres, France; writer on dance; 1519-95) 1588

Archangel on the White Sea as a trading post 1584

Archimbaldo, Giuseppe (Italian painter) 1591

Ardabil carpets begun in Persia 1539

Ardres, Peace of 1546

Aretino, Pietro (Italian journalist and publicist; 1492-1557) 1524, 1525, 1527

Ariosto, Lovovico (Italian poet; court poet in Ferrara; 1473-1533) 1515, 1518. 1566

Arras, treaty of 1579

Art of War, The (Libro dell' arte della guerra by Niccolò Machiavelli) 1521, 1560

Arthur Tudor, Prince of Wales, heir to the English throne (1486-1502) 1501, 1502

Articles of Religion in England 1562

Ashikaga shogunate ends in Japan 1573

Ascham, Roger (English scholar; c.1515-68) 1570

Aske, Robert, leader of Pilgramage of Grace English Catholic uprising 1536, 1537

Askew, Anne, burned at the stake 1546

Asuncion founded by the Spanish 1536

Attaignant, Pierre (French music printer; printer and bookseller in music for the King of France from 1537; c.1494-c.1551) 1527, 1537

Audiencia of New Granada created 1549

Augsburg submits to HRE Charles V 1547

Auto-da-fé, first held in Mexico 1574

autograph album 1554

Aztec/Spanish dictionary 1555

Aztec gold 1520

Babbington, Anthony (English conspirator; 1561-86) 1586

Babbington Plot 1586

Babar "the Tiger" (first Mughal Emperor of India; 1483-1530) 1525, 1526, 1530

Bacon, Francis, Baron Verulam of Verulam, Viscount St. Albans (English philosopher, essayist and statesman; 1561-1626) 1597

Bagdad captured by the Turks 1534

Balboa, Vasco Nunez de (Spanish explorer; 1475-1519) 1513

Baldwin, William (English writer; d. 1563) 1553, 1559, 1570

Banco di Rialto of Venice 1584

Banco Sant'Ambrogio of Milan 1593

bankruptcy in France 1558

bankruptcy in the Papal States 1521
bankruptcy in Spain 1557, 1575, 1597
Baptists in Zurich, Switzerland 1527
Barbaro, Daniello (Italian architect) 1556
Barbary States of Algiers and Tunis founded 1518
Barcelona, Treaty of 1529
Barclay, Alexander (Scottish poet and author; c.1475-1552) 1509
Bardi, Giovanni de', Count of Vernio (1534-1612) 1573
Barents, William (Dutch navigator; d.1597)) 1596
Baronius, Caesar (Cesare Baronio; Italian Church historian; 1539-
    1607) 1596
Baros, Joao de (Portuguese historian; 1496-1570) 1552
Barrow, Henry, Puritan martyr in England 1593
Bartas, Seigneur du (Guillaume de Salluste; 1544-90) 1578
Barton, Elizabeth ("The Nun of Kent") 1534
Basel canton, Switzerland 1501
Basenose College founded at Oxford University, England 1509
Basil (see Vasili) III (Grand Duke of Moscovy and Ruler of Mos-
    cow to 1533) 1503, 1504, 1505, 1514, 1533
Bassano family of musicians 1540
Bassi, Matteo, founder of the Capuchin Order 1525
Bastides, Rodrigo de (Spanish explorer) 1501, 1524
Batavia, Java, founded 1597
Bathory, Sigismund, Prince of Transylvania from 1581-1597
    (nephew of Stephen Bathory; 1572-1613) 1581, 1597
Bathory, Stephen, Hungarian King of Poland, 1575-86; Prince of
    Transylvania from 1571; 1533-86) 1575, 1586
Bavarian Royal Library founded 1558
Bayard, Chevalier de (Pierre du Terrail, q.v.; French military hero:
    "the knight without fear and without reproach"; 1476-1524)
    1512, 1515, 1524
Bearn annexed to the French crown 1592
Beatus Thenanus (Bild aus Theinau; German historian; 1485-
    1547) 1531

Beaujoyeulx, Balthasar de (Baldassare de Belgioioso; "Baltazarini"; Italian Ballet master and violinist, resident in France; b. before c1535—c1587) 1581"

Beaulieu, Edict of, grants toleration to French Huguenots 1576

Beddingfield, Thomas (English translator) 1595

beer brewed in Roanoke Colony, North America 1587

Belgrade taken by Turks 1521

Bellay, Joachim du (French poet and prose writer; member of "La Pléiade" 1522-60) 1549

Bellini, Giovanni (Italian painter; c. 1430-1516) 1502

Belon, Pierre (French icthyologist; 1517-64) 1551

Bengal becomes a Portuguese trading station 1579

Benten, Peace of 1589

Berwick, Treaty of 1560, 1586

Bess of Hardwick (Elizabeth Talbot, Countess of Shrewsbury) 1597–XE "1597"

Best, George (English navigator) 1578

Beware the Cat (A Marvellous History intituled Beware the Cat) the first English novel, 1570

Beyezid, Sultan of Turkey (r. 1481-1512) 1512

Bigges, Walter (English writer on Drake's voyages) 1589

billiard 1550, 1565

Biocca, Battle of 1522

Blackfriars Theatre, London 1596

Blois Treaty of 1505, 1572

Blundeville, G. (English writer on veterinary science) 1566

Bodin, Jean (French political philosopher; 1530-96) 1587

Bodley, Sir Thomas (English scholar and diplomat; 1545-1613) 1598

Bogota, Colombia, founded 1538

Bohemia's Crown proclaimed hereditary under Habsburgs 1547

Boleyn, Anne (daughter of Sir Thomas Boleyn; Queen of England 1533-36; mother of Queen Elizabeth I; c1504-36) 1532, 1533, 1536

Bologna, Concordat of 1516

Bologna, Giovanni da (Italian sculptor) 1594

Book of Common Prayer, England, revised 1552

Borgia, Caesare (Italian soldier; illegitimate son of Pope Alexander VI; onetime Cardinal, captain-general of the papal army , and Duke of Romagna; 1476-1507) 1503, 1507

Borgia, Lucretia (sister of Caesare; Duchess of Este from 1501; 1480-1519) 1500, 1501

Bornu Empire, Sudan 1571

Borromean League (Swiss Catholic canton group) 1586

Borromeo, Cardinal Carlo (Italian churchman; cannonized 1610; 1538-84) 1570, 1578

Bosch, Hieronymus (Netherlandish painter; c.1460-1516) 1500, 1504

botanical gardens founded 1543, 1545, 1593

Botero, Giovanni (Italian writer on city planning; 1544-1617) 1588, 1589

Bothwell, James Hepburn, 4th Earl of, 3rd husband of Mary Queen of Scots; (1537-78) 1567

Botticelli, Sandro (Italian painter; 1444-1510) 1500, 1502

bottled beer 1568

Boulogne captured by King Henry VIII 1544

Boulogne, Peace of 1550

Boulogne under seige by French 1549

Bourgeois, Loys (French music theorist and composer; c. 1510-15-c.1560) 1550

Bourne, William (English writer on navigation and gunnery) 1574, 1587

bow and arrow abandoned as a weapon by the English army 1595

Brahe, Tycho (alt Tyge; Danish astronomer; 1546-1601) 1569, 1572, 1576, 1598, 1599

Bramante, Donato (Italian sculptor; 1444-1514) 1506

Brandenburg Duchy formed 1525

brandy 1537, 1596

Braun, Georg, and Hagenberg, Frans (German cartographers) 1572

Bronzino, Agnolo (Italian painter; 1502-71) 1530, 1545, 1552

Brazil colonized by Portuguese 1531

Brazil discovered by Portuguese 1500

Breda Conference 1575

Bright, Timothy (English writer on shorthand; 1551?-1615) 1588

Brindal, Edmund, Archbishop of Canterbury 1575-83 1575

"broken consort" first used in England 1575

"Bronzino, Il" (Agnolo di Cosimo di Mariano; Italian mannerist painter; 1502-72) 1530, 1552

Browne, Robert (English Protestant Separatist leader) 1580

Brueghel, Jan the Elder (alt. Breughel; Flemish artist; younger son of Pieter the Younger; 1568-1625) 1600

Brueghel, Pieter the Elder (alt. Breughel; Flemish artist; c.1520-1569) 1559, 1562, 1564, 1565, 1566, 1567, 1568

Brunei, Africa 1522

Brunfels, Otto (German botanist; 1488-1534) 1530

Bruno, Giordano (Italian philosopher and scientist; c1548-1600) 1584, 1589, 1591, 1592, 1600

Brussels, Peace of 1516

Brussels, Treaty of 1522

Buda, Hungary, captured by Turks 1529

Budé, Guillaume (Budaeus; French scholar; 1467-1540) 1508, 1520

Buenos Aires, Argentina 1583

Bull of Deprivation 1585

Bull, John (Jan; Jean Bonville; Jean Bouville; English composer, virginalist, organist, and organ builder; c1563-1628) 1586, 1589, 1597

Bullinger, Heinrich (Protestant leader) 1566

Burbage, James, constructs the first English theatre (English actor; d.1597) 1576

Burbage, Richard (English actor and theatre builder; son of James; c1567-1619) 1594, 1599

Burghley, William Cecil, Lord (see Cecil) 1572, 1587, 1598

Burrows, Sir John (English soldier) 1592

business fair 1579

Byrd, William (English composer; c.1540-1623) 1563, 1572, 1575, 1578, 1588, 1591

Cabezon, Antonio de (Spanish composer; 1510-66) 1578

Cabeza de Vaca, Alvar Nunez (Spanish explorer) 1536

Cabot, Sebastian (Venetian navigator and cartographer; second son of John Cabot; Pilot Major for HRE Charles V; inspector of the Royal Navy for King Edward VI; c.1475-1557) 1512, 1526, 1527, 1544, 1548, 1551

Cabral, Pedro Alvars de (Portuguese navigator; 1467-c.1520) 1500

Cabrillo, Juan Rodriguez (Spanish explorer; c.1500-1543) 1542, 1543

Caccini, Giulio (called Giulio "Romano"; Italian composer of songs and operas; 1514-1618) 1600

Cadamosto, Alvise (Italian explorer) 1507

Caesarian operation 1500

Cadiz, Spain, taken by the English 1596

Cairo captured by Turks 1517

Caius, John (English physician; 1510-73) 1552

Calais taken by the French 1558

Calais taken by the Spanish 1596

Calderia, Antonio (Portuguese explorer) 1544

Calvin, John (French Protestant theologian and reformer; 1509-64) 1536, 1537, 1538, 1540, 1541, 1542, 1559

Calvinist refugees from Flanders settle in England 1561

Cambrai, League of 1508, 1509

Cambrai Peace Conference 1558

Cambrai, Peace of 1529

camerata founded in Florence, the beginnings of opera 1573

Campion, Father Edmund, S.J. (martyred English Jesuit; 1540-81; canonized 1970) 1580, 1581

cane sugar refinery in Augsburg 1573

Cano, Juan Sebastian del (Basque navigator; d. 1526) completes Magellans's voyage of circumnavigation 1522

Canterbury Cathedral, England 1503

Canton, China 1513, 1517

Capuchin Order organized 1528

Caravaggio, Michelangelo Merisi da (Italian painter; 1573-1610) 1594, 1599,1600

carbuncular fever epidemic in Lisbon 1569

Cardano, Giralomo (Italian physician, naturalist, philosopher, gambler and astrologer; 1501-1576) 1545, 1551, 1554

Cardenas, Garcia Lopez de (Spanish explorer; first to reach the Grand Canyon) 1540

Cardinals' number set at seventy 1586

Carew, Richard (English translator) 1600

Caroso, Fabritio (Italian dancing master and writer on dance; c,1527-35-after 1605) 1581, 1600

carrier pigeons 1572

Cartagena, South America, founded 1533

Carthusian monks executed in London 1535

Cartier, Jacques (French navigator; 1491-1557) 1534, 1535, 1541

Carvahal, Luis de ("El Mozo"; a martyred Mexican Jew) 1596

Casa de la Contratacion (House of Commerce) 1503

Casimir, John, Elector Palatine (d1592) 1567, 1578, 1580, 1590, 1592

Castiglione, Count Baldassare (Italian courtier and writer; 1478-1529) 1528, 1561

castrati used in Papal choir 1563

cat, first North American 1500

catacombs beneath Rome discovered 1578

Catalogue of All the Principal and Most Honorable Courtesans of Venice (Catalogo de tutte le principali e piu honorate cortigiane di Venezia) 1565

Cateau-Cambrésis, Treaty of 1559

Cathedral of Milan consecrated 1577

Cathedral of St. Basil erected in Moscow 1534

Cathedral of Salamanca, Spain, begun 1514

Cathedral of Seville, Spain, completed 1517

Catherine de' Medici (see Medici; Queen of France; wife of King

Henri II; mother of 3 Kings of France; 1519-89) 1531, 1547, 1533, 1560, 1563, 1564, 1586, 1589

Catherine of Aragon (Queen of England 1509-33; daughter of Queen Isabella and King Ferdinand of Spain; 1st wife of King Henry VIII; 1485-1536) 1501, 1503, 1509, 1531

Catholic League of France 1585, 1588, 1589, 1594, 1596

Catholic League of Nuremberg 1538

Catholic legislation repealed in England 1558

Catholic priests expelled from Japan 1587

Catholic uprising in northern England 1569

cattle introduced in South America 1550

Cavendish, Thomas (English navigator; c1555-92) 1586

Cecil, Sir William (English statesman; knighted 1551; Chief Secretary of State for England from 1558; Master of the Court of Wards from 1561; Baron Burghley from 1571, q.v.; Lord High Treasurer from 1572; 1520-1598) 1550, 1558, 1560, 1561, 1571, 1572, 1587, 1598

Celebes Islands 1511

Cellini, Benvenuto (Italian goldsmith, sculptor and engraver; 1500-71) 1534, 1540, 1543, 1558, 1570

Cenci, Count Francesco and family 1599

Cerignola, Battle of 1503

Cervantes, Miguel de Saavedra (Spanish novelist; 1547-1616) 1585

Ceulen, Ludolph van (Dutch mathematician; 1540-1610) 1596

Chancellor, Richard (English explorer; d.1556) 1553

Chamber of Commerce founded in Marseilles, France 1599

Chambord, Chateau of 1519

Chambre Ardente (Burning Chamber) created in Paris for trials of heretics 1547

Charles, Archduke of Inner Austria 1589

Charles of Habsburg (1500-1558; King Charles I of Spain from 1516; Holy Roman Emperor Charles V from 1520) 1504, 1507, 1515, 1516, 1517. 1519. 1520, 1521, 1522, 1524, 1526, 1528, 1530, 1532, 1535, 1540, 1541, 1543, 1544, 1547, 1549, 1552, 1553, 1555, 1556

Charles of Valois, King Charles IX of France from 1560 (1550-1574) 1560, 1563, 1564, 1570. 1574

Charles Vasa, Karl of Sodermanland, King Charles IX of Sweden from 1599-1611 (1550-1611) 1599, 1600

Charron, Pierre (French theologian and philosopher; 1541-1603) 1594

Chastel, Jean, would-be assassin of King Henri IV of France 1594

Chaucer, Geoffrey (English poet; c.1345-1400) first collected edition of works published 1532

Chester, England, annual football game banned 1540

Chettle, Henry (English dramatist and pamphleteer; d. c1607) 1592, 1593

chiaroscuro 1600

Chile explored by Spaniards 1535

China defeats the Mongols for the first time 1532

China expels Portuguese 1523

China first visited by Portuguese 1516

Chinese at war with Mongols 1528

Chinese first use cannon 1520

Chinese laws 1551

Chinese Mongols converted to Buddhism 1575

Chinese porcelain imitated in Europe 1575

Chinese use movable type for printing 1574

Chios 1566

Christian II, King of Sweden, Denmark and Norway (var. Kristian; deposed as King of Sweden in 1523; 1481-1559) 1513, 1515, 1520, 1522, 1523, 1531

Christian III, King of Denmark and Norway (var. Kristian; 1502-1559; King from 1533) 1533, 1543, 1537

Christian IV (var. Kristian; King of Denmark and Norway from 1588; 1577-1648) 1588, 1596

Christian I, Elector of Saxony from 1586 1586. 1590

Christian II, son of Christian I, King of Saxony from 1591 1591

Christian missionaries executed in Japan 1597

Christ's College, Cambridge University, England 1505

Christ's Hospital, London, founded 1552

Christian catechism printed in China 1584

Christians persecuted in Japan 1593

Christmas tree in Strasbourg, Germany 1539

chocolate brought to Spain 1520

Cicero's complete works published in Venice 1537

Cieza de Leon, Pedro del (Spanish historical writer; 1518-60) 1553

Claude de Valois, daughter of King Louis XII of France 1514

Clouet, François (French portrait painter; son of Jean; c.1516-1572) 1560

Clouet, Jean (French portrait painter; 1485-1541) 1529

coal mining in the Ruhr valley, Germany 1590

coffee 1517, 1580

coinage of the Holy Roman Empire is standardized 1559

Colet, John (English humanist philosopher and theologian; 1466-1519) 1509

College of France founded 1529

College de Trois Langues (College of Three Languages), Louvain 1517

Collegio Romano founded as a Papal University in Rome 1551

Collegium Germanicum established in Rome 1573

Colombo, Ceylon 1517

Colona, Vittoria (Italian poet; c.1492-1547) 1538

Columbus, Christopher (Genoese explorer working for Spain; 1451-1506) 1502

Cambrai, League of 1508

Commentary on the most notable and monstrous things in Italy 1550

Compromise of Breda 1566

Comuneros revolt in northern Spain 1520, 1521

Condé, Prince of 1561

Condéll, Henry (English actor) 1599

Confederation of Vilna 1599

Congress of Ghent 1576

Confession of Augsburg 1530

Consensus Tigurnus agreement among Swiss Protestants 1549
conservatories of music founded in Venice and Naples 1537
Constantinople, Peace of 1573
Consulado in Seville, Spain 1543
Contarini, Giovanni (Italian cartographer) 1506
Copernicus, Nicolas (Polish astronomer; 1473-1543) 1503, 1543
copyright library established in Paris 1537
Cordova, Gonzalo de (Spanish military commander) 1503
Corfu beseiged by Turks 1537
Cornysh, William (English musician and composer; d.1523) 1509,
    1513, 1520
Coronado, Francisco Vasquez de (Spanish explorer; 1510-54) 1540,
    1541
Corporation of Trinity House founded in London 1514
corral (dramatic performance) in Madrid 1568
Correggio, Antonio Allegri da (Italian painter; c.1494-1534) 1515,
    1530
Corte Real, Gaspar and Miguel (Spanish explorers) 1500
Cortes, Hernan (var. Hernando; Cortez; Spanish explorer. 1485-
    1547) 1519, 1521, 1522, 1532, 1536
Cortes, Martin (Spanish writer on navigation) 1551
Corpus Christi College, Oxford University, England 1516
Cosa, Juan de la (Spanish explorer; c. 1460-1510) 1500
Coucy, Edict of 1535
Council of the Indies established by Spain 1511
Council of the North created in England 1537
Council of Ten's powers limited in Venice 1682
Council of Trent convened (through 1563) 1545
Council of Trent denounced by Protestants 1546
Council of Trent moved to Bologna 1547
Council of Trent reconvened 1562
Cranach, Lucas the Elder (German painter; 1472-1553) 1502,
    1504, 1508, 1510, 1520, 1521, 1524, 1527, 1530, 1532
Cranmer, Thomas, Archbishop of Canterbury from 1532 (1489-
    1556) 1532, 1533, 1548, 1550, 1554

Crépy, Peace of 1544

cricket, first mention 1550

criminal code established in Holy Roman Empire 1530

Cromwell, Thomas, Earl of Essex and Lord Privy Seal of England
(English statesman; c.1485-1540) 1536, 1540

Cuba 1511

Cuba annexed by Spain 1538

Cunha, Tritao da (Portuguese explorer) 1506

Curtain Theatre, London, opened 1578

Cusa, Nicholas of (Nicolaus Cusanus; German Cardinal, philosopher and scientist; 1401-64) 1565

Dallam, James (var. Dalham; Dallum; English organ builder;
c.1570-after 1614) 1599

Danish ballad collection 1591

Dare, Virginia (first English child born in America) 1587

Dasypodius , Conrad, builds Strasbourg clock 1574

Damville, Marshal of France 1574

Danish nobles revolt 1522

Darnley, Henry Stuart, Lord (2nd husband of Mary Queen of
Scots; d.1567) 1565, 1567

David, Gerard (Flemish painter; c1450-1523) 1509

Davidson, William, English Secretary of State 1587

Davila y Padilla, Augustin (Spanish historian) 1596

Davis, John (English navigator) 1585

Daza, Diego (Archbishop of Seville, Grand Inquisitor of the Faith,
Confessor to the Spanish Royal Court; 1444-1523) 1517

Dee, Dr. John (English alchemist, geographer, mathematician and
astrologer; 1527-1608) 1558, 1564, 1595

De impressione librorum 1515

Delorme, Philibert (French architect; c.1510-70) 1552, 1564

Der Goldfaden (The Gold Thread) 1557

Diane de Poitiers, Duchess of Valentinois (mistress of King Henri
II of France; 1499-1566) 1559

Diaz del Castillo, Bernal (Spanish soldier and historian; c.1492-

1581) 1576

Diaz, Diego (Portuguese navigator) 1500

Diaz de Solis, Juan (Pilot Major of Spain; 1471?-1516?) 1516

Diet of Augsburg 1500, 1530, 1555

Diet of Constance 1507

Diet of Ratisbon 1532, 1541, 1576, 1594

Diet of Schmalkalden 1535

Diet of Speyer, Second 1529

Diet of Speyer 1570

Diet of Worms 1521, 1545

Digby, Everard 1587

Digges, Thomas (English scientist and military scholar; c.1546-95) 1576

Dilligen University founded in Bavaria 1554

dissection of human corpses 1565

Ditchley Manor, Oxfordshire, England 1592

Diu, Battle of 1509

Dmitri, son of Tsar Ivan "the Terrible" of Russia 1591

Dolet, Etienne (French scholar and printer of scholarly books) 1546

Don Antonio of Portugal 1581

Don Juan of Austria (illegitimate half brother of King Philip II of Spain; 1547- 78) 1569, 1573, 1577, 1578

Dominican Colegio de San Tomas established in Seville, Spain 1517

Donne, John (English poet; c1572-1631) 1596

Dossi, Dosso (Italian artist; court painter at Ferrara; 1486?-1542) 1516, 1523

Douglas, Archibald, Earl of Angus, Scotland 1514

Dowland, John (English lutenist and songwriter; c1563-1626) 1597, 1600

Drake, Sir Francis (English navigator and pirate; 1540-96) 1567, 1572, 1573, 1577, 1579, 1580, 1585, 1587, 1589, 1595, 1596

Drury, Sir William (English army commander) 1573

Durazzo 1501

Dürer, Albrecht (German painter and engraver; 1471-1529) 1500,

1502, 1504, 1505, 1507, 1511, 1513, 1518, 1519, 1520, 1522

Durham Cathedral sacked 1569

Dutch East India Company founded 1594

Earl of Leicester's Men theatrical company licensed 1574

earthquake in Constantinople 1509

earthquake in London 1580

earthquake in Shansi, China 1556

earthquake in Santiago, Guatemala 1541

East Asian porcelain imported to Europe 1518

East India Company of England incorporated 1600

Eden, Richard (English translator) 1596

Edict of Orleans 1561

Edict of St. Germain 1562

Edict of St. Germain-en-Laye 1594

Edinburgh burned by English 1544

Edinburgh, Treaty of 1560

Edmund, Earl of Suffolk 1506, 1507

Edo becomes the capital of Japan 1600

Edward Tudor (son of King Henry VIII of England and Queen Jane Seymour; King of England from 1547; 1537-53) 1537, 1547, 1553

Egmont, Lamoral, Count of, Prince of Gavre (heroic Flemish states-man and soldier; 1522-68) 1564, 1565, 1568

Elector of Brandenburg 1539

Elector of Saxony 1508

Eleonore of Habsburg, Queen of Portugal, later of France 1530

Elisabeth of Austria, wife of King Charles IX of France 1570

Elisabeth of Valois, Queen of Spain from 1559 (Fr. Isabelle; third wife of King Philip II; d.1570) 1559

Elizabeth Tudor, Queen Elizabeth I of England from 1558 (daugh-ter of King Henry VIII and Queen Anne Boleyn; 1533-1603) 1533, 1544, 1548, 1554, 1558, 1559, 1562, 1563, 1570, 1575, 1581, 1585, 1587, 1588, 1591, 1600

Elyot, Sir Thomas (var. Eliot; English scholar and diplomat; c.1490-1536) 1531, 1538, 1542
England aids Protestant rebels in the Netherlands 1572, 1584
English acting company visits Germany 1587
English College of Douai removed to Rheims 1578
English College removed from Rheims to Rome 1579
English currency reformed 1560
English-Dutch military alliance 1579
English Eastland Company 1579
English House of Commons 1589
English Levant Company 1579
English merchants expelled from the Holy Roman Empire 1598
English Muscovy Company 1555
English Parliament laws 1512, 1534, 1535, 1536, 1539, 1543, 1547, 1563, 1572, 1575, 1576, 1581, 1584, 1593, 1597
English plantations in Ireland 1586
English Royal Navy 1511, 1512, 1582
English royal succession 1544
English battleship "Mary Rose" sinks immediately after launching 1545
English Star Chamber 1586
English weavers 1528
Erasmus, Desiderius, of Rotterdam (Netherlandish humanist and scholar; 1466-1536) 1500, 1504, 1509, 1515, 1516, 1517, 1528, 1530, 1531
Erik Vasa, Crown Prince of Sweden 1559
Erik XIV, King of Sweden 1560-69 (1533-77) 1560, 1561, 1569
Erikszen, Barent 1593
Ernest of Habsburg, Archduke of Austria, Governor of the Spanish Netherlands 1594, 1595
Escorial, El (San Lorenzo del Escorial) 1563
Essex, Robert Devereux, 2nd Earl of (English soldier and favorite of Queen Elizabeth; 1566-1601) 1596, 1599, 1600
Este, House of 1597
Ethiopia visited by Portuguese 1520

Eustachio, Bartolomeo (Italian anatomist; 1520-74) 1552

Everyman 1515

"Evil May Day" riots in London 1517

Eworth, Hans (Flemish painter; c.1520-after 1573) 1562, 1563, 1569

Fabricius, Hieronymus (Girolamo Fabrici; Italian anatomist; 1537-1619 1574

Fairfax, Edward (English scholar; c.1580-1635) 1600

faience pottery first manufactured in France 1578

Famagusta, Cyprus, people massacred by Turks 1571

Farmer, John (English composer c1570-fl.1570-1601) 1599

Farnese, Pier Luigi (Duke of Parma 1545-51) 1545, 1551

Fathers of the Oratory formed 1540

Ferdinand of Aragon (King of Spain; 1452-1516) 1500, 1501, 1504, 1505, 1506, 1507, 1511, 1514, 1516

Ferdinand of Habsburg (younger brother of HRE Charles V; King of Austria, 1521; King of Bohemia, 1526; King of Hungary, 1527; HRE as Ferdinand I from 1558; 1503-64) 1521, 1526; 1527, 1530, 1533, 1538, 1540, 1551, 1553, 1555, 1556, 1557, 1564

Ferdinand of Habsburg, grandson of HRE Ferdinand I; HRE Ferdinand II from 1637; 1578-1637) 1590

Fernandez de Oviedo y Valdes, Gonzalo 1526

Fernandez, Juan (Portuguese navigator) 1563

Ferreri, Zacharie 1525

Ferro, Scipione del (Italian mathematician; 1465-1526) 1505

Field of the Cloth of Gold 1520

field hospitals and dispensaries 1597

Fifth Council of the Lateran 1513, 1515

firearms introduced to Japanese 1543

First Blast of the Truompet Against the Monstrous Regiment of Women 1558

first Christian baptism of Native Americans 1540

first Christian religious service in California 1579

first Protestant Christian baptism of a Native American 1587
first Protestant university founded 1527
first swimming treatise in English 1587
Fischart, Johann (German satirist; c.1545-90) 1573, 1575, 1580
Fisher, John, Cardinal (English churchman and humanist; Cardinal 1535; 1469-1535; canonized 1935) 1509, 1521, 1527
Fitch, Ralph (English merchant and traveler) 1583, 1594
Fitzgerald, James Fitzmaurice, Irish rebel leader 1579
Fitzherbert, Anthony (English writer on agriculture) 1523
Flanders Galleys 1532
Flodden Field, Battle of 1513
Florida colonized by French 1562
Florio, John (English translator of Montaigne's essays; c1533-1625) 1598
flying machine designed by Albrecht Dürer 1522
Folembray, Decrees of 1596
Folz, Hans, Mastersinger of Nuremberg (1450-1515) 1500
Fontainbleau, Edict of 1540
forks 1589
Forman, Simon (English astrologer and unlicensed doctor; 1552-1611) 1591
Fortune Theatre opens, London 1600
Fox, Richard, Bishop of Winchester, England 1517
Foxe's Book of Martyrs 1563
Foxe, John (English writer on religion; 1516-87) 1563
François de Valois, Duke of Angoulême, King François I of France from 1515 (1494-1547)1514, 1515, 1516, 1518, 1519, 1520, 1524, 1526, 1527, 1528, 1530, 1532, 1534, 1535, 1536, 1537, 1538, 1540,1541,1545,1547
François de Valois, King François II of France 1559-60 (first husband of Mary Queen of Scots; 1544-60) 1559, 1560
Francanzano de Montalboddo 1507
France nationalizes some factories 1515
Francis Xavier, Saint (Francisco de Xavier; Spanish missionary and co-founder, with Ignatius Loyola, of the Jesuits; "Apostle of

the Indies"; 1501-1552; canonized 1622) 1534, 1542, 1545, 1549, 1552

Franciscan mission to Mexico 1529

Franciscan mission to Japan 1592, 1593

Franck, Sebastian (German humanist; 1499-1542) 1528

Frankfurt, Treaty of 1539

Frederick I, King of Denmark and Norway from 1523 (Duke of Schleswig-Holstein; 1471-1533) 1523, 1533

Frederick II, King of Denmark from 1559 (1534-88) 1559, 1588

Frederick III, Elector Palatine (d.1576) 1562, 1576

Frederick IV, Elector Palatine, leader of the German Protestant princes 1592, 1594

Frederick the Wise, Elector of Saxony 1502, 1508, 1515

Freiburg, Treaty of 1516

French colonies 1555

French States-General 1561, 1588, 1593

French Fury—sacking of Antwerp 1583

French replaces Latin as official language of France 1547

French wars of religion 1560, 1562 1570, 1572, 1573, 1574, 1575, 1576, 1577, 1580

Frisius, Reinerus Gemma (1508-55) 1530

Frobisher, Sir Martin (English navigator; 1535-94) 1576, 1588, 1594

Fuca, Juan de (Spanish navigator) 1592

Fugger, House of (Augsburg merchant bankers) 1514, 1519, 1546

Fugger, Anton (Augsburg merchant banker) 1530

Fugger, Jakob (Augsburg merchant banker ; 1459-1525) 1506, 1508, 1509, 1518

Fugger, Raimund 1530

Fuenterrabia, Spain 1513, 1521

furniture 1581

Fyodor I, Tsar of Russia to 1598 1584, 1598

Gabrielli, Andréa (Italian composer and organist, active in Venice; c.1510-86) 1571

Gabrielli, Giovanni (Italian composer and organist, active in Venice; nephew of Andréa; c1553-1612) 1587

Galilei, Galileo (Italian astronomer, mathematician and natural philosopher; 1564-1642) 1583 , 1588, 1589, 1592, 1593, 1596

Galla, Orlando, of Venice, glass mirror maker 1507

Gama, Vasco da (Portuguese navigator; 1469-1525) 1502, 1503, 1524

Ganassi dal Fontego, Sylvestro di (Italian instrumentalist and author of treatises on musical performance; 1492-d.mid century) 1542

Garamond, Claude (French printer and designer of type; c.1480-1561) 1530, 1545

Gardiner, Stephen, Church of England Bishop (c.1483-1555) 1551

Garig, battle of 1503

Garray, Blasco da 1543

Gasca, Pedro de la 1548

Gascoigne, George (English poet and dramatist; c.1525-77) 1566. 1575

Gasparo da Salo (Bertolotti; Italian maker of violins, violas and other bowed string instruments; 1540-1609) 1562

Gebhard, Archbishop of Cologne, Germany 1583, 1589

Geneva Academy (later University) founded in Switzerland 1559

Geneva Bible published 1560

Genoa becomes a republic 1528

Gentlemen and Choristers of the English Chapel Royal founded 1532

Gera, Agreement of 1599

Gerard, John (English herbalist and barber-surgeon; 1545-1612) 1597

Germaine de Foix, neice of King Louis XII of France 1506

German Palitinate becomes Protestant 1545

Gerusalemme Liberata (*Jerusalem Liberated* or *The Liberation of Jerusalem*; also *Godfrey of Bulloigne*) 1575, 1581, 1594, 1600

Gessner, Conrad (Swiss natural scientist and physician;1516-65)

Gosson, Stephen (English pamphleteer) 1579
Granada, Treaty of 1500
graphite pencil 1565
Gravelines 1558
Greco, El (Domenico Theotocopoulos; Cretan painter resident in
    Spain; 1541-1614) 1577, 1582, 1587, 1590, 1593, 1595
Greek printing press in Rome 1513
Greene, Robert (English writer; 1558-92) 1589, 1591, 1592
Greensleeves 1580
Greenwich, Treaty of 1543
Gregorian calendar adopted by Catholic countries 1582
Granada Cathedral begun in Spain 1528
Grenville, Sir Richard (English soldier) 1591
Gresham College, London 1597
Gresham, Sir Thomas (English financier and philanthropist; founder
    of the Royal Exchange; 1519-79) 1548, 1558, 1571, 1597
Gresham's Law 1558
Grey, Lady Jane (Queen of England for nine days in 1553; 1537-
    54) 1553, 1554
Grey's Inn Hall 1555
Grijalva, Juan de (Spanish explorer) 1518
Grindal, Edward, Archbishop of Canterbury 1577
Groswardein, Peace of 1538
Grunewald, Mathias (German painter; c.1480-1528) 1511, 1515,
    1516
Guatemala conquered by Spanish 1522
Guadaloupe, Our Lady of, appears to Juan Diego 1531
Guarini, Battista (Italian poet;1538-1612) 1585
Guatemala City founded by Spanish 1524
Guazzo, Stefano (Italian writer on manners; 1530-94) 1574
Guicciardini, Francesco (Italian historian; 1483-1540) 1509, 1534,
    1561, 1565
Guise, François, Duke of 1556, 1563
Guise, Henri, Duke of (leader of the French Catholic League) 1576,
    1584, 1587, 1588, 1596

Guinea Coast of Africa settled by the Dutch 1595
Gustavus Vasa, King Gustav I of Sweden from 1523 (1496-1560)
    1523, 1527, 1550, 1560
Gwalior, India, conquered by Akbar the Great 1558
Gyalu, Treaty of 1541

Habsburg family 1551
Hague, Treaty of the 1596
Hake, Edward 1567
Hakluyt, Richard (English navigator and geographical writer;
    c1553-1616) 1581, 1589, 1600
Halle, Edward (var. Hall; English historian; c.1499-1547) 1512
Halley's Comet appears 1531
Hall of the Middle Temple erected in London 1562
Hamburg, Germany, becomes a free city 1510
Hamburg, Germany, library founded 1529
Hamburg, Germany, stock exchange founded 1558
Hampton Court Palace completed 1515
Hampton Court, Treaty of 1562
Hansa trading organization 1552
Hanseatic League 1598
Harington, Sir John, the Elder 1550
Harington, Sir John (the Younger; English courtier and writer;
    godson of Queen Elizabeth I; 1561-1612) 1591, 1596
Hariot, Thomas 1588
Harrison, William (English historian; 1534-93) 1577
harvest failures in England 1594
Hatton, Sir Christopher, Lord Chancellor of England from 1587
    (English courtier, and favorite of Queen Elizabeth; 1540-91)
    1587, 1588
Havana, Cuba, sacked by the French 1556
Hawkins, Sir John (English navigator and naval commander; 1532-
    95) 1562, 1565, 1568, 1573, 1588, 1595
heels on shoes 1595
Heidelberg Catechism 1562

Heidelberg, League of 1553

Helmstedt University, Brunswick, founded in Gremany 1567

Helsinki, Finland, founded 1550

Hemand, Urbain (writer on teeth) 1582

Heminge, John (English actor) 1599

Henlein, Peter, of Nuremberg 1502

Henri of Navarre, King of Navarre, King Henri IV of France from 1589 (first Bourbon King of France; 1553-1610) 1572, 1576, 1577, 1585, 1586, 1589, 1591, 1593, 1594, 1595, 1596, 1597, 1598, 1600

Henri of Valois,Duke of Orleans, King Henri II of France from 1547 (1519-59) 1531, 1547, 1551, 1552, 1556, 1559

Henri of Valois, King Henri III of France from 1574 (son of King Henri II and Queen Catherine de' Medici; 1551-89) 1574, 1575, 1576, 1577, 1585, 1587, 1588, 1589

Henry Fitzroy, Duke of Richmond, illegitimate son of King Henry VIII of England (d.1536) 1525

Henry Tudor, King Henry VII of England from 1585 (1457-1509) 1501, 1502, 1504, 1507, 1509

Henry Tudor, Prince of Wales (later King Henry VIII of England) 1502, 1503, 1505, 1506

Henry Tudor, King Henry VIII of England from 1509 (1491-1547) 1509, 1510, 1511, 1512, 1513, 1519, 1520, 1521, 1522, 1525, 1527, 1528, 1530, 1531, 1532, 1533, 1534, 1535, 1536, 1538, 1539, 1541, 1542, 1543, 1544, 1547

Henry, Cardinal and King of Portugal from 1578 to '79 1578, 1579

Henry VI, Part III, by Shakespeare performed in London 1592

Henslowe, Philip, manager of the Rose Theatre, London 1592

Heptameron 1558, 1559

Herberstein, Siegmund freiherr von (Austrian scientist and writer; 1486-1566) 1549, 1550

Herculaneum uncovered 1594

Heredia, Pedro de (Spanish explorer) 1533

Hernandez de Cordova , Francisco (Spanish explorer) 1517

Heywood, John (English epigrammatist, playwright and musician; 1497c.1580) 1534

Hideyoshi, Toyotomi (Japanese warlord; ruler of Japan; 1537-98)
1582, 1583, 1587, 1588, 1590, 1591, 1592, 1593, 1597,
1598

Hilliard, Nicholas (English painter and goldsmith; 1537-1619)
1572, 1577, 1588, 1600

Hindu temples in Goa destroyed by Portuguese 1540

Hoby, Sir Thomas (English courtier and diplomat; 1530-66) 1561

Hofman, François (French political philosopher) 1573

Holbein, Hans the Younger (German painter; 1497-1543) 1515,
1523, 1526, 1527, 1532, 1533, 1535, 1536, 1537, 1539,
1543

Holinshed, Raphael (English historian; d. c1580) 1577, 1587

Holy League 1510, 1511, 1512

Hongzhi, 10th Emperor of the Ming Dynasty, China, from 1488
to 1505 1505

Hooker, Richard (English theologian) 1594

hop culture manual written in England 1573

hops introduced to England 1525

Hormuz captured by Portuguese 1514

horserace meetings in Chester, England 1500

Hotel de Bourgogne, first roofed theatre, opened in Paris 1548

hottest summer in England 1540

Howard, Catherine, Queen of England 1540-42 (fifth wife of Henry
VIII; d.1542) 1540, 1541, 1542

Howard, Charles, Baron of Effingham, English Lord High Admiral from 1585; Earl of Nottingham from 1597; 1536-1624)
1588, 1596, 1597

Hsu Wei (Chinese writer) 1560

Hubblethorne, Martin, English dyer 1579

Humayun, Mughal Emperor of India (d. 1556) 1530

Hungary restored to Archduke Ferdinand 1547

iconoclasm 1538

MOSH

Joinville, Treaty of 1585

Jonson, Ben (English dramatist; 1572-1637) 1598, 1599

Josquin Despres (var. Juschino; Josse; Josquin des Prés; Jodocus Pratensis, etc. Northern French composer; c.1440-1521) 1500, 1502, 1512

Journey to the West, The (Chinese novel) 1570

Juana the Mad ("la loca"; Countess of Flanders and Queen of Castile; daughter of Queen Isabella and King Ferdinand of Spain; mother of HRE Charles V) 1500, 1504, 1505, 1506

Julian calendar reformed 1582

Kalsburg, Treaty of 1551

Kandahar, India 1594

Kempis, Thomas à (German religious writer; 1379-1471) 1503, 1567

Kepler, Johan (German astronomer; 1531-1630) 1596, 1600

Keresztes, Battle of 1596

Kett, Thomas 1588

Kiev Academy founded in Russia 1589

Kildare, James Oge, Earl of 1534

Kircher, Athenasius 1600

Knights of St. John (after 1530, Knights of Malta) 1522, 1530

Knights of Malta 1522, 1530

Knollys, Lettice, Dowager Countess of Essex; Countess of Leicester from 1578 1578

Knox, John (Scottish Protestant reformer; c.1513-1572) 1541, 1554, 1555, 1558, 1559

Koh-i-noor (mountain of light) and Agra diamonds acquired by Emperor Babar 1526

Koller, Gaspard, invents rifling 1520

Kyd, Thomas (English dramatist; 1558-94) 1587

Labé, Louise (French poet; c.1520-1566) 1555

Lachrimae (Flow My Tears) by John Dowland 1600

Lancaster, Sir James (English navigator and merchant; c1554-

1618)) 1591, 1592, 1594

Lando, Ortensio (Italian writer) 1550

Longleat House manor completed in England 1574

Laocoön sculpture found in Rome 1506

Las Casas, Bishop Bartholome de (Spanish missionary; Bishop of Chiapas, Mexico; "the Apostle of the Indians"; 1474-1566) 1509, 1552

Lassus, Orlande (Roland) de (Orlando di Lasso; Franco-Flemish composer; 1532-1594) 1555, 1556, 1570, 1573, 1574

Latin Vulgate Bible 1590

lead pencils 1500

League of Native American Nations (Iroquois Confederacy) 1550

League of Cognac 1526

League of Gotha 1526

League of Torgau 1576

Lécluse, Charles de (Carolus Clusius; French botanist; 1525-1609) 1576

Lee, Sir Henry (Queen Elizabeth I's "Champion"; 1530-1610) 1592

Le Havre 1562, 1563

Lehmann, Caspar 1600

Leicester, Robert Dudley, Earl of (favorite of Queen Elizabeth I; Earl of Leicester from 1564; c1532-88) 1575, 1578, 1586, 1588

Leiden, John of, Anabaptist leader 1534

Leland, John, Chaplain to King Henry VIII of England 1533

Leonardo da Vinci (Italian artist and polymath; 1452-1519) 1502, 1503, 1510, 1512, 1516, 1518, 1519

Lepanto 1503

Lepanto, Battle of 1571

Le piacevole notti (The Pleasing Nights; the first published fairy tale) 1550

Lescot, Pierre (French architect) 1546

Levant Trading Company founded in London 1578

Leyden, Lucas van (Netherlandish painter; 1494-1533) 1520

Libavius, Andréas (Libau; German alchemist; c1560-1616) 1597

licencing of ale houses and taverns in England 1551

life insurance in England 1583

lighthouse at Cordanau, France 1584

Ligorio, Piero (Italian architect) 1549

Lima, Peru, founded 1535

Linacre, Thomas (English humanist and physician to Kings Henry VII and VIII; c.1460-1524) 1500, 1518

Linshoten, Jan Huygen van Huyghen; Dutch traveler and writer; c1563-1611) 1596, 1598

Lippershay, Hans (Dutch optician; c1570-1619) 1600

Lippi, Fra Filippo (Italian painter; c.1458-1504) 1501

Lipsius, Justus (Joest Lips; Flemish humanist; 1547-1606) 1574, 1583, 1584, 1590, 1598

Lisbon spice market closed to English and Dutch merchants 1594

Lithuania 1503

Liu Chin 1515

Livonia 1561, 1563

Livonian War 1557

Locke, John (English explorer) 1554

Lockey, Roland (posthumous painter of Sir Thomas More's family) 1593

Lodge, Thomas (English pamphleteer) 1579

London Company of Mercers 1510

London theatres closed 1593

London, Treaty of 1518

Longleat House, England 1568

Lonjumeau, Treaty of 1568

Lopez, Roger (physician to Queen Elizabeth I of England) 1594

Lopez de Gomara, Francisco (Secretary to Hernan Cortez; historian of the Indians) 1551, 1578

Lopez de Sequeira, Diego (Portuguese explorer) 1508

Lord Admiral's Company (English acting company) 1585

Lord Chamberlain's Men (English acting company) 1594

Loredon, Leonardo, Doge of Venice 1501

lottery in London 1569

Lotto, Lorenzo (Italian painter; c. 1480-1556) 1505, 1507, 1529, 1533, 1550

Louis XII, King of France (1462-1515; King from 1498; "Father of the People") 1500, 1501, 1504, 1506, 1510, 1514, 1515

Louis II, King of Bohemia and Hungary 1521, 1526

Louis VI, Elector Palatine, 1576-80 1576

Louis of Nassau 1574

Louise de Vaudemont of Lorraine, wife of King Henri III of France 1575

Louise of Savoy, Queen Mother of France 1525

Louis, Prince of Condé 1576

Louvre Palace begun 1546

Lusiades, Os (The Lusiads) 1572

Luther, Martin (German Protestant reformer; translator of the Bible into German; 1483-1546) 1505, 1507, 1510, 1517, 1519, 1520, 1521, 1522, 1525, 1526, 1529, 1534, 1542, 1566

Luther's catechism 1529

Luther's *Table Talks* 1566

Lutheran Book of Concord 1577

Lutheran martyrs 1523

Lyly, John (English dramatist and novelist; the "Euphuist"; c.1554-1606) 1578, 1580, 1584, 1591, 1592, 1597

Lyons, France 1594

Lyons, Treaty of 1504

Macao obtained as trading post by Portuguese 1537

Macao trading factories established at Portuguese settlement 1556

Machiavelli, Niccolò (Italian statesman, writer and political philosopher; 1469-1527) 1506, 1513, 1521, 1525, 1532, 1560, 1595

Madeleine de Valois, wife of King James V of Scotland 1537

Madre de Dios treasure ship 1592

Madrid as capital of Spain 1560

Madrid, Treaty of 1526

Madrid University (College of Dona Maria de Aragon) 1590

Magdalen College of Cambridge University founded 1542

Magellan, Fernando (Fernao de Magalhaes; Portuguese navigator
    working for Spain; c.1480-1521) 1519, 1520, 1521

magic lantern invented 1600

maize cultivated by the Chinese 1573

Major, John (var. Mair; Scottish scholastic theologian and histo-
    rian; c.1470-1550) 1521

Malabar coast of India 1505

Malacca 1511

Malmö, Treaty of 1524

Mameluke Empire ends in Egypt 1517

Malta attacked by Turks 1551, 1565

Manoel I (Manuel), King of Portugal (r.1495-1521) 1513

manual for production of paints and inks 1533

Manifest detection of the most vile and detestable use of Dice-play , *A*
    1552 (apx)

Manila founded in the Philippines 1571

Mar, Earl of, Regent of Scotland 1570, 1572

Marbeck, John: *The Booke of Common Praier Noted* 1550

Marenzio, Luca (Italian composer and singer; c1553 1599) 1580

Mareshal, Abbé Philibert (Sieur de la Roche; French writer on arts
    and sciences) 1598

Margaret of Austria (Duchess of Savoy; daughter of HRE
    Maximilian I; Regent of the Netherlands from 1509; 1480-
    1530) 1506, 1507, 1508, 1509

Margaret, Duchess of Parma; (illegitimate daughter of HRE Charles
    V; Regent of the Netherlands from 1559; 1522-86) 1559

Margaret of Hungary (sister of HRE Charles V; Regent of the
    Netherlands from 1531 to 1552) 1531

Margaret, Countess of Richmond and Derby 1502, 1505

Margaret of Parma, Regent of the Netherlands 1564, 1566, 1567

Margaret Tudor (1489-1541) eldest daughter of King Henry VII
    of England, Queen of Scotland 1503, 1513, 1514

Marguerite d'Angoulême (Queen of Navarre; sister of King François

from 1508; 1459-1519) 1505. 1507, 1508, 1509, 1510, 1513, 1514, 1515, 1519, 1520

Maximilian of Habsburg (Holy Roman Emperor Maximilian II from 1564; eldest son of HRE Ferdinand I; 1527-76) 1548, 1549, 1563, 1564, 1576

Maximilian I, Duke of Bavaria, son of William V 1597

Mayan uprising in Mexico put down by Spanish 1545

Mayenne, Duke of, Leader of the French Catholic League 1588, 1589

Mechlin, Treaty of 1513

Mecklenburg, Defensive League of 1550

Medici, Alessandro de', Duke of Florence 1537

Medici, Catherine de' (see Catherine; Queen of France; 1519-89) 1531, 1533, 1547, 1560, 1563, 1564, 1586, 1589

Medici, Cosimo de' ("the Great"; Duke of Florence from 1537; Grand Duke of Tuscany from 1569; 1519-74) 1537, 1547, 1555, 1569

Medici family 1527

Medici, Lorenzo de' , Duke of Urbino 1521

Medici, Maria de' (1573-1642) marries King Henri IV of France 1600

Medina-Sidonia, Alonzo Perez de Gusman el Bueno, 7th Duke of (Commander of the first Spanish Armada; 1550-1619) 1588

Mendana de Neyra, Alvaro (Spanish explorer; 1541-95) 1567

Mendoza, Antonio de (Viceroy of New Spain, 1535; Viceroy of Peru, 1551; 1490-1552) 1535, 1551

Mendoza, Bernardino de, Spanish Ambassador to England 1574, 1584

Mendoza, Diego Hurtado de (Spanish politician; 1503-75) 1553

Mendoza, Pedro de (Spanish explorer) 1536

Menendez de Aviles, Pedro (Spanish explorer) 1565

Mercator, Gerardus (Gerhard Kremer; Flemish cartographer; 1512-94) 1537, 1538, 1541, 1544, 1546, 1569, 1585

Merchant Taylor's School founded in London 1561

Meres, Francis (English anthologist) 1598

Merisi, Angela, founds Ursuline order 1535
Mesopotamia captured by the Turks 1534
Metsys, Jan (Flemish painter; 1509-75) 1564
Miguel of Portugal, Dom 1500
Michelangelo Buonarotti (Italian painter and sculptor; 1475-1564)
    1500, 1504, 1505, 1508, 1512, 1513, 1514, 1520, 1529,
    1534, 1536, 1546, 1550
Mildmay, Sir Walter 1584
Military Order of St. John of Jerusalem suppressed 1540
milled coins in England 1562
mining for copper and lead in England 1561
Mirror of a Sinful Soul, The (Le Miroir de l'ame Pecheresse) 1531
Missale Romanum (Roman Missal) 1570
Modon passes from Venetian to Turkish control 1500
Mohacs, Battle of 1526
Mohammed III, Sultan of Turkey 1595-1603 1595, 1596
Mohammed Khudabanda, Shah of Persia from 1578 1578
Moldavia occupied by Turks 1546
Molina, Alonso de (Spanish lexicographer; d.1585) 1555
Molina, Luis de (Spanish Jesuit theologian; 1535-1600) 1588
Mona Lisa 1503
monasteries suppressed in England (to 1539) 1536
Montaigne, Michel de (French essayist; 1533-92) 1580
Montalboddo, Francanzano de (writer on geography) 1507
Montano, Francisco (Spanish explorer) 1522
Monteverdi, Claudio (Italian composer; 1567-1643) 1587, 1588
More, Sir Thomas (English statesman and scholar; 1478-1535;
    canonized in 1935) 1516, 1529, 1532, 1535, 1543
Mor, Antonio (var. Moro; Sir Anthony More; Anthonis; Dutch
    portrait painter; 1519-75) 1553, 1554, 1555
Moray, James Stewart, Earl of; Regent of Scotland from 1567 (var.
    Murray; 1531-70) 1567, 1570
Morgues, Jacques LeMoyne de (French cartographer) 1564
Morley, Thomas (English composer; 1557-1603) 1593, 1597,
    1599, 1600

Morton, Earl of, Regent of Scotland 1572
Moscow destroyed by fire 1547
Moscow, Russia 1510
Mota, Antonio de (Portuguese explorer) 1542
Mountjoy, Charles Blount, 8th Lord, Earl of Devonshire (Commander of the English forces in Ireland;1563-1606) 1599
Muhlberg, Battle of 1547
Mulcaster, Richard (Headmaster of Merchant Taylors' School in London; c.1530-1581) 1582
Munday, Anthony (English poet and playwright; 1553-1633) 1590
Munzer, Thomas (leader of the German Anabaptist Protestant movement, and of the Peasants' Revolt; 1489-1525) 1520, 1525
Murad III, Sultan of Turkey from 1574 (d1595) 1574, 1595
muskets first used in battle 1525
Muskovite state church 1551
Muscovy Company founded 1553
Muslims persecuted in Spain 1502
Muslims revolt in Spain 1568
My Ladye Nevells Booke 1591
"mystère" performances banned in Paris 1548

Nabunaga, Oda (Japanese ruler; 1534-82) 1568
Nagasaki opened to foreign trade 1570
Nagashino, battle of 1575
Nantes, Edict of 1598
Naples, Kingdom of 1500, 1501, 1504, 1570
Naples, royal palace construction 1600
Nash, Thomas (var. Nashe; English dramatist and satirist; 1567-1601) 1592,1594, 1597
Navarre, Kingdom of 1515, 1591
Navaez, Panfilo de (Spanish explorer; 1480-1528) 1527
Navarro, Pedro 1503
Nemours, Treaty of 1585

Netherlands come under English protection 1585
Netherlands provinces annexed by HRE Charles V 1548
Netherlands provinces declared independent by HRE 1549
New Guinea visited by Portuguese 1526
Newfoundland 1567, 1583
New Testament printed in English 1526
Nice captured by French and Turks 1543
Nice, Truce of 1538
Nicocia, Cyprus, sacked by Turks 1570
Nicolas, Thomas 1578
Nicot, Jean 1561
Niehoff, Heinrich (var. Nyhoff; Nyeuwenhoff; Niegehoff; Neuhoff;
    German organ builder; member of a family of organ builders
    active in the Low Countries; c.1495-1560) 1520
Nobunaga, Oda (Japanese warlord, ruler of Japan) 1575, 1582
Nonsuch Palace, England 1538, 1592
Nonsuch, Treaty of 1585
Noort, Olivier van (Dutch explorer) 1598
Norfolk, Thomas Howard, 4th Duke of (1536-1572) 1572
Norris, Sir John (English soldier) 1591, 1595
North, Sir Thomas (English translator of *Plutarch's Lives*; 1535?-
    1601?) 1579
Northumberland attacked by Scots 1541
Northumberland, John Dudley, Duke of from 1551 (Earl of
    Warwick; Lord Protector from 1549; father of Robert Dudley,
    Earl of Leicester; executed 1553) 1549, 1551, 1553
Northumberland, Henry Percy, 8th Earl of (d. 1585) 1585
Norton, Thomas 1561
Nostradamus (Michel de Notredame; French prophet; 1503-1566)
    1529, 1555, 1558, 1559, 1563
Notizie Scritte newspaper in Venice 1566
Nova, Joao de (Portuguese navigator) 1502
Novarra, Battle of 1513
Novgorod's people massacred 1570
Nowell, Alexander 1568

Noyon, Peace Treaty of 1516
Nun of Kent, The (see Elizabeth Barton) 1534
Nuñes, Pedro (Cosmographer to the Portuguese crown; 1492-1577) 1537
"Nuremberg Egg," the first watch 1502
Nuremberg, Peace of 1532

Olivarez, Spanish ambassador to Pope Sixtus V 1586
O'Neill, Sean (Irish rebel leader; 1530-67) 1567
Ordaz, Diego de (Portuguese explorer) 1531
Orellana, Francisco de (Spanish conquistador) 1537, 1541
oriental languages professorship at College de France, Paris 1538
Orinoco River, South America, explored 1531
Orlando Furioso 1515, 1516
Orozo, Alfonzo (Spanish university founder) 1590
Ortelius, Abraham (Flemish editor and publisher of maps; "father of modern geography"; 1527-98) 1570, 1575
Orviedo y Valdes, Gonzalo Fernandez (Spanish historical writer) 1535
Oursian, Nicholas (clockmaker) 1540
Oxford, Edward de Vere, 17th Earl of (English poet, playwright and reputed author of the plays and poems of William Shakespeare; 1550-1604) 1573, 1576, 1580, 1599

Pacification of Boulogne ends fourth French war of religion 1573
Pacification of Ghent unites Netherlands provinces 1576
Pacific Ocean 1513, 1572
Padilla, Father Juan de (missionary with Coronado's expedition) 1542
Padilla Manrique, Don Martin de, Commander of the Second Spanish Armada 1596
Padron Real 1508
Palatinate 1503
Palace of Westminster , England 1512
Palazzo Strozzi completed in Florence 1507

Palestrina, Giovanni Pierluigi da (Italian composer; c.1525-94) 1551, 1554, 1567

Palissy, Bernard (French potter; c.1510-after 1586) 1566

Palladio, Andréa (Italian architect; 1508-1580) 1538, 1549, 1550, 1554, 1556, 1560, 1565, 1570, 1576, 1579

Panama colony founded 1519

Panipat, Battle of 1535

paper mill in England 1590

Paracelsus (Theophrastus Philippus Aureolus Bombastus von Hohenheim; Swiss alchemist and physician; 1493-1541) 1527, 1528

Paradise of Dainty Devices, The 1576

Paré, Ambroise (French surgeon; c.1510-90) 1572, 1575

Parke, Robert (English translator) 1588

Parker, Archbishop Matthew (English churchman; 1505-75) 1575

Parma, Duke of 1578

Parmigiano (also "Parmigianino"; Girolamo Francesco Maria Mazzola; Italian painter; 1503-1540) 1524, 1529, 1531, 1535

Parr, Catherine, Queen of England 1543-47 (6th wife of King Henry VIII; 1512-48) 1543

Parsons, Father Robert, S.J. (English Jesuit) 1580

Passau, Treaty of 1552

paupers' settlement founded in Augsburg 1519

Peace of Bergerac ends sixth French War of Religion 1577

Peace of Monsieur ends fifth French War of Religion 1576

Peake, Robert (English painter) paints "Blackfriars Portrait" 1600

peasants revolt in Austria 1526

peasants revolt in Hungary 1514

peasants revolt on the island of Majorca 1521

peasants revolt in Oxfordshire, England 1596

peasants' revolt in Speyer, Germany 1502

peasants revolt in Southern Germany 1524

peasants revolt in Upper Austria 1595

Peking (Beijing), China beseiged by Mongols 1550

Pen-ts'ao kang-mu, Chinese treatise on pharmacopoeia 1578

pepper plant grown in England 1548

Perez, Antonio (private secretary to King Philip II of Spain) 1591

Peter Martyr Anglerius (Pietro Martire d'Anghiera; Italian geographical writer resident in Spain; 1459-1525) 1530, 1547

"Peregrina , La" pearl pendant 1554, 1558

Peri, Jacopo ("Zazzerino"; Italian composer of songs and operas,
singer and instrumentalist; 1561-1633) 1598, 1600

Perigord annexed to the French crown 1592

Peru conquest gets underway 1530

Peru under complete Spanish control 1538

Peter Apian (writer on geography) 1524

Petrie, Olavus (Swedish dramatist; 1493-1552) 1550

Petrucchi, Ottaviano dei (Italian music printer; 1466-1539) 1501

Pfyffer, Colonel (Swiss Catholic leader) 1586

Phalèse, Pierre, the Younger (music publisher; 1550-1629) 1582

Philippine Islands 1564

Philip of Habsburg , King Philip II of Spain from 1556 (son of
HRE Charles V; King of England, 1554-58; 1527-98) 1543,
1551, 1553, 1554, 1555, 1556, 1557, 1563, 1564, 1570,
1573, 1576, 1589, 1590, 1595, 1596, 1597, 1598

Philip of Habsburg, King Philip III of Spain from 1598 (son of
King Philip II and Elisabeth of Valois) 1598

Philip "the Handsome" of Habsburg ("le Bel"; King of Castile;
husband of Juana of Castile; 1478-1506) 1504, 1505, 1506

Philip, Landgrave of Hesse 1540, 1541

Philips , Peter (var. Phillipps, Phillips; Pierre Philippe; Pietro
Philippi; Petrus Philippus; English composer resident in the
Spanish Netherlands; c.1560-61-1628) 1596

"Pilgrimage of Grace," English Catholic uprising 1536

pineapples imported to Europe 1514

piquet first played 1526

Pizarro, Francisco (Spanish conqueror of Peru; c.1478-1541) 1530,
1531, 1532, 1538, 1541

Pizarro, Gonzalo, son of Francisco 1548

plague epidemics 1523, 1528, 1537, 1562, 1563, 1575, 1592,

Pope Paul IV (Giovanni Pietro Caraffa; Pope from 1555; d. 1559) 1555, 1556, 1557, 1559

Pope Pius III (Francesco Todeschini-Piccolomini; elected and d. 1503) 1503

Pope Pius IV (Giovanni Angelo de'Medici; Pope from 1559; d.1565) 1559, 1564, 1565

Pope Pius V (Michiele Ghislieri; Pope from 1566; canonized 1712; 1504-72) 1566, 1570, 1572

Pope Sixtus V (Felice Peretti; Pope from 1585; d.1590) 1585, 1586, 1590

Pope Urban VII (Giovanni Battista Castagno; Pope for 13 days) 1590

Popocatepetl, Mount, Mexico, first climbed by a Spaniard 1522

populations of European countries 1600

porcelain, East Asian, imported to Europe 1518

Porta, Giovanni Battista della (Giambatista; Italian natural philosopher; c.1535-1615) 1558, 1589, 1593

Portugal absorbed into Spain 1580

Portuguese Cortes submit to King Philip II of Spain 1581

postal services established 1500, 1504, 1570

potato 1553, 1566, 1580

Prague as capitol of Holy Roman Empire 1576, 1583

Praise of Folly (Moriae Encomium) 1515

Price List of the Whores of Venice (La tariffa delle puttane di Venegia) 1535

Prince, The (*Il Principe*) published posthumously 1532

printing introduced in India 1561

printing introduced in Ireland 1551

printing presses in Russia 1563

proclamation to restrict growth in London 1580

Protestant Reformation in Denmark and Norway 1536

Protestant Reformation in Geneva, Switzerland 1536

Protestant Reformation in Scotland 1528

Protestant Reformation in Sweden 1527

Protestant revolt in Scotland 1557

Protestant uprisings in the Netherlands 1566
Ptolemy's *Geographia* 1508, 1511
public lottery in France 1539
Puerto Rico settled by Spanish 1510
Purana Pul bridge, India 1593
Puritan first used as a designation 1563
Puritan party in England 1576
Puritan religion in England 1593
Puttenham, George (English writer; d.1590) 1589
Pynson publishers, London 1518

Quechua/Spanish dictionary published 1584
Queen's Men, The, theatre company of Queen Elizabeth I 1589

Rabelais, François (French satirist; c.1494-1553) 1534
Raleigh, Sir Walter (var.Ralegh; English courtier, navigator, and
    poet; 1552-1618) 1595, 1596
Ralph Roister Doister comedic play 1567
Ramusio, Giambattista (Italian travel writer; 1485-1557) 1559
Rape of Lucrece, The 1594
Raphael (Raphael Sanzio; Italian painter; 1483-1523) 1500, 1504,
    1505, 1507, 1508, 1509, 1512, 1513, 1514, 1515, 1516,
    1518
rebellions and uprisings 1549, 1551, 1553, 1554, 1595
Red Lion, a building for staging plays, built in London 1567
"Reformation" Parliament in England 1529, 1534, 1536
Regius Professorships founded at Oxford and Cambridge 1540
Regnans in excelsis Papal Bull excommunicating Queen Elizabeth I
    of England 1570
Religious Peace of Augsburg 1555
Reuchlin, Johann (German Christian humanist and scholar of Ju-
    daic language and the Kabbalah; 1455-1522) 1506, 1509,
    1517
Rhaeticus (Georg Joachim von Lauchen; German astronomer and
    mathematician; 1514-74) 1540, 1550, 1596

Rhodes captured by Turks 1522

Rialto Bridge, Venice 1587

Ribero, Diego (Portuguese cartographer working for HRE Charles V) 1529

Ricci, Matteo (Jesuit missionary to China where he was known as Li-ma-teu; 1552-1610) 1582, 1598

Riccio, David (secretary and musician to Mary Queen of Scots) 1566

Ridolfi, Roberto (Florentine banker) 1572

Ridolfi Plot against Queen Elizabeth I of England 1572

Rinuccini, Ottavio (Italian poet; 1562-1621) 1600

Rio de Janiero, Brazil 1567

Rippon, Walter (Dutch coach builder resident in London) 1555, 1564

Roanoke Island colony, Virginia 1585, 1590

Robinson, Ralph, translates More's *Utopia* 1551

Robsart, Amy, wife of Robert Dudley (d.1560) 1560

Rogers, John, first Protestant martyr under Queen Mary I 1555

Roman Catholic bishops restored to power in England 1553

Roman Catholicism restored as state religion in England 1554

Roman type 1518

Rome sacked 1527

Romoli, Domenico (author of *The Steward*) 1560

Ronsard, Pierre de (French poet; member of "La Pléiade"; 1524-85) 1550, 1552, 1560, 1572, 1578, 1586

Rose Theatre, London 1587

Royal College of Physicians founded, England 1518

Royal Commission on enclosure of common lands, England 1517

Royal Exchange at Cornhill, London, opened 1571

Royal Library of France founded 1520

Royal Order of the Holy Spirit founded in France 1578

Rubens, Peter Paul (Netherlandish painter; 1577-1640) 1600

Ruckers, Hans (Flemish harpsichord maker; c.1540-98) 1581

Ruckers, Johannes (Flemish harpsichord maker; eldest son of Hans; 1578-1643) 1595

Rudolf of Habsburg , Holy Roman Emperor Rudolf II from 1576
    (1552-1612) 1576, 1583, 1590, 1592, 1594, 1597
Rugby School founded in England 1567
Rupert, son of the Elector Palatine 1504
Russia invades Siberia 1581
Russian reign of terror 1564
Russians at war with Mongols 1558
Ruthven, Raid of 1582, 1583
rutter first published in English 1528

St. Andrew's Castle, Scotland, captured by French 1547
St. Andrew's Golf Club, Scotland, founded 1552
St. Augustine, Florida, founded 1565
St. Bartholomew's Hospital, London, refounded 1544
St. Bartholomew's Day massacre 1572
St. Cecilia, body of 1599
St. George's Chapel at Windsor Castle, England, completed 1519
St. John Lateran Basilica, Rome 1587
St. John's College founded at Cambridge University, England 1509
St. Paul's Cathedral, London, damaged by fire 1561
St. Paul's School founded in England 1509
St. Quentin, Battle of 1557
Ste. Aldegande, Marnix de, composes *Wilhelmuslied* 1568
Sachs, Hans (German poet and dramatist; 1494-1576) 1523, 1553
Sack-Full of Newes is first play to be censored in England 1557
Sackville, Thomas 1561
Sahugun, Father Bernardino de 1529
Salamanca, Treaty of 1505
Sales, St. François de (French Catholic cleric; canonized in 1665;
    1567-1622) 1598
sales tax adopted in France 1596
San Juan Pueblo 1598
Sansovino (Jacopo Tatti; Italian sculptor and architect; state archi-
    tect in Venice from 1529; 1486-1570) 1537
Sancy diamond 1589

Santa Maria, Tomas de (var. Sancta Maria; Spanish friar, music theorist and composer; d.1570) 1565

Santa Trinita bridge, Florence, constructed 1567

Santiago becomes the capital of Cuba 1513

Santiago, Chile, is founded 1541

Santo Espiritu, Paraguay, fortified 1527

Sanudo, Marino (Italian historian) 1535

Sao Paolo, Brazil, founded 1554

Sao Salvador founded 1549

Sarto, Andréa del (Andréa d'Agnolo; Italian painter; 1486-1531) 1517

Saxony invaded by Bohemians 1546

Saxton, Christopher (English atlas compiler; c1544-c1611) 1579

Schaffhausen canton, Switzerland 1501

Schlick, Arnolt (German organist and composer; c.1560-c.1521) 1511, 1512

Schmalkaldic League of Protestants 1531, 1532, 1538, 1546, 1547

Scipione del Ferro (1465-1526) 1505

Scotland abolishes Papal jurisdiction 1560

Scotland's first printed book 1508

Scott, Sir Reginald (English writer; c.1538-99) 1573, 1584

Scottish College founded in Rome 1600

scourer of drains and pipes for English royal palaces 1533

Scrots, William (Netherlandish painter; court painter to King Henry VIII from 1545) 1545

sealing wax first used 1550

Sebastian I, King of Portugal from 1557 (1554-78) 1557, 1578

Second Helvetian Confession 1566

Sekigahara, Battle of 1600

Selim I "the Grim," Ottoman Sultan of Turkey from 1512 (1467-1520) 1512, 1514, 1515, 1516, 1517

Selim II, Ottoman Sultan of Turkey from 1566 (1524-74) 1566, 1568, 1574

Serrao, Francisco (Portuguese explorer) 1513

Seymour, Jane (Queen of England from 1536; c.1509-1537) 1536,

1537

Seymour, Lord Thomas, of Sudeley (younger brother of the Duke of Somerset; Lord High Admiral of England from 1547; c.1508-1549) 1549

Sforza, Francesco Maria, Duke of Milan, son of Lodovico; duke from 1522; 1492-1535) 1535

Sforza, Lodovico, Duke of Milan (1452-1508) 1500

Shakespeare, William, of Stratford-upon-Avon (var. Shaksper, Shakspere, Shaxpere; actor and theatrical manager; reputed poet and dramatist;1564-1616) 1585. 1592, 1593, 1594, 1596, 1599

Sher Shah, Emperor of Delhi 1540

Ship of Fools English translation 1509

Shute, John (English painter and architect; d.1563) 1563

Sidney, Sir Philip (English poet, patron of the arts and courtier; 1554-1586) 1586, 1590, 1591

Sidney Sussex College of Cambridge University founded 1589

Siena, Italy 1555

Sigismund I ("the Old"), King of Poland from 1506, Grand Prince of Lithuania (1467-1548) 1506, 1548

Sigismund II, Augustus, King of Poland from 1548 (son of King Sigismund I; 1520-72) 1548

Sigismund III, Vasa, King Sigismund III of Poland from 1587 to 1632; King of Sweden from 1592 to 1599 (son of King John III of Sweden and nephew of King Sigismund II, Augustus, of Poland; 1561-1632) 1587, 1592, 1593, 1595, 1599

Signorelli, Luca (Italian painter; c.1441-1523) 1508

silk manufacture introduced in France 1521

silver 1570

silver discovered in Potosi 1544

silver guilders 1500

silver mines opened in China 1514

silver mined in Zacatecas and Guanajuato, Mexico 1548

Simier, Jean de, representative of the Duc d'Alençon 1579

Sistine Chapel, Rome 1508

"Sixteen, The" (French revolutionary group) 1586
slavery 1547, 1582
slavery abolished 1582
slaves and slave trade 1503, 1518, 1581
Smith, Sir Thomas (English classical scholar and statesman; 1513-77) 1561, 1583, 1589
snuff 1558
Socinus, Faustus 1579
Solway Moss, Battle of 1542
Somerset, Edward Seymour, 1st Duke of (Lord Protector for King Edward VI of England; 1506-52) 1547, 1548
Somerset House in the Strand begun in London 1547
"Sommerville" Plot 1583
Songhai Empire, Africa 1591
Soto, Hernan de (var. Fernando; Spanish explorer; c.1496-1542) 1539, 1541, 1542
Southwell, Robert (martyred English Jesuit priest; beatified 1929; c1561-1595) 1595
Souza, Thome de (Portuguese explorer) 1549
Spanish attack in Cornwall, England 1595
Spain at war with England 1585
Spanish Armadas 1588, 1596, 1597, 1599
Spanish coinage devalued 1596
Spanish Council of the Indies 1524
"Spanish Fury" 1576
Spanish law bans attendance at non-Catholic foreign universities 1559
spectacles 1518
Spem in alium motet by Thomas Tallis 1573
Spenser, Edmund (English poet; c.1552-99) 1579, 1590, 1596
spot removal manual 1596
Staden, Hans 1557
steamboat design 1543
Stephanus (Robert Estienne; French lexicographer; printer to King François I of France; 1502-59) 1531, 1540

Stephen Bathory of Transylvania, King of Poland 1575-86 1575, 1577

Straparola, Giovanni Francesco (Italian collector of fairy tales; 1490-1557) 1550

Stapleton, Thomas (English religious writer) 1588

Stationers Company of London 1556

Stettin, Peace of 1570

Stevens, Father Thomas 1579

Stevin, Simon (Stevinus; Flemish mathematician; 1548-1620) 1585

Stocking frame invented 1589

Stow, John (English tailor; writer of a survey of London; 1525-1605) 1598

Strasbourg clock built 1574

Strasbourg submits to HRE Charles V 1547

Suez Canal proposed by Venetians 1504

sugar cane first cultivated in Brazil 153

Suleiman I "The Magnificent"; Ottoman Sultan of Turkey from 1520 (var. Suleyman; 1494-1566) 1520, 1521, 1522, 1524, 1525, 1526, 1528, 1529, 1532, 1535, 1540, 1541, 1552, 1553, 1566

Suleiman I's mosque in Constantinople 1556

Sully, Duke of, French Superintendent of Finances 1599

sumptuary laws in England 1510, 1559

sumptuary law in Venice 1562

Surrey, Henry Howard, Earl of (c.1517-47) 1557

Swan Theatre, London 1595

"sweating sickness" 1507, 1508, 1517, 1528, 1551, 1552

Sweden declared an hereditary kingdom 1544

Swedish Diet 1599

Swedish persecution of Catholics 1600

Sweelinck, Jan Pieterszoon (var. (Swelinck, Zwelinck, Sweeling, Sweelingh, Sweling, Swelingh; Netherlands composer, organist and teacher; 1562-1621 1594

sweet potatoes in England 1565

Swiss Catholic cantons form alliance with Spain 1587
Swiss Protestant cantons allied against Savoy 1584
Swiss civil war between Catholic and Protestant cantons 1531
syphilis 1506

Table fork depicted in a painting 1599
Tahmasp I, Shah of Persia (1514-1576) 1524
Tallis, Thomas (English composer; c.1505-85) 1573, 1575
Tartaglia, Niccolò (Niccolò Fontana; Italian mathematician; 1499-
    1557) 1535, 1537
Tasso, Torquato (Italian poet; 1544-95) 1575, 1581
Taverner, John (English composer; c.1490-1545) 1526
Taverner, Richard, translates Erasmus' *Adagia* 1539
Taxis, Franz von, Postmaster-General of Netherlands 1516
tea 1559
Teatro Olympico, Vicenza, Italy 1585
Teerlinc, Lavina (Netherlands miniature painter; c.1510-76) ap-
    pointed English court miniaturist 1546
telescope experiments begun 1600
tempered scale defined by Chinese Prince 1584
tennis 1522
Teresa of Avila, Saint (Spanish mystic and saint; canonized 1622;
    1515-82) 1562, 1568
Terrail, Frederick, Chevalier de Bayard, q.v. (French hero; 1473-
    1524) 1512, 1515, 1524
Tetzel, Johann (German monk; c.1465-1519) 1516
Teusina, Treaty of 1595
theatres in London reopen after plague epidemic 1594
thermometer 1596
Thevet, André (French biographer; 1502-90) 1584
Thirty-Nine Articles 1552, 1571
Thirty-one Articles 1563
"Three Brethren" jewel 1547
"Throckmorton Plot" (var. Throgmorton) 1583
Tiepolo Pisani Land Bank of Venice 1584

Till Eulenspiegel 1500

Tilney, Sir Edmund, Master of the Revels for The Queen's Men 1583

Timbuctoo, Africa 1590

Tintoretto (Jacopo Robusti; Venetian painter; 1518-94) 1548, 1557, 1560, 1564, 1574, 1588

Titian (Tiziano Vecellio; Venetian painter; c.1488-1576) 1515, 1520, 1523, 1530, 1531, 1533, 1534, 1538, 1539, 1540, 1543, 1545, 1546, 1548, 1550, 1552, 1559. 1565, 1570

tobacco 1555, 1558, 1561, 1565, 1586, 1595

Tobia Commedia , earliest Swedish stage play 1550

Tokugawa Ieyasu (ruler of all Japan from 1600; d.1616) 1575, 1589, 1598, 1600

Tokugawa Shogunate Period 1600

Toledo, Francisco de, Viceroy of Peru 1569

Toledo, Treaty of 1539

tomatoes introduced in England 1596

tomb of Chinese Emperor Wan-li 1584

Torrigiano, Pietro (Italian sculptor) 1512

Tottel's Miscellany 1557

Transylvania 1597

treasure from the Americas 1544

Tridentine decrees (promulgated at Council of Trent) 1564

Tridentine Index of Forbidden Books (Council of Trent) 1564

Trinity College, Cambridge University, founded 1546

Trinity College, Dublin, founded 1591

Trinity College, Oxford University, founded 1554

Tripoli taken by Turks 1551

Tritheim (Johannis Trithemius; German expert on cyphers; 1462-1516) 1518

Troyes, Peace of 1564

Tuilleries Palace, Paris 1564

tulip 1559

Tunis captured by the Turks 1534

Tunis comes under Turkish control 1574

Tunis founded 1518
Turin the capital of Savoy 1562
turkeys 1524
Turner, William 1562
Tye, Christopher (English composer; c.1505-c.1572) 1553
Tyndale, William (English Protestant; translator of the Bible into
    English; 1494-1536) 1525, 1526, 1530, 1534, 1535, 1536
typhoid fever 1567
Tyrone, Hugh O'Neill, 2nd Earl of (Irish rebel leader; c.1540-
    1616) 1562, 1594, 1595, 1596, 1597, 1598, 1599, 1600

Udall, Nicholas (English dramatist; 1504-1556) 1533, 1553,
    1567
Ulloa, Alfonso de (Italian historian; d. c.1580) 1570
Union of Lublein unites Poland and Lithuania 1569
Union of Utrecht 1579, 1581
University of Alcala, Spain 1508, 1514
University of Berlin 1574
University of Edinburgh , Scotland 1582
University of Frankfurt an der Oder, Germany 1506
University of Granada , Spain 1531
University of Konigsberg, Germany 1544
University of Leiden , Netherlands 1575
University of Lima , Peru 1553
University of Lisbon transferred to Coimbra, Portugal 1537
University of Messina, Italy 1548
University of Paris reorganized 1598
University of Santiago de Campostela, Spain 1504
University of Seville, Spain 1504
University of Valencia, Spain 1500
University of Warsaw , Poland 1576
University of Wittenberg, Germany 1502
Uppsala, Convention of, upholds Martin Luther's doctrines 1593
Upper Austria becomes Catholic 1597
Uraniborg (Castle of the Heavens) Observatory founded 1576

usury forbidden by papal bull 1586
Utopia 1516, 1551
Utrecht Library founded 1582
Ursuline Order founded in France 1535

Valdivia, Pedro de (Spanish explorer) 1541
Varthema, Ludovico de (Italian traveller and writer; c.1465-c.1510)
   1510
Vasa, Gustavus (King Karl IX of Sweden from 1604; 1550-1611)
   1595
Vasari, Giorgio (Italian artist and art historian; 1511-74) 1558
Vasili III (see Basil; Grand Duke of Muscovy and Ruler of Moscow; 1479-1533) 1503, 1504, 1505, 1514, 1533
Vasquez de Ayllon, Lucas 1526
Vatican Council 1515
Vatican Library opened in Rome 1588
Vaz de Camoens, Luiz (Portuguese poet; 1524-80) 1572
Vega, Lope de (Lope Felix de Vega Carpio; Spanish dramatist and
   poet; 1562-1635) 1598
Velasquez de Cuellar, Diego de 1511
Venetian Council of Ten 1582
Venice Arsenal 1530
Venice at war with Turks 1570
Venice, first commercial colleges 1500
Venus and Adonis 1593
Vere, Sir Francis (English soldier; c.1560-1609) 1589, 1596, 1600
Vergil, Polydore (De Castello; Italian-born English historian;
   c.1470-c.1555) 1501, 1534
Vervins, Treaty of 1598
Verzellini, Jacob (Venetian glass maker resident in London) 1574
Verrazano, Giovanni da (Florentine navigator sailing for France;
   c.1480-c.1527) 1522, 1524
Veronese, Paolo (Paolo Calieri; Venetian painter; c.1528-1588)
   1553, 1572, 1573
Vesalius, Andréas (Belgian anatomist; 1514-1564) 1543

Vespucci, Amerigo (Italian-born Spanish explorer; 1451-1512) 1501, 1502, 1505
Victoria, Tomas Luis de (Spanish composer; 1548-1611) 1576
Vienna beseiged by Turks 1529
Vienna, Treaty of 1515
Viète, François (French mathematician; 1540-1603) 1591
Villa de la Vega , Jamaica, founded 1523
Villa d'Este at Tivoli 1549
Vincent de Paul (French Catholic cleric; founder of the "Congregation of Priests of the Mission"; 1576-1600; canonized 1737) ordained priest 1600
Vives, Juan Luis (Ludovicus; Spanish philosopher and humanist; 1492-1540) 1522, 1524, 1531

Waghenaer, Lucas Janszoon (Dutch compiler of a seachart atlas; 1534 or 35-1606) 1583, 1585, 1586, 1588
Waldseemuller, Martin (German cartographer; c.1480-1521) 1505, 1506, 1507, 1513
Wales incorporated with England 1536
wallpaper 1509
Walsingham, Sir Francis (English statesman; principal Secretary of State from 1573; c.1530-90) 1573, 1590
Wan Li, 13th Emperor of the Ming Dynasty, China from 1573 to 1620; 1563-1620) 1573
War of the German Knights 1522
"War of the Three Henry's" 1585
wardrobe of Queen Elizabeth I of England 1600
Warner, William (English poet; c1558-1609) 1586
Warsaw the capital of Poland 1595
water closets (toilets) installed at Richmond Palace, England 1596
waterworks in London 1582
Welser merchant bankers of Augsburg 1528, 1586
Welsh language book is printed for the first time 1546
Welsh translation of the Bible 1588
Wenden, Battle of 1578

Westminster Palace, London, destroyed by fire 1512
whalebone used for skirt hoops in England 1580
wheel-lock musket invented in Germany 1517
Whetstone of Wit, first English treatise on algebra 1557
Whitehall Palace, London 1530
Whitgift, John, Archbishop of Canterbury to 1604 (c1530-1604)
    1583, 1586
Whithorne, Peter (English translator and soldier) 1560
Whythorne, Thomas (English lutenist and composer; 1528-96)
    1571
Willaert, Adrian (Flemish composer; c.1490-1562) 1527
William V, Duke of Bavaria (to 1597) 1579, 1597
William of Orange ("William the Silent"; leader of Protestant rebels
    in the Netherlands; Prince of Orange; Count of Nassau; 1533-
    84) 1574 ,1575, 1576, 1577, 1582, 1584
Willoughby, Sir Hugh (English explorer; d. c.1554)) 1553
Willoughby d'Eresby, Peregrine Bertie, Baron (1555-1601) 1589
Wimpfeling, Jakob (German historian; 1450-1528) 1505
windmills in the Netherlands 1592
Windsor, Treaty of 1506
Winkyn de Worde 1524
Wittenberg Nightingale, The (Die Wittenbergisch Nachtigal) 1523
Wolsey College, Cambridge University, refounded as Christ Col-
    lege 1545
Wolsey, Thomas (English cleric and statesman; Cardinal and Lord
    Chancellor of England from 1515; 1475-1530) 1514, 1515,
    1525, 1528, 1529, 1530
women first appear on stage in Italy 1529
women first appear on London stage 1600
Wright, Edward (English explainer of Mercator's projection) 1599
Wyatt, Sir Thomas(English soldier; ?1520-1554) 1554

Xaquixaguane, Peru, Battle of 1548

Yellow Ford, Ireland, Battle of 1598

York Conference, England 1568

York Palace, London, completed (later Whitehall Palace) 1525, 1530

Yonge, Nicholas (var. Young, Younge; English music editor and singer; ?-1619) 1588

Yoshishige, Otomo, Japanese warlord 1578

Yucatan coast of Mexico conquered by Spanish 1533

Yucatan coast of Mexico discovered 1517

Zacconi Lodovico (Italian music theorist and priest; 1555-1637) 1592

Zanzibar becomes a Portuguese colony 1503

Zapolya, John, King of Hungary (1487-1540) 1526, 1528, 1530, 1538, 1540

Zapolya, John Sigismund, King of Hungary (1540-71) 1540

Zaragosa, Treaty of 1529

Zeeland falls to Dutch rebels 1574

Zeno of Venice 1555

Zhengde (Cheng Tih) 11th Emperor of the Ming Dynasty, China, from 1506 to 1521 1506

Zwingli, Huldreich (Latin: Ulricus Zuinglius; Swiss Protestant reformer; 1484-1531) 1519, 1522, 1524, 1529, 1531